Turning Freud Upside Down 2

Turning Freud Upside Down 2

More Gospel Perspectives on Psychotherapy's Fundamental Problems

edited by Lane Fischer
and Aaron P. Jackson

BYU Studies
Provo, Utah

To contact BYU Studies, write to 1063 JFSB, Provo, Utah 84602, or visit http://byustudies.byu.edu.

Library of Congress Cataloging-in-Publication Data

Names: Fischer, Lane, 1955– editor. | Jackson, Aaron P., 1960– editor.
Title: Turning Freud upside down 2 : more Gospel perspectives on psychotherapy's fundamental problems / edited by Lane Fischer and Aaron P. Jackson.
Description: Provo, Utah : BYU Press, [2017] | Includes bibliographical references and index.
Identifiers: LCCN 2017029503| ISBN 9781942161479 (pbk.) | ISBN 9781942161486 (ebook)
Subjects: LCSH: Pastoral counseling. | Pastoral psychology. | Psychotherapy--Religious aspects--Christianity. | Psychotherapy.
Classification: LCC BV4012.3 .T87 2017 | DDC 253.5/2--dc23
LC record available at https://lccn.loc.gov/2017029503

Printed in the United States of America

Contents

Once More unto the Breach, Dear Friends

Lane Fischer

Turning Freud Upside Down (2005) began a process of considering fundamental issues in psychotherapy through the lens of the restored gospel of Jesus Christ. It was well received and continues in publication. We were grateful to BYU Studies for its willingness to publish and distribute the book. We were grateful to the authors who generously contributed their thoughts and insight. We knew the task was far from complete.

When *Turning Freud Upside Down* was first conceived, we had concerns that we could easily go astray. There were so many pitfalls. We are not authorized to define the gospel. We have limited wisdom. I was particularly concerned that simply applying the labels "gospel" or "BYU" or "Freud" would inadvertently stop people from thinking. I was concerned that positive stereotyping would be as detrimental as negative stereotyping. Based on the reception of the book and general feedback we have received, my particular concerns were unfounded. Readers have been thoughtful and reflective about the work. Students especially have studied the text and been forthright in their challenges and questions about the concepts. Readers have not seemed to accept or reject the text wholesale or to assume that we have presented an authorized completion of the entire question. It has stimulated further thought and discussion.

The overall objectives have remained the same. We recognized that psychotherapy is built on philosophical foundations that are often unspoken but nevertheless omnipresent. Many of those assumptions, when elucidated, were not consistent with the restored gospel of Jesus Christ. It seemed that we had enough understanding to begin to build our psychotherapy from the foundation of the restored gospel. Richard Williams's (2003) essay "The Restoration and the 'Turning of Things Upside Down': What Is Required of an

LDS Perspective?" was a seed crystal and an impetus to begin. But it is not as easy or concrete a task as it might seem. Having some understanding and faith in the restored gospel is necessary but insufficient for the task at hand. There is the ongoing need to deepen and refine our understanding of and faith in the gospel. There is also the simultaneous demand to deepen and refine our observation of how humans develop. There is the sequential demand to then integrate the best of our understanding into interventions that are well founded and efficacious. Continuing forward to address those demands requires humble gumption. This volume of essays represents the ongoing exploration, questioning, contemplation, and courageous efforts by our contributors to step into that complex gap.

We structured the first volume of *Turning Freud Upside Down* around five very specific topics: the nature of law, the nature of suffering, the nature of agency, the nature of truth, and the nature of being. We invited authors to respond to one of those topics. We were much more open-ended in this volume. We asked authors to continue their thinking in the same area or respond to other constructs according to their preference. Hence, this volume ranges a bit more broadly around the common theme of exploring the foundation of psychotherapy through the lens of the gospel. There is notable diversity among the authors' ideas. We certainly have not come to a consensus view. Nevertheless, the consistency within these faithful essays is significantly higher than would be found in a potpourri of ideas not based on the restored gospel.

It is overly simplistic to summarize any of the essays as having a unitary focus. As they examine primary areas of interest, they invariably reference other correlated concerns. The original five topics are inextricably intertwined, and to ask one is to eventually ask them all. Two of the essays, by Tim Smith and by Matt Draper and Mark Green, deal with issues of faith. They range in their definitions and applications but are working to understand similar constructs. Three of our authors, Lane Fischer, Jeffrey Reber, and Richard Williams, engage in the issues that surround moral agency, and a fourth author, Kristin Hansen, considers moral agency and its implications for practice. Two essays (one by Ed Gantt and Stan Knapp and the other by Aaron Jackson) focus on the fundamental issues embedded in relationships, Jackson at an ontological level and Gantt and Knapp at a more applied level. Robert Gleave focuses on justice and forgiveness. Throughout all of the essays, the issues of being, truth, agency, suffering, and law interplay with each other.

In the end, I am left with admiration for the intelligence and faith of the authors. I have never constructed a bifurcation between faith and intelligence. Nor do I see that the restored gospel should not be considered as a viable philosophy. My opinion is that the restored gospel has more intellectual heft than any other philosophy. Similarly, the prophets, while being holy, also tend to be brilliant thinkers. I don't restrict the implications of their writings to "religious" issues. I find that they have wrestled with the same fundamental issues as any other so-called philosopher. I am impressed by their inspired answers to fundamental questions. Treating them as philosophers does not discount their holy callings as prophets, seers, and revelators.

I have always been deeply impressed by Mormon. He was perhaps one of the most brilliant people to ever live on earth. He was identified by age ten as the next keeper of the national archive. By age fifteen, he was appointed as the military leader of the nation's armies. He simultaneously then led the military, abridged a thousand years of records, and was the prophet and spiritual leader of the church. He was brilliant! Given all of Mormon's brilliance, I have no problem trusting his approach to fundamental questions that must underlie our psychotherapy. For example, one of the curative factors in group psychotherapy is "instillation of hope." When people experience hope through group psychotherapy, they tend to improve their lives. Mormon had ample reason to lose hope. His sad task was to watch his culture self-destruct. If anyone had justification to become cynically despairing, it would have been Mormon. He had to wrestle with the nature of life and hope. He asked, certainly from his own pondering and grief, "What is it that ye shall hope for?" His response was, "Ye shall have hope through the atonement of Christ and the power of his resurrection, to be raised unto life eternal, and this because of your faith in him according to the promise" (Moro. 7:41). Mormon was no modern existentialist dealing with despair and the nothingness of death. He understood human existence very deeply with all of its anguish and terror, and he resolved our common plight with a philosophy that rested on the Savior and the universal resurrection. I find that the truths of the restored gospel are more powerful foundations for life than any others. I am grateful to the authors in this book for their faith and intelligence.

Richard N. Williams

The Freedom and Determinism of Agency

It has been suggested, with good reason, that of all the profound and marvelous doctrines of the restored gospel, agency (what we often call "free agency") is most fundamental. While this essay does not defend this claim, there is a good case to be made for the centrality of agency to any understanding of the meaning and purpose of the plan of salvation and the Atonement of Jesus Christ, which is its essential core. After all, if we were not moral agents, no atonement would be necessary, because we could not really sin, since sin requires purposive action. Simple behavioral control would be sufficient to overcome or prevent negative comportment and its consequences. Indeed, if there were no agency, controlling or preventing anyone's behavior could take one or more of three forms: (1) intrusive control of persons' spheres of action exercised in the world where behavior takes place, (2) somewhat less intrusive control of all the environmental circumstances that produce behavior, or (3) control of the biological makeup of persons so that only certain behaviors are produced. By the same token, if we were not moral agents, we would not be the sort of beings that are perfectible in the first place—unless by "perfectible," we are content to mean something like "without design flaws," or "perfectly (re)engineered." Indeed, if human beings are simply natural organisms, created or evolved, parts of a completely deterministic natural material universe, "free will" could only be, at best, a comforting illusion, and, at worst, a significant design flaw.

If we were not morally perfectible agents, no "infinite and eternal" sacrifice (Alma 34:14) would be necessary. It is even unclear how Christ's sacrifice might affect us under such circumstances unless it were something like a cosmic force able to control all our behaviors in the way just discussed. Indeed, one wonders why a certain quantity of suffering might be necessary to "pay for" behaviors that were the inevitable products of that same cosmic force or one very much like it. The whole language of redemption becomes a hollowed-out metaphor. The best we could hope for would be to not be who (or what) we have been due to the operation of forces we do not control, but rather to be subject to other forces we do not control but which do not make God angry with us.

It seems that, while perfection may be a contextual state (because we never live completely alone but are always with others and among things), it is certainly not a contingent state (one dependent on the existence of some other independent state)—since contingent beings arise out of and are dependent on extraneous originating conditions. No "infinite and eternal" atonement (Alma 34:14) would be necessary to make us contingently "good,"—control of contingencies would suffice. And any type of "contingent perfection" is a logical contradiction, especially if we take into account the notion of perfection as "completeness," or "lacking nothing." As contingent beings, we would lack autonomy and the power to *be* perfect rather than to simply be *made* perfect by contingent circumstance. In such a case, it would be the contingencies that were first perfect, and we would be just their product. This argument goes at least as far back as the early Patristics and their reading of Aristotle.

Finally, if we take seriously one of the defining characteristics of "intelligence," that it is "independent in that sphere in which God has placed it, to act for itself" (D&C 93:30), moral agency is integral to intelligence, sin, and perfectibility. It is the real possibility of both sin and perfection that makes necessary the supreme atoning act of our Savior. Nonintelligent (nonagentic) beings need no Savior, but they do require a good technician. The fact is that in a completely determined (and therefore closed) universe, it is not at all clear what sin, justice, or mercy could mean. It does not make a lot of intuitive sense to thank a Savior for suffering for sins that absolutely could not have been avoided or thank him for his gift of mercy to compensate for acts that were not my fault and to which I made no meaningful contribution. At best, such thanks would be perfunctory; after all, someone apparently had to do the suffering. It is not even clear to whom—or to what—suffering and atonement are owed when predetermined "sins" are committed. If the answer is "law," then one wonders what sort of cosmic reality could or would exact payment for inevitable acts, or how such acts could offend a cosmic reality responsible for the hard determinism of those very acts in the first place. Clearly, we can do better than this in our understanding of the moral character and quality of mortality. And the key to such understanding is agency.

Any serious discussion of agency must be clear about what agency is—and what it is not. While this is not a simple matter, I want to begin with a fairly generic sense of agency. That human beings are agents means that we—and, importantly, our actions—are not just products of substances, forces, or other things extraneous to us, whether these things be outside us or inside us. It is in being agents that we make intentional and definitive contributions to those actions and to who and to what we really and fundamentally are at every moment present and future. In other words, agency must affirm profoundly that "people are not things."

This is not to say that we must stand apart from all forces or "things" or be totally unaffected by them, nor is it to say that there is nothing "thinglike" about us (such as our weight). It is to say, however, that whatever things may be influential in our lives, and however they may affect us, this whole process of influence and effect cannot be sufficiently understood by theories, models, or constructs that are adequate to understanding nonagentic things and how forces act upon them. For the most part, we are not affected by the same kinds of forces or factors that affect mere things. But, more importantly, not being mere things, we are not affected by what is around us and in us *in the way* (nonhuman) things are thus affected—by what is around and in them. The processes, models, and theories that describe things (animate or inanimate), and what works in them or on them, don't suffice for us, and in the most fundamental sense, they don't apply to us. Mere things have some types of contingent relationships with the things that affect them and determine them. Agents do not have those same sorts of contingent relationships with any things. We relate to what is around us and in us very differently from the way nonagentic things do. Relations of mere things to their environments do not hold for us. A man and a stone caught in the same landslide do not relate to the event and the environment of gravity and other rocks and trees the same way. There is an undeniable qualitative difference. Human beings and their experiences are, unlike rocks and the things that happen to them, "saturated" phenomena (Marion, 2002). There is an "overflowing" in our humanity that cannot be captured by a complete list of physical, environmental, and biological factors even though such a list suffices for natural objects and events. This overflowing is the manifestation of agency, not only our own agency but also the agency of others because we experience them as overflowing as well.

It is the rejection of the thesis that all human action can be wholly explained by extraneous contingent relationships that leads people to conclude that agency stands in opposition to determinism. They suppose that to claim human agency is real is to claim that human actions are not determined (especially by things outside human beings themselves). We cannot circumvent this problem by claiming that we are agents in that we are determined by things *inside* us because the principle at stake here is not the *source* or *origin* of the causes and influences that may affect our lives, but the nature of the causes and influences and the *way* they affect our lives—in other words, the nature of determinism itself. Whether from outside or inside, if our actions arise from factors or causes that are thinglike, or if the actions are affected by the same kinds of processes by which mere things are affected, or in the *way* mere things are affected, agency is impossible. It cannot exist. Thus, it seems reasonable to conclude (wrongly) that agency and determinism cannot both be operative in genuinely human activity. The reasonable (though wrong) conclusion from this analysis is, then, that agency requires, or that it just *is,* indeterminism.[1]

Indeed, most textbooks in the social sciences—if they deal with agency at all—deal with it as a species of indeterminism. This makes agency seem unscientific, mystical, and indefensible, totally incompatible with an empirically minded, scientific psychology. And I must agree that they are right about that—if agency is indeterminism, it is indeed mystical and indefensible. This is also why agency has been so hard to defend—and thus why the agentic side loses so many arguments about agency. Indeterminism is an indefensible position. It must ultimately hold that there are no causes of actions or events—that is, no strong ties between events and their antecedents. Any conceptually consistent indeterminism must hold, therefore, that events are ultimately just random.[2]

This equation of agency with indeterminism is problematic on two accounts. First, even casual observation is sufficient to persuade us that events in the world are not random. There are indeed strong relationships between events and their antecedents. It also seems like a weak argument to hold that while most or all of the

1. In fact, this essay will argue that it is precisely in human activities that both agency and determinism operate, even though they both do not operate in such a way in the nonhuman world—the world of nonhuman things.

2. We will leave aside here any facile indeterminism (or any soft determinism) that holds that mere ignorance of the causes of events is sufficient to make a place for agency. If the causes are not known, then there is room for freedom. However, this makes agency just a form of ignorance, and freedom an illusion. Albert Bandura (1989) among others has actually made this argument.

physical/observable world is deterministic, human action is not. Our observations, not to mention our reflective sense of ourselves, tells us that our actions are indeed tied to meaningful antecedents. This leads us to the second problem. It is that, even if it were true that indeterminism rules in the sphere of human action, this would not allow for any meaningful agentic human action. If human actions have no antecedents, then they have no context, they reveal no order, and tend toward nothing and have no meaning. This is not the sort of agency that any rational human being might want. If, as our scriptures and doctrine suggest, a war was fought in heaven over the issue of agency, it was a senseless war if the outcome is merely the right and privilege to behave randomly and without regard for history, context, or even desire.

There have been many arguments to the effect that freedom (or agency) is not only compatible with determinism, but that it requires determinism (see, e.g., an example in the work of Foot, 1957). All such arguments must be based in, and then offer a response to, some form of the two arguments noted above. If there is no determinism (of any sort), then acts have no meaningful antecedents; they come from nowhere and lead nowhere and are thus not agentive—produced by agents—since, in the act of production, the agent becomes the antecedent. Agency under an indeterminist regime might be adequately modeled by an unpredictable nervous twitch that interferes with otherwise normal stimulus response sequences.

Because of this line of analysis, I have argued (Williams, 1992) that agency should not, indeed must not, be tied to indeterminism. Positions arguing that agency is compatible with determinism are known as "compatibilist" positions. In assessing whether compatibilist positions preserve genuine agency, everything depends on how "determinism" is understood. Most positions that seek to reconcile agency and determinism end up redefining agency to be compatible with a classically hard form of determinism, but lose what is essentially agentic in the process.

I submit that rather than redefining agency, trying to make it compatible with a classically hard mechanical determinism, we need to re-understand determinism in such a way that it is compatible with agency—without losing what is essential in determinism. I have suggested (e.g., Williams, 1992) that the solution to this problem lies in carefully examining what a deterministic understanding of life and world really requires. I believe it is simply this: that there is meaning, order, and continuity in the world manifest in the fact that all events (including acts) have meaningful antecedents. Without these antecedents, the events would either not occur or would not be what they are.

What is at issue in an adequate conceptual understanding of agency, then, is not whether all events have such antecedents, but rather to understand the nature of the relationship between particular events and their antecedents. In the realm of human action, I submit, the relationships between acts/behaviors and their antecedents are strong, but also subject to change and alteration, and they are contextual, historical, and open-ended—among other things. Significantly, and in an important way, these relationships are also to be understood as the acts of the human beings who carry out the behaviors—sometimes simultaneously with the antecedent acts themselves.[3] Sometimes an entire network of antecedents solidify for the first time as an agent simultaneously acts and understands the meaning and purpose of his or her own act. We might refer to such agentive acts as "investments" in the present, in the sense that to invest is to "grant . . . control or authority over," or to "furnish with power or authority" (Webster, 1965).

This act of investiture endows life and acts with meaning and context, not after the fact as I might endow a good book with a favorable review. Rather, the sort of endowment of meaning and context that is the heart of agency is immediate and creative "in the moment." To return to the example of reading a book, I endow the book with meaning *as I read it,* not afterward. The book exists for me as I am reading. It, like life itself, does not just wait around to be endowed. So my endowment of meaning is neither determined by things outside me or outside the book, nor is it arbitrary or untethered from the book itself. However, we must be careful about how we understand such agentic acts. They are fundamental to our being the kind of meaning-making beings we are, but they cannot be understood merely as cognitive deliberation and decision making—for reasons to be taken up below. Such investments in the present, as is true of all investments, are oriented toward the future where they either come to fruition or fail. They create (or determine) the future in a

3. See Slife's (1993) helpful discussion of simultaneous causality and Rychlak's (1988) discussion of formal and final causes.

way, but do not control it in the classical mechanical sense. They "put up" the future in the present, as one may "put up" fruit that is consumed later.

This creative quality of agency is obvious to all who think seriously about it. It is this sense of agency that leads some compatibilists to conclude that agency is dependent on—or manifest in—deliberative cognitive acts, particularly choices. While choosing is clearly a reflection of agency and cognitive deliberation is generally a good thing and certainly descriptive of human agents, it is a serious question whether deliberative choices constitute the essence, or the "test case," of agency. There are several problems inherent in conflating agency with the making of choices. I will briefly mention only three.

First, this position contradicts our experience. Most of our day-to-day living does not reflect careful cognitive deliberation. For example, reaching across the table to pick up a drink—while absorbed in conversation on other matters—most often does not reflect rational deliberation, but we do not want to conclude that it is not an agentive act just because there was little if any deliberation. The same observation might be made about the acts of placing the tongue in just the right spot in the mouth and turning the vocal chords on and off in just the right way for intelligible, purposeful, and meaningful speech. The muscular aspect of speech does not seem to need much deliberation, and, in fact, deliberation will just interfere with the process. One might argue that in these kinds of actions we are just not mindful of the deliberating process or that the act is so practiced that the deliberation is not necessary any longer. This is to say that there *must have been* deliberation at some point, but it was either always "unconscious," or it was conscious and we have forgotten. Either of these alternatives, of course, begs the question by assuming precisely what is in question, by invoking another realm of mind to do the deliberating (either now or in the past) without our present awareness or deliberation. Such a solution explains merely by defining the process in such a way as to fit the model that requires that the process exist. But even if it is so, in any case it would be hard to argue convincingly that if the deliberation attending our actions is so easily set aside, so evanescent, and so completely forgotten, it is nonetheless the *essential defining feature* of the agentic act. It is certainly hard to argue that such deliberation is the defining test case for *all* agentic acts. At least this line of analysis brings one to wonder at this point just what agency is, and what it is good for if it is simply a consequence of situated, contingent reason.

This brings us to the second point, which is that to make agency dependent on another more fundamental principle or process—such as rationality (manifest as deliberation)—really destroys what is most agentic about agency. In this case, then, agency is not really fundamental to our nature. Rather, rationality is. Now the analysis must shift to a defense of rationality and whether or not it is genuinely fundamental—or agentic. So, agency is explained as a manifestation of "how the mind works."[4] It may be derivative of some other fundamental process, such as synapses and sodium uptake. Rationality may also be a historical byproduct of being born into a culture with a heritage that includes Greek philosophy. Pretty soon, however, agency *qua* agency is gone. We can then debate about what processes really are fundamental, but agency certainly does not qualify. Thus, depending on other things over which we have virtually no controlling input (such as our powers of rationality based on intellectual aptness, cultural history, or the quality of our synapses), there are varying amounts of agency. This produces, in my view, significant conceptual problems, such as making agency not fundamental but contingent. If it is contingent, it isn't really agentic. In addition, such an analysis requires that an understanding of agency must wait until after a full analysis and understanding of rationality. I do not believe we can afford to wait that long.

Third, if rationality—the process of logic and analysis that produces good decisions and deliberate actions—is really fundamental, and if rationality and "making sense" are powerful forces (as we hope they are), then one might argue that the choices and actions that proceed from rational deliberation are not really free precisely because rationality and logic are so powerful and compelling, so fundamental. Rationality can be seen, and indeed has been seen, this way—as heavy-handed—in much contemporary scholarly work of what is often called the "postmodern era" (see, e.g., the discussion in Baynes, Bohman, & McCarthy, 1987). This position also has

4. This style of theorizing and explaining is known generally as "psychologism." See entry for "psychologism" in the *APA Dictionary of Psychology* (American Psychological Association, 2007).

a corollary disadvantage, namely, that if agency is really deliberated action, and if the rationality behind such action is strong and compelling, then perhaps all real acts of freedom must be the ones that resist or defy the overwhelming rational thrust of reasoned action and must be, therefore, irrational, and in that sense, deviant or pathological. This is very close to the indeterminist position.

For these and other reasons that cannot be taken up here, I have argued elsewhere (Williams, 1992; Williams, 2005) that whatever we ultimately understand agency to be, it cannot exist simply as "free choice." Choice cannot be the fundamental and defining manifestation of our agency. I have instead offered an alternative account or understanding of agency as "having the world truthfully" (Williams, 1992). I have also tried to distinguish agency from other types of purposeful actions (Williams, 1994) and to suggest what may be the conditions of human being and human life necessary for agency to exist (Williams, 2005). I should note here, however, that phenomena of "choice," while they do not constitute the defining and fundamental test case for agency, are nonetheless important to understanding agency. Choices reflect our agency as well as any human action does.

Agency at Three Levels of Analysis

Given the foregoing analysis, some attention must be turned to how—*other than as deliberative choice*—agency is likely to be manifest in human action and how it can be understood from different explanatory perspectives. I believe that sorting out this multilayered aspect of agency is very important if agency is to be understood and incorporated into clinical practice. Finally, I will attempt to extend my own sense of what might be the most clinically important manifestation of agency.

I turn attention first to understanding agency at three conceptually (and clinically) relevant levels of analysis: the ontological, the phenomenological, and the pragmatic. The *ontological level* of analysis is the most fundamental. Understanding agency at this level is to understand it in terms of what it *fundamentally* is and *must be,* and, which is to say the same thing, at the level of what we fundamentally *are* as human beings. The *phenomenological level* of analysis is the level of lived experience. Agency may look and feel different at the level of our own experience of ourselves and our world than it looks (or than it really is) at the ontological level. This is simply to say that even if at the ontological level I am first and foremost an agent, it is not obvious what it will "feel like" to be an agent at the level of my own experience of life, self, and world. It may be the case that I really don't "feel like" an agent much if at all—but all the same, I may be the sort of being for whom agency is possible. I might not feel like an agent, because I am living untruthfully and maintaining too many falsities about life and the world. It is the phenomenological level that may be of most interest and importance to clinicians. The *pragmatic level* is the level on which we must take account of practical constraints and conditions. Agency *per se* is not likely to make me rich, handsome, or a first baseman for the Los Angeles Dodgers. We live in a world of facticity, of "things in themselves," of what John-Paul Sartre (1956) referred to as the "in itself." While I am convinced that such pragmatic givens neither create nor destroy agency, I am also convinced that they will have a profound effect on how agency will be manifested in actions, feelings, and thoughts. It should be noted here that questions regarding agency at the level of pragmatics and givenness are not "whether questions" (whether agency exists), but rather "how questions" (how it works and how it will be manifest).

Agency at the Ontological Level. For reasons illustrated above, I submit that agency, if it is genuine, cannot be the result of other processes or conditions. It must exist as "what we are" (moral agents), or it is not really agency and will not reveal itself in us in ways that produce meaning in our lives or in ways that make contact with the restored gospel. If we are not agents at the ontological level (where there is nothing behind it or underneath it), then we cannot be agents at all because all our acts will be contingent on the existence and relative magnitude of factors and forces in which we do not meaningfully and creatively participate. Perhaps the most succinct description of agency at this level is in 2 Nephi 2:14, where we learn that creation consists of "things to act and things to be acted upon." We are the former and can never become the latter in the ontological sense. We can never become—or be made to become—merely things to be acted upon. While my body may be acted upon, and while I may be acted upon in some sense by trials, tribulations, illnesses, and other persons, the effect of these things on me will not be exactly like how brute *things* are acted upon. And therein is the guarantor of our agency, our humanity, and our essential being-in-the-world. It is important in education, in human relations, in families, and in therapy that we be clear about whether we are dealing with an agent or some other sort of living *thing.* As a discipline, we have only begun to explore in preliminary ways the profound difference this makes. I wish to offer a call to action in regard to this most essential and meaningful question. If we don't know who we are (or what we are), how will we really know how to help ourselves or help each other?

Agency at the Phenomenological Level. Even if at the fundamental (ontological) level I am an agent—"not created or made" (D&C 93:29)—how or whether I am aware of that fact may vary considerably according to many things in my world, including my own experience. My fundamental agentic nature may or may not manifest itself in the exercise of my capacity to make choices, especially good ones. So many things in my proximal world of experience may mask the distal reality of my intrinsically agentic character. This is certainly not to say that I am caused to act in certain ways by the kinds of natural forces that act on things, nor is it to say that the effects my world of experience may have on me are similar to the effects present in the world of mere things. It is simply to say that as a meaning-making moral agent, trapped in facticity, and participating with others in actively creating my world and my life, many things—including my truly agentic essence—can become overlain by layers and layers of more immediate and seemingly more demanding concerns. The fact that I do not stand against the crowd, that I do not make choices, that I "am lived" in certain ways, or that I do not feel much in control of my life, are *not* evidence that I am *not* an agent, but mere testament to the often overwhelming reality of the mortal world and my own embodiment. That we cannot find recognizable evidence for some kinds of freedom of the will in our clients or in ourselves is not evidence that it does not exist. Rather, much of what we see in others and experience in ourselves are sediments laid down over the top of our essential agentic character, over time, by facticity and a history of our responses to it.

Therapy with moral agents is carried out almost exclusively at the phenomenological level. It will deal with life as experienced and will work to carve out effective life strategies in a world of facticity, or even enhance the agentic quality of our actions. However, I submit that it makes all the difference in the world whether in the therapeutic work at the phenomenological level we understand—and believe—that we are, in truth, working with a real, irreducible, honest-to-goodness moral agent, and not a "thing to be acted upon." I can think of no more intriguing or more worthwhile endeavor than to explore what a grand and glorious difference it can make in what we are doing, to know the real nature of the being we are working with—that this being, in the most profound sense and at the most fundamental level, is a moral agent animated by and sensitive to truth, and that many of the things we take to be causes and immutable psychic realities are mere sediments, artifacts of facticity.

Agency at the Pragmatic Level. At the pragmatic level we take note of many things in our lived world that are outside our control and do not depend on our experience—and are not particularly influenced by it. Existentialists and other theorists have spoken of this quality of the world as "facticity," or givenness, and about our realization of our sometimes impotent immersion in such a world as "throwness" (e.g., Heidegger, 1962; Sartre, 1956). We find that we cannot conjure the world to be as we want it to be. No amount of positive thinking, or affirmation, or choosing, no amount of believing in ourselves, can change certain brute realities. This leads some to conclude either that there is no such thing as real agency, because it is impotent in this way, or, even if there is agency, that it doesn't really matter. We can grant that it is true that there are certain things which, in the natural course of things (barring supernatural intervention), can be influential in our lives and immune to our best efforts to change them. However, we should not make the mistake of concluding therefrom that agency does not exist or that it doesn't matter. While, as I suggested above, I cannot necessarily, by agentive acts, change my physical stature, cure a disease, straighten my teeth, or change my economic circumstance, this does not mean that I am not an agent. We often recognize this by saying something like: "We can't choose our circumstances, but we can choose how we *react to* them." Unfortunately, this sometime rings a bit hollow and sounds facile to people engaged in real struggles with circumstance. (See Rychlak, 1979, for a careful, sophisticated, and nonshallow treatment of this approach to agency at the pragmatic level.)

The problem with this analysis of our relation to facticity is that it relies too much on an understanding of agency as mere choosing, which, as I argued earlier and in other places, is not an adequate account of agency. While it may be true that choices are frequently impotent, this does negate real agency. What we can say is that genuine agentic beings—beings whose agency is self-existent at the ontological level—will likely not experience (or at least *do not need to* experience) the world of facticity at the pragmatic level as purely material organisms and other kinds of "things" may experience it. Even more importantly, truly agentic moral beings have a formidable arsenal of modes of being within and from which to confront the world of stubborn facticity—not the least of which are the mode of meaning-making, creativity, commitment, resistance, and volition. This theme is repeated over and over in various life-affirming approaches to psychology and psychotherapy such as Logotherapy (e.g., Frankl, 1959) and many others. As was true of therapy at the phenomenological level, I am convinced that therapy aimed at helping clients live fulfilling lives at the pragmatic level will be very different when it is directed—or driven—by a keen and clear vision that every client, at the ontological level, is a moral agent. I hope scholars can come together to explore the depth and breadth of this possibility and its impact on therapy, education, and family relations.

Agency as Persuasibility—as Being Influenced

If we grant that agency fundamentally consists of having the world truthfully, and that it does not manifest itself first and foremost as choosing and "taking charge" through cognitive deliberation and control of behavior or outcomes, we are left with the question, How, then, will agency manifest itself in its purest form? The answer, I believe, will take us not only to enhanced understanding and appreciation of agency, but also to a concomitant understanding and appreciation of virtue. The fundamental insight leading to our understanding that agency cannot simply be manifest as choice is that choices are always grounded in reasons, desires, myriad other aspects of facticity, and our mode of being in the world. If we conclude that this is true of acts of agents, then we conclude that it is also true of agency itself. Agency, as an attribute of agents manifest in their actions, is always grounded—contextual—taking account of reasons and realities. Because of this, there is no absolute objectivity—no space where we can stand uninfluenced by grounds, facticity, reasons, desires, experience, etc. Therefore, the real test case of agency is not to be found in escape from these things or in decision making from presumably influence-free grounds. Ironically, it is found, rather, in active, participatory persuasibility—the ability to be persuaded or convinced of truth.

This stands in contrast to the common notion that agency must be understood as resistance to enticement and persuasion. To the extent we can be persuaded by (or to) truth and to the Good, we are "having the world" truthfully, and our agency is manifest and operative. This may be what Alma was trying to teach us by encouraging us to try an experiment with the word of Christ and, over time, to be persuaded that this experience is good (Alma 32).

The prophet Lehi taught: "Wherefore, the Lord God gave unto man that he should act for himself. Wherefore, man could not act for himself save it should be that he was enticed by the one or the other" (2 Ne. 2:16), "the forbidden fruit in opposition to the tree of life; the one being sweet and the other bitter" (2 Ne. 2:15). The irony here rises nearly to the level of paradox (but not quite). Agency requires humility rather than "taking charge"—at least not a self-conscious, self-assertive kind of taking charge. Rather than cognitive assertion, the hallmark of agency may be a sense of our own nothingness (Mosiah 4:11), a clear sense of our dependence on the Lord. At the same time, from a religious perspective, agency seems ultimately to require an active God to intervene in our lives, testifying by various means, and influencing (or enticing) us. For the nonreligious, it requires simply that we have sensitivity to truth and a capacity to recognize the good and the true and distinguish them from the bad and the false. More concisely, we need to be able to know what is really the case, and what is not. Freedom in this context of enticement is a yielding, a giving of oneself (Williams, 2002). Virtues that are seemingly inimical to agency as "taking charge"—humility, responsiveness, yielding, giving oneself to others—provide the foundation for agency as living truthfully, which often takes the form of acceding to truth, giving oneself over to what is good and right, committing one's own life, or submitting to circumstances, but which may also take the form of holding firm, being solid and unwavering, and doing what one feels compelled to do (a wholly different type of "taking charge"). I am hopeful that work on this aspect of agency can bring us and those whom we serve in closer and fuller contact with our agency and establish the foundation for a virtuous and flourishing life.

References

American Psychological Association (2007). *APA dictionary of psychology*, G. R. VandenBos, Ed., Washington, D.C.: American Psychological Association.

Baynes, K., Bohman, J., & McCarthy, T. (1987). *After philosophy: End or transformation?* Cambridge, MA: The MIT Press.

Bandura, A. (1989). Human agency in social cognitive theory. *The American Psychologist, 44*(9), 1175–1184.

Foot, P. (1957). Free will as involving determinism. *The Philosophical Review, 66,* 439–450.

Frankl, V. (1959). *Man's search for meaning.* New York: Pocket Books.

Heidegger, M. (1962). *Being and time.* (J. Macquarrie & E. Robinson, Trans.). New York: Harper and Row.

Marion, J. L. (2002). *Being given: Toward a phenomenology of givenness.* (J. L. Kosky, Trans.). Stanford, CA: Stanford University Press.

Rychlak, J. F. (1979). *Discovering free will and personal responsiblity.* New York: Oxford University Press.

Rychlak, J. F. (1988). *The psychology of rigorous humanism.* New York: New York University Press.

Sartre, J. (1956). *Being and nothingness.* (H. Barnes, Trans.). New York: Philosophical Library. (Original work published 1943.)

Slife, B. D. (1993). *Time and psychological explanation.* Albany, NY: State University of New York Press.

VandenBos, G. R. (2007). *APA dictionary of psychology.* Washington, DC: American Psychological Association.

Webster, N. (1965). *Webster's seventh new collegiate dictionary.* Springfield, MA: G. C. Merriam Company.

Williams, R. N. (1992). The human context of agency. *The American Psychologist, 47*(6), 752–760.

Williams, R. N. (1994). The modern, the post-modern, and the question of truth: Perspectives on the problem of agency. *Journal of Theoretical and Philosophical Psychology, 14*(1), 25–39.

Williams, R. N. (2002). On being for the other: Freedom as investiture. In E. E. Gantt, & R. N. Williams (Eds.), *Psychology for the other: Levinas, ethics, and the practice of psychology* (143–159). Pittsburgh: Duquesne University Press.

Williams, R. N. (2005). Agency: Philosophical and spiritual foundations for applied psychology. In A. P. Jackson, L. Fischer, & D. Dant (Eds.), *Turning Freud upside down: Gospel perspectives on psychotherapy's fundamental problems* (pp. 116–142). Provo, UT: Brigham Young University Press.

Kristin Lang Hansen

The Relational Moral Agent and Its Implications for Practice

Introduction

In the last half century, as social scientists and psychologists have developed prominent voices in defining the causes of emotional suffering, spirituality and religion have often been subtly and even intentionally squeezed out of psychological theories, treatment, and research (Slife and Reber, 2009). In recent decades, many have defended religion and spirituality's foundational role in mental health (Bergin, 1980, 1985, & 1991; Miller, 2015; Richards & Bergin, 2005; Slife & Reber, 2009).

In considering how to address values in psychotherapy, for example, religiously oriented mental health professionals have realized that the ideal of the therapist as an objective observer or a "blank slate" to receive the client's projections was simply an impossible standard, and because of the power differential between therapist and client, therapists cannot help but play an important role in influencing clients' values. Since religiously oriented therapists gained a voice in the increasing secularization of the mental health field, they have been able to acknowledge openly the role of values in therapy, but the difficulty in determining how to do so has also come to light. It has become apparent that trying to "add on" religion and spirituality to theories of human nature that have naturalistic assumptions does not work. Richards and Bergin (2005), among others, have highlighted the underlying set of assumptions necessary for a psychology that acknowledges a moral and spiritual/religious foundation, which they call a theistic approach to psychotherapy. Their work, along with the work of others, has given a voice to mental health professionals who want to acknowledge spiritual and religious values in psychotherapy.

Theistically oriented psychotherapists—that is, those grounded in a religious/spiritual perspective—describe humans as being spiritual, created by God, and in an unseen relationship with him (Richards & Bergin, 2005). This perspective cannot be captured by the naturalistic philosophical assumptions that ground much of psychological theorizing, which include: determinism (forces outside our control cause behavior), universalism (context-free natural laws guide behavior), reductionism/atomism (all behavior can be divided into smaller parts), materialism (human behavior has a mechanical or material basis), ethical relativism (all values are culture-bound), ethical hedonism (humans only act to be rewarded and to avoid pain), and classical realism/positivism (science is the only means for understanding the universe) (Richards & Bergin, 2005).

A psychology that acknowledges our spiritual nature must see a role for free will (the ability to make choices independent of biology and social forces), contextuality (the role of context in who we are, and that private phenomena can be experienced and not viewed empirically), holism (that we are more than the sum of our parts), transcendent spirit/soul (we can't reduce our spirits to biology and social forces), universals (some values are more healthy and moral than others), altruism (humans can forgo pleasure for the welfare of others), and theistic realism (God is the ultimate creative and governing force in the universe) (see Richards & Bergin, 2005, p. 11). Richards and Bergin refer to these later assumptions as a spiritual worldview. I like to refer to them as spiritual assumptions in contrast to naturalistic assumptions used for explaining human nature. Paul the Apostle makes a similar distinction when he refers to "the things which are not seen" which are "eternal" (2 Cor. 4:18) in contrast to the things which are seen which are of a temporal nature.

Psychology, in turning to naturalistic assumptions, continually tries to ground its understanding of human nature in the things that "are seen" or are temporal. Aspects of human nature that are of an eternal nature—such as agency, the learning and values we acquire on our mortal journey, and the character we develop—cannot be explained only by naturalistic assumptions. Spiritual assumptions such as the ones Richards and Bergin identify are needed.

Nevertheless, there seems to be continued confusion in our field and conflict between naturalistic assumptions and spiritual assumptions. In addition to the conflict between differing worldviews (naturalistic vs. spiritual), sometimes theistically oriented therapists unknowingly utilize therapies with naturalistic assumptions that lead them to undermine their spiritual beliefs. Cognitive behavioral therapy, for example, can be practiced in a way that sets up the therapist's organization of reality against the client's and undermines the client's agency and the therapist's respect for that client's agency. This can occur as a therapist tells his or her client what his or her core beliefs are and how to change them. A client who is working with a therapist who respects his or her agency should not have to wonder, "Is my therapist correct or am I?" Additionally, the pitting of naturalistic and spiritual assumptions against each other can often cause the value conflicts that arise in therapy. The fact that theistically oriented therapists turn to therapies that have underlying naturalistic assumptions and struggle with the dilemma of how to deal with value conflicts in therapy suggests an underlying confusion in our field. It gives evidence that therapists are often unaware of the underlying assumptions that guide their theories and practice and the role that these different assumptions play in theorizing and practice. The assumptions that underlie our psychological theories take us to different places in how we practice therapy, so it matters that we understand what assumptions underlie the theories we use (Slife & Williams, 1995).

The problems that theistically oriented therapists have of utilizing theories based on naturalistic assumptions or getting into value conflicts with clients reflect a paradox. To solve this paradox, I suggest that we not only discuss which assumptions are more correct—spiritual or naturalistic—but that we recognize a model of human nature that can incorporate an understanding of what both of these assumptions are addressing in our nature. Such a theory helps us better conceptualize our spiritual nature and acknowledge it by grounding that understanding in spiritual assumptions governed by spiritual laws, and, at the same time, such a theory allows us to acknowledge the influence of mortal conditions, governed by naturalistic laws, on our spiritual nature. Difficulties that lead to emotional suffering can be found in how we are engaged spiritually, or as a result of our unique mortal conditions, or some combination of both. The role of the therapist is to make an assessment that can help clarify where the problems or opportunities for growth are and to provide treatment targeted to address these problems or opportunities for growth specific to our spiritual and/or mortal natures. Depression due to a spiritual trial, for example, is handled in therapy much differently from depression that appears to have a biological basis. If a client's problem involves having a boss who is limiting his or her agency, leading to sorrow in his or her spirit, using medication for depression would not be effective or necessary. Working, instead, with the client's agency would be more effective.

A model that acknowledges both spiritual and naturalistic assumptions recognizes that whether or not we believe in a spiritual reality influences how we are grounded and affects the extent to which we can recognize the presence of both spiritual and naturalistic assumptions or whether we simply rely only on naturalistic assumptions. A religiously oriented person, for example, who believes that true altruism is possible, might be able to access realms of reality in a way that someone who is more hedonistic or who denies the existence of the spiritual aspect of our nature cannot. In contrast, someone who denies that we have a spiritual nature and who chooses to ground all of our spiritual and psychological nature in naturalistic rather than spiritual assumptions, will most likely see only the mortal aspects of our nature. *Our nature is designed such that we can attribute either spiritual, naturalistic, or both sets of assumptions to explain human nature.* For those who acknowledge that we have a spiritual nature, grounding our mental life in an eternal spiritual nature situated in mortal conditions changes our understanding of the work of therapy and better captures the complex etiologies of emotional suffering.

Psychology needs a way to understand those aspects of our nature that are spiritual without accidentally relying on naturalistic assumptions to do so. For this reason, I have found Joseph Rychlak's (1994) reliance on formal and final causality useful for not only changing how we describe aspects of our spiritual nature such as agency, meaning, values, belief, and faith, but also for giving us a theory of our nature that is more consistent with the complexity of our spiritual and mortal nature. In order to discuss formal and final causality we must first consider our perspective or the grounds upon which we are standing. Once clarifying how perspective matters in our theorizing, the groundwork will be laid to describe formal and final causality and how it allows for (1) grounding the spiritual aspects of our spiritual nature, such as agency and meaning making, in a way that more accurately explains them; (2) describing a meaning-making capacity not possible without agency that can create different views of reality, including the view that we do not have a spiritual nature; (3) addressing the fact that our nature includes both eternal and mortal components in dialectic relationship with each other and our relational context; and (4) developing different therapeutic methods to target differently the mental aspects of our spiritual nature, such as our agency and how we make meaning, and the mental aspects affected by our mortal conditions, such as a biologically based mental illnesses like schizophrenia.

I will unfold a model of the relational moral agent and how this model addresses the above-described complexity in our nature and helps theistically oriented therapists practice therapy in a way that is more consistent with their underlying spiritual and religious beliefs. In discussing spirituality and religion, I take a Judeo-Christian perspective, but my hope is that the ideas presented here will also resonate with those of other faiths.

With the model of the relational moral agent in mind, the work of the therapist is to help clients practice their agency in consideration of their mortal conditions, context, and journey. First, therapists assess, address, or rule out mortal influences on the clients' presenting problems, such as the role of biology (perhaps some forms of OCD, bipolar disorder, schizophrenia, and developmental disorders) in producing emotional suffering. If problems seem more related to a client's spiritual nature, there are many things therapists can do to work on this level with clients. Therapists, for example, can help clients look at their unique way of organizing their experience. Therapists can observe patterns of behaving, patterns of thinking, and patterns of regulating emotion and reflect them back to clients. Clients, then, can more intentionally observe their own patterns and direct these toward ends that the clients choose, create, or submit to. Therapists can help clients reorganize their experience or create new organizations aligned with their values. A therapist works as a witness, a guide, and a resource for the client. Value conflicts diminish, because both therapists and clients have similar goals of helping clients understand how they have made choices and meaning in the past, how they do so in the present and intend to in the future, and how they can do this in ways that are more aligned with what they hope to create in their lives going forward. They have this focus because therapists can teach clients that they have agency, which allows them the opportunity to become aware of how they make choices and create meaningful lives.

Perspective Matters

Our perspective influences how we view the potential realities in which we participate. Research in the area of positive psychology, for example, shows that having gratitude and a positive attitude can increase happiness in our lives (Seligman, 2002). Another way that our reality is influenced is whether we believe that God is the ultimate creative and governing force in the universe and the ultimate reality, or whether we believe that there is nothing more to the universe than what we can see with our eyes and prove with our scientific theories. Those who rely only on science will agree with the latter. Those who turn to scripture and to God's word to answer this question and to determine what they believe will acknowledge that not only is God the ultimate reality and creator of this universe (Gen. 1 and 2), but that he teaches us there are different levels of closeness we humans can have with him. In the Christian tradition, for example, it is written that there are different degrees of glory that can be obtained, depending upon our righteousness on the earth (1 Cor. 15:40–42; D&C 76:50–79). God states that there are some who draw near unto him with their mouths, but their hearts are far from him (2 Ne. 27:25). Jesus claims to be "in" the Father and beckons us to join him by observing and following his example (John 10:38; 14:10; 1 Jn. 2:24). Likewise, a Book of Mormon prophet, Lehi, in his vision, stands at the tree of life partaking of Christ's atonement and calls his family, who are not at the tree, to come closer, implying that they are not as close to Christ (1 Ne. 8). God teaches through his holy word that there are different perspectives to be experienced and enjoyed depending upon our faithfulness and on our willingness to have hope in unseen things of a spiritual nature (Heb. 11:1). We have the ability to choose the course we will follow, whether we strive to be "in the Father" and at the tree of life or instead turned toward the great and spacious building referred to in Lehi's vision in the Book of Mormon. The assumptions that we hold closely motivate our actions and consequently affect the realities we experience, as well as what we can have a hope of experiencing. The assumptions that underlie our theorizing in psychology can and do have the same impact.

There are different assumptions that cause us to see different realities. Much of psychology has relied on naturalistic assumptions to theorize about human nature. These assumptions are based on scientific studies that have approached an understanding of human nature from a third-person perspective, or by viewing people at a distance or "from over there" (Rychlak, 1994). From a third-person perspective, what we learn about what it means to be human is limited to what we can observe and study scientifically, which falls into two categories: nature and nurture, or biology and social context, respectively. Behavioral scientists, studying human nature from a third-person perspective, do not take context-specific information to be most relevant. They assess, instead, group behavior and norms. Since spiritual possibilities cannot be observed, these behavioral scientists do not consider them. From this perspective, a person's *active involvement* in thinking, feeling, and behaving is inferred only from *outside* the person, and so these behavioral scientists have not considered that they are not focused on the individual. They have not focused on how the individual is uniquely organizing experience from the presented possibilities in his or her unique context; nor have they considered that the individual is capable of imagining new possibilities that might or might not become real or that the individual can have faith in the existence of spiritual possibilities and realities (Rychlak, 1994).

Because behavioral scientists and mental health workers subscribing to approaches based on third-person theorizing essentially see people as objects and interchangeable, psychological treatment approaches based on such theories leave therapists and clients looking for answers to clients' problems in what is observable with the human senses; that is, nature or nurture. From such a perspective, it is easy to see how blaming families of origin or social contexts, or suggesting medication seem like the only answers for emotional suffering. While many individuals' emotional struggles will have etiologies in biology or social context, they may also have psychological problems that are related to their eternal nature, such as spiritual trials and how they direct their agency. If all of our emotional problems are reducible to forces beyond our control, as naturalistic assumptions have us believe, there is no reason to hope that we can sometimes transcend biology or circumstance or even have the possibility of help from unseen spiritual realities and resources. It is possible, because of this perspective, that our commitment to the reality of naturalistic forces might even sometimes get in the way of allowing God's healing influence in our lives. While God can intervene in human life at any time (see Paul the Apostle [Acts 9], Alma the younger [Mosiah 26–28; Alma 36], and Laman and Lemuel [1 Ne. 3]), our theories can keep us from recognizing spiritual possibilities available for healing from some forms of emotional suffering. A strict reliance on naturalistic assumptions to understand human nature gives us only a partial picture of the etiology of emotional suffering and neglects the important role spirituality can play as both a resource for healing, such as when God intervenes to connect a client with a therapist who is uniquely prepared to help that particular client, or as a possible source of pathology, such as when spirituality and religion are misused to abuse others or when they become part of a schizophrenic's delusions or lead to a limiting phobia.

A First-Person Perspective Changes How We View Our Nature and the Role of Agency

Agency Is Active, Not Passive. In contrast to an external, naturalistic perspective, we are more able to learn about our spiritual nature when we view it from the first-person perspective or an introspective approach (Rychlak, 1994). We therapists take a different position theoretically in order to move from seeing people as objects that are controlled by biological or social forces to considering each individual as though "we are 'in the heads or hearts' of . . . [the person] we are observing" (Rychlak, 1994, p. 10). We are not literally getting into someone's else head, but rather we are creating a theory about how our psychology works from the perspective of being within the individual engaged in a dialectical relationship with his or her own body situated in a unique social environment. "An introspective approach leads us into a place of action, where we come to recognize—not only that we *have* agency—but that we *are* agents" (Rychlak, 1994, p. 10).

Using the introspective point of view to theorize shifts our thinking from seeing the mind as only a repository of information or containing an organizing ability (e.g., found in the frontal lobe) to seeing individuals as organizers, framers of experience, or creators having a unique mortal experience. In the former, responsibility is abdicated by seeing the mind in a passive way, while in the latter, responsibility for what choices are made because we have agency lies with the agent.[1] When we theorize in this way, we are led to put agency at the center of our theorizing in dialectical relationship with our embodied mortal situatedness. In so doing, we can better account for the spiritual and mortal complexity of our nature.

Agency Is Both Free and Determined at the Same Time. Agency, a part of our eternal nature, is involved in how we make meaning, make choices, have faith, believe, value, etc. When described using naturalistic assumptions, agency is reduced to a brain function or, according to some postmodernists, is the result of social forces. Such views see agency as strictly determined, remove the possibility of human control and freedom, and make agency a small part of our theory of human nature. In contrast, a first-person perspective is needed to see the interaction between agency and its dialectical interface with the mortal conditions the agent faces. With this change in perspective, it becomes clear that both freedom and determinism are part of how agency can be understood (see Williams, 2005).

Some recent authors on agency capture the paradox of how it is both free and determined by describing agency as underdetermined (Sugarman, 2008); that is, agency is *influenced* by biology and social context but is *not determined* by them. The meaning we create and the choices we make because of our agency are intimately connected to the contexts in which we live and grow. We need both the freedom to take responsibility for our choices in order that agency be free, and yet we are not entirely free because we act as agents from within a mortal body, within unique moral contexts and relational histories. We don't have control over which bodies we have, the unique contexts in which we have been placed and how they have influenced us, or the consequences of our choices in how they open up or close down possibilities in our specific relational contexts. Spiritual assumptions, such as final and formal causality, allow us to explain how agency can be free, allowing us to choose from among

1. However, in the case of some forms of mental illness that are clearly biologically based, like schizophrenia, the ability to make choices or exercise agency has been impaired such that the person is not competent to be responsible for their choices.

possibilities with moral implications within the embodied reality of the human mortal experience, the latter of which makes agency, in part, determined.

Spiritual Assumptions Needed to Explain Moral Agency

Aristotle's formal and final causality grounded in what Rychlak (1994) refers to as the "logos" can be used to describe our agency and other aspects of our spiritual nature, such as how we make meaning from our experience. Formal causes describe patterned meaning. These meanings are extended for the sake of ends, such as God's creations and his divine plan for mankind. The extension of meaning "for the sake of an end" is the final cause. Taken together, formal and final causality can describe agency's role in creating and organizing experience in the "logos" (what I refer to as spiritual assumptions) in contrast to the "bios" or "physikos" groundings (what Rychlak uses to describe our mortal conditions governed by natural laws). Interestingly, *logos* translates from the Greek to mean, among other things, "the word of God," which is what the Gospel writer John calls Jesus when he says, "In the beginning was the Word" (John 1:1). For me, formal and final causality can better capture the eternal part of our nature and can help us spiritually ground our agency without needing to reduce it and other aspects of our eternal nature to something found in our physical world.

As agents, we are constantly bringing what we know to what we are newly experiencing. We affirm one thing and not another based on what we have already learned and where we are directing our behavior. We create meaning in patterns that are extended conceptually, rather than chronologically, toward different ends that we choose (Rychlak, 1994). Formal and final causality gives us a language for describing agency's ability to make meaning, organize, imagine, create, believe, dream, and have faith in a way that naturalistic assumptions could not. First, I will describe in more detail *formal causality,* then *final causality,* and finally, how they work together through *oppositionality* to help us understand a spiritually grounded moral agency in a mortal context that can better account for the spiritual and mortal complexity of our nature.

Formal Causality. Having agency gives us the opportunity to create and organize meaning from our experience. Because meaning is not something that we can locate in the brain, we must, instead, appeal to a different way of describing meaning. Formal causality is useful for this purpose. A formal cause refers to the shape, pattern, or ordering of elements that describes the essence of an object or event (Rychlak, 1994). The fact that Martha is recognizable at age forty by an old friend from age twelve is not reflective of biology, since all the cells in Martha's body have changed, and at forty she appears to be much different than she was at age twelve. Her essence or "spirit," however, has a quality of sameness that makes it recognizable. The plans or blueprint for a home about to be built would also be an example of the formal cause (Slife & Williams, 1995). Formal causality suggests that there is some order or organization that transcends biological substance and its movements.

Formal and final causes can account for meaning and, more specifically, how meaning is organized and how it is directed (Rychlak, 1994). Formal causes capture *meaning's patterns,* while final causes capture *intentionality or direction* of our actions for the sake of which meaning is extended without being dependent on the passage of time (Rychlak, 1994). Research supports the conclusion that the better we elaborate or organize meaning, the better we will remember it, implying the importance of our being agents with the ability to create and organize meaning and not passive recipients of information (e.g., the "self-generation effect") (Nairne, Pusen, & Widner, 1985; see also Bruner, 1990).

Final Causality. Final causality explains how behavior is made for the sake of a goal or an end. Behavior is purposive, and goals and actions happen simultaneously as opposed to happening in a linear fashion over time. Williams (this volume) refers to such simultaneous goals and actions as "investments" in the present that create the future depending on the direction in which they are oriented. Actions and intentions work together. "To have an intention is to act for the sake of it" (Slife & Williams, 1995, p. 113). No passage of time is required if an intention or action is changed. In one moment, a mother could intend to start cooking, and in the next instant she could help a crying baby. "The goal never has to be completed in any final cause relationship. The final cause merely determines our actions while we maintain the goal. Theoretically, we can change our intentions and actions at every moment of the day" (Slife & Williams, 1995, 114). To change an intention will always be the instantiation of, or investing in, another intention or action. Choosing is essentially a process of "final cause replacement" (Williams, 2016, personal communication). Reaffirmation of intention and holding it in mind is required to keep action aligned with it. For example, the addicted person may state his intention to give up an addiction when really holding in his mind an intention to continue the addiction. Therapists often bring to light such competing intentions, stated versus actual, and can facilitate the realization of the actual intention, which in turn gives the client increased possibility to act differently. The client, for example, could learn to direct his intention to noticing and experiencing an emotion in his body, with the final end of integrating rather than avoiding the emotion; this could help the client act less impulsively whenever the unwanted emotion surfaced.

Final cause theorizing is referred to as a teleological approach. It is "the view that events are predicated according to plan, design, or assumptions—that is, based on purposive meanings or reasons—and therefore directed to some intended end" (Rychlak, 1994, p. 322). Teleologies deal with final causes. Rychlak (1994) suggests three possible forms teleological theorizing can take—"*natural teleology, human teleology, and deity teleology*" (see p. 8). A divine plan reflected in events would be a *deity* teleology. Rychlak (1994) writes, "The plan per se is a formal cause, but the presumption that the deity designed it and now creates a reality 'for its sake' (based on it) brings in the final-cause meaning as well" (p. 8). For example, a deity teleology might be reflected in the Latter-day Saint view that God's desire is that "men [and women] are, that they might have joy" (2 Ne. 2:25) and that God's purpose is "to bring to pass the immortality and eternal life of man [and woman]" (Moses 1:39). While Latter-day Saints believe God has instituted the sacrament as a part of his plan to help humankind receive an eternal inheritance with him (a deity teleology), they engage in a human teleology when they take the sacrament following a promise to "always remember" the Savior, Jesus Christ. From this perspective, they are creating an organization of thought and action intended toward always placing Jesus Christ at the forefront of their thoughts and actions. This intention is reaffirmed weekly so that the goal or intention stays steady and becomes well organized.

A person can also attribute all that happens in reality to natural events and deny a "deity" teleology. A person who does not believe in God and believes life is only about how much money one makes might have a human teleology intentionally directing thought and behavior toward making money. Such a patterning of thought would involve reaffirming this intention until making money becomes a focus for this person. Similarly, a person who believes that science is the only pathway for understanding reality will organize and direct thought and action toward learning about and understanding reality only in this way. Describing agency based on final and formal causality can allow for people to have different perspectives on what reality is (Rychlak, 1994). This theory seems to capture our nature better, rather than a theory that gives only one view of our nature.

Oppositionality. Formal and final causality change how we view human nature and how we create meaning in terms of patterns that are extended toward ends in a time-independent way, limiting or closing off options as we affirm some meanings and not others. Our ability to make meaning from experience must take into account this oppositional quality (Rychlak, 1994). We see in our language, for example, the presence of oppositional reasoning in examples such as healthy vs. sick and tall vs. short. In both examples, healthy also implies not sick, and tall implies not short. This human quality, where one meaning also includes what it is not, is something a computer cannot simulate (see Rychlak, 1991). From an introspective perspective, the agent organizes meanings in a particular way, and in affirming one way of organizing, *at the same time* other ways are not affirmed but nonetheless implicated. Meaning extended in one direction replaces other possible directions to which meaning could have been extended. Without the ability to reason oppositionally, for example, I could not choose one career direction over another, or limit time with one friend to open up time for another. I could not focus on time spent with my children to nourish those relationships rather than spending that time on media or superficial acquaintances. I could not focus on fostering loving thoughts rather than fearful ones. Oppositional reasoning allows for morality. There is an inherent asymmetry in that some meanings that we affirm hold greater value for us and will open up more possibilities and freedom in our lives than others. Formal and final causality help capture the quality of oppositional reasoning that is fundamental to our eternal nature (2 Ne. 2:11). They also make it more correct to speak about our agency as *moral agency* because how and what we affirm and how we organize our experience matters for our eternal happiness and is thus a moral endeavor (Alma 42:8, 16).

The Moral Agent in Dialectic Relation with Its Embodied, Embedded Mortal Conditions

Each of us, as moral agents, inhabits a body and lives in a unique relational space from moment to moment. We experience emotions and physical and perceptual sensations from our bodies that are interwoven with the meanings we organize and create (see Stern, 1985). We always find ourselves in the midst of a world informed by our relationships and social context. We are, in every moment, organizing and making meaning (formal causes) and directing (final causes) meaning toward ends that we choose from our experience and that are made available to us from our biological (or embodied) condition and our relational context. There is an interweaving or a dialectical relationship between our moral agency and its embodied, contextually situated mortal condition (see Frie et al., 2008).

There are myriad ways that we can experience, organize, and make meaning from our reality in any given moment. Our relational context not only includes other living humans, but also can include our interactions with God, our past experiences, such as with deceased relatives, and meaningful projections onto others. God himself is not contextless, unchangeable, and passive (Slife & Reber, 2005). He is actively engaged in our specific contexts in a very real way, and a change in our context can change how he ministers to us (Slife & Reber, 2005). From the Christian perspective, Jesus Christ, the Son of the Father, came to earth to dwell in a mortal tabernacle and live an embodied, contextually situated life so that he might have perfect empathy for us. We, as agents, can interact with possibilities that are imagined or not visible to our natural eyes but nevertheless real (i.e., spiritual realities), such as God's promise that we might have an eternal heritage with him if we endure our mortal journey well (Heb. 6:15, 17; 1 Ne. 13:37). Our human nature is to be relationally oriented, and we are ever in a dialectical relationship with our relational context (Frie, 2008; Martin, 2008; Stern, 1985; Slife & Reber, 2005; Sugarman, 2008).

While our ability to affirm and organize meaning from a wealth of possibilities, seen and unseen, gives us our freedom, agency is determined by what we organize. What we have organized becomes the context or background knowledge that we bring to bear on new learning (Rychlak, 1994). Our actions are based on meaningful antecedents, which make them meaningful (Williams, 1992). We could not acquire knowledge or meaningful information *unrelated* to anything that we have experienced (or even imagined) in the past (Williams, 2005). Agency does not come from "indeterminism," which proposes that events and human actions have no meaningful antecedents and arise for no particular reasons (Williams, 2005, p. 126). Williams (1992, p. 756) states, "There is an intimate relationship, not a dualism, between agents and grounds." Sauvayre (2008), who has written on the dialectical relationship between agency and context, explains that the self as an agent is both apart from and a part of the determining context. Quoting Merleau-Ponty (1966), he writes, "My self and these determining factors are therefore best seen not as separate but as an 'inextricable tangle' (p. 454): a dialectic" (p. 146).

Sauvayre (2008) gives a clinical example to illustrate the point that we cannot shift the direction of our agency without embracing and acknowledging determining contexts that we bring to bear on how we organize experience. He describes a client who moved from France to the U.S. in an attempt to escape his overbearing parents but was unable to extricate himself from his own psychological history to which he once surrendered and against which he was now attempting to rebel. In the U.S., he found relationships that recreated the same dynamics that he was trying to escape. It was only when he acknowledged and accepted the "determining contexts" that have made him who he is that he was able to reconfigure how he construes meaningful relationships in his life going forward (p. 145). He recognized that he could not escape the fact that he had organized his experience all along in ways that influenced his capacity to create new learning; but in recognizing how he had been organizing his experience, he was able agentically to create a new direction for organizing, replacing both his reactionary approach (i.e., where his determining context was influencing his behavior without conscious awareness) and his rebellious approach (i.e., his conscious denial of his determining context, rather than his recognition of his ability to transcend his context as he acted from within it). Our agency is clearly not independent of past learning, but it is not determined by it (in the sense that we generally use that term—as pure automatic necessity) (Williams, 2016, personal communication). When we can make this past learning more conscious, we can gain more control over the ways we can direct our agency in the present.

Contextuality, which provides the knowledge base that becomes interwoven with how we direct our agency, is one key to understanding agency. It does not determine, however, the meanings that we affirm and organize. While recognition of the contextuality of life makes us less judgmental or more empathic to individual and cultural differences, contextuality should not negate the awareness that we live in a moral world where we can direct our agency in many different ways, within any of a number of "determining contexts" (sometimes only with a recognition of what these were, or with spiritual help). Psychological theories that appreciate the role of contextuality as a fundamental reality of our nature sometimes fall into two traps. One is that we cannot escape our determining contexts, which Sauvayre's (2008) example shows is possible, and the other is ethical relativism.

The contextuality of our nature does not mean that everything we affirm and organize from our experience is of equal value (i.e., ethical relativism). Our agency is not completely free, because there are both contexts and consequences for our actions. For this reason, Latter-day Saint scriptures refer to agency as moral agency or in terms of the accountability attached to our being agents (D&C 58:27; 101:78; Christofferson, 2009; Judd, 2005). Research supports a world with moral agency rather than free agency, showing that some values promote positive mental health and harmonious relationships better than other values (Bergin, 1980, 1985, 1991; Doherty, 1995; Richards & Bergin, 2005). For example, addictions, negative thinking, boasting to cover feelings of insecurity, intellectualizing, getting angry, or staying busy to avoid feeling sadness, etc., keep us from growing and can hurt and dampen our relationships. Choosing to work things out in a relationship rather than relying on the "silent treatment" or on "intrusive complaining" *could* reflect valuing growth and courage as opposed to choosing to stay stuck and valuing fear. Our choices, and how we choose, take us in different directions in terms of the personal growth and types of relationships that we can potentially cultivate. Specific to each individual are better ways of creating meaning that will bring greater happiness, meaning in life, and closeness with God.

There are two things to consider. As agents, we are in a dialectical relationship with our social context and embodied condition. And while we have freedom to organize and affirm meaning as we wish in our unique contexts, what we affirm has meaningful consequences and influences what we can affirm in the future. Having agency is an ontological reality: it can never be lost, changed, or stolen from us (Williams, 2005). Williams, however, notes that it is "our freedom, not our agency, that is a fragile thing" (p. 135). How we direct our agency matters.

Morality

What meaning we create or organize from experience determines our possibilities and constraints and our opportunity for long-term joy. Agency operates in "a moral sphere" where truth and falsity are continually before us (Williams, 2005, pp. 114–115; 2 Ne. 2:11–30). To understand agency, therefore, one must see its link to morality (Williams, 2005). Agency is not only about the freedom to choose but also about what we choose. Agency provides us with the opportunity to learn how to discern truthful from nontruthful ways of living (Oaks, 1996) within the tension of abiding universal truth with respect to the individual's situated contextuality.

There are consequences for how we organize and affirm meaning. For example, if I decide to steal money and go to jail, the window of possible meanings available to me to organize suddenly decreases. On the other hand, obtaining an education might open possibilities that I might otherwise not have had. Choosing to have faith in a living God might open up possibilities for affirming new meanings, while experiencing God as harsh and judgmental might limit my ability to receive of God's love. Latter-day Saint and nearly all other Christian doctrines teach that if we direct our agency toward God's truth, it will bring us promised blessings, happiness, and peace

(Christofferson, 2009). Intending to live according to the Savior's example will cause more *possibilities to be open before us,* and our agentic capacity *increases* (Christofferson, 2009). Choosing contrary to this (D&C 88:38; 122:9) binds us because we experience a decrease in both meaningful possibilities and the ability to direct our agency. Williams (2005) explains, "Agency does not consist chiefly in doing or being able to do what we want; rather it consists in doing or being able to do what we should—in living truthfully" (p. 118). For believers, emotional suffering, not due to biological causes, comes when we live in "false" ways either by our own choices or because of the choices of others (Williams, 2005; Warner, 2001).

Because of agency, we can create righteous patterns of thinking, regulating emotion, and behaving (e.g., developing self-regulation skills such as the ability to feel emotion and to choose our reaction to it), and we can recognize how we sometimes affirm and organize meanings that bind us by limiting our freedom and the possibilities for growth (e.g., such as addictions or passive-aggressive behavior). Learning how to direct our agency in wise ways takes effort. The scriptures make numerous references to training our desires and asking for spiritual help to shift our intentions in righteous ways (e.g., Luke 17:5). Therapists can be instrumental in helping clients recognize their intentions (motivations) and patterns of thinking, behaving, and regulating emotion; they can help clients practice directing their agency to create and organize in ways that will bring emotional health and joy into their lives. Sometimes, however, clients need help from therapists to learn how to remove themselves from an agency-limiting, emotionally abusive situation.

The Christian tradition teaches us that God gives humanity its agency that we may overcome fear and motivation for reward to demonstrate instead, through giving up our selfish desires, that we will turn our agency towards loving God; to learn about his ways; and to learn how to love him and to love others as he does. Because he knows that men and women will be in a constant struggle with the desires of the embodied mortal state and they will err many times in the process of learning to love God and others with their whole hearts, God allowed his Only Begotten Son to make his life an offering for men and women to escape the punishment of divine justice (the breaking of spiritual laws) for their sins (Mosiah 3:19).

God the Father and his Son, Jesus Christ, give everything to humanity, hoping for our returned love. They have taught us that this is in our best interest and will allow us to experience the greatest amount of happiness if we learn to love as God loves, because loving in this way embodies a perfect love that surpasses all understanding (Eph. 3:19; Philip. 4:7).

Agency and Our Moral Obligation to God and Each Other

From the Christian tradition, God's plan was to give us our agency, which would allow us to keep and break spiritual laws, and to provide a Savior to pay the consequences for our unwise choices and unintentional errors. For Christians and Latter-day Saints, agency is all about "the other." The kind of charitable love that the Savior gives to humankind, something we have the opportunity to learn to emulate, is a reflection that God's work is all about us. He loves us with his whole heart, and we are here to learn to love him and to love others as he does.

We have been placed in an embodied mortal condition not only to experience our bodies and this earth, but also to be confronted with a relational context. For Christians and Latter-day Saints, this relational context is a classroom for learning how to love like God. We cannot avoid paying attention to our moral indebtedness to each other if we are to maximize the happiness that we can find and not shy away in the false safety of self-focus. Life is challenging because it takes effort to relate to each other in principled ways that take context into account. Loving well cannot be simplified into generalities that either entirely respect someone's agency or, on the other hand, do not take agency into account at all. Relating requires understanding the tension or dialectic between agency and the relational context. If an eight-year-old child, for example, appeared to be drowning in the deep end of a swimming pool, I would feel a moral obligation to jump in and save him, regardless of whether he actually needed the help. I would not waste time wondering if he could swim. If my eight-year-old son, however, wanted help getting dressed, I would encourage him to do this by himself. I would feel a moral obligation to help him learn how to direct his agency toward being increasingly responsible for himself (doing it for him would take away that opportunity). This analogy could be applied to anyone suffering from other serious emotional afflictions, such as a person who has suicidal ideation, where therapists have been trained to make educated determinations about when to jump in the pool and rescue and when to allow someone to sit with painful emotion, imagery, or thoughts.

The Judeo-Christian scriptures provide a handbook of stories on moral decision making in relationships, showing us individuals' and groups' choices, their relational consequences, and God's responses. In the biblical story of the Garden of Eden (Gen. 2:17), Adam and Eve are taught not only that there are consequences for their individual choices, but that they are morally indebted to each other. We see this emphasized in what follows from Eve's partaking of the forbidden fruit. She forces Adam into a choice, to stay alone in the garden or to leave with her so that they can have children together. This story reminds us that we have moral obligations to each other because, through our agency, we necessarily close off the possibility of other choices, which affects our own and others' choices in positive and negative ways.

We are continually engaging in moral decision making about when to act and when to withhold action in relation to ourselves and to others. Sometimes our choices are motivated by moral obligation and concern for others or for ourselves, and at other times we are motivated by selfishness rooted in conscious choice or past wounds. Our psychology must have a theory of human nature that can describe the interrelationship between our accountability for our choices and the moral obligations we have because of our dependence and reliance on each other. In living, we are and we become "the guardians and nurturers of others' agency" (Williams, 2005, p. 137). With this important responsibility, it is incumbent upon us to learn what truth is, or for those from a Judeo-Christian perspective, we might ask, What is God's will for me? What are his rules, and our promises to each other? How do we abide them?

In summary, theorizing from an introspective perspective allows the dialectic between the embodied moral agent and his unique embeddedness in a particular context to come into view. Formal and final causality provides a spiritual grounding that accounts for agency's meaning, creating organizing capacity, which is both determined and open to possibility. It is determined because what is learned is brought to bear on further learning (which is necessary to make knowledge meaningful) and open to possibility because agency can be directed toward different ends simply by holding an intention in mind (which allows for freedom). Oppositional reasoning and an asymmetry in what is chosen demonstrate that not all choices are equally meaningful or desirable. This is necessary for an understanding of agency and its link to morality.

Placing agency at the center of our psychological theorizing about our nature allows us to acknowledge the spiritual and biological complexity of our embodied, contextual situatedness. We can embrace both spiritual and natural assumptions to understand this complexity, and in doing so we can better understand that emotional suffering can occur because of how we direct our agency, because of biological illness, because of interpersonal dynamics in the relational context, or because of some combination of difficulties in all these areas. A more complex understanding of our nature is revealed when theorizing from an introspective perspective, which allows us to realize that we must use a different set of assumptions from naturalistic assumptions to describe the mental aspects of our eternal nature. From this viewpoint, describing us as moral agents in dialectical relationship with our own embodied, mortal situatedness provides a better and more accurate way to capture the complexity of our eternal and mortal natures and inform psychotherapy treatment.

How an Agentic Model Informs Psychotherapy Treatment

The holistic model presented in this chapter brings clarity to the complex roles that the spiritual and mortal aspects of our nature can play in emotional suffering and mental-health-related concerns. It attempts to capture the tension between our moral agency and our embodied relational contextuality and, in so doing, shifts the work of therapy and gives therapists a clearer model for addressing the different concerns that clients bring to therapy. Approaches based on models grounded in naturalistic assumptions have tended to view therapists as value neutral and clients as having "values." Postmodern approaches, which have reacted against naturalism, slip into relativism with the overvaluing of the client's uniquely culture-bound reality. In addition, while many therapists currently address spiritual, emotional, cognitive, behavioral, and relational problems, there is confusion about how these different aspects are grounded, and there is a lack of clarity in their relationship to each other.

The holistic model presented here makes us aware that therapist and client not only *are valuing*, but also *have values*. When viewing therapist and client as both valuing and having values, the valuing aspect reflects an appreciation for our client's capacity to direct his or her agency, which is often neglected when we focus only on client values (what the active agent creates in dialectical relationship with his or her situated embodied condition). With the framework of the relational embodied moral agent in mind, the therapist can instead focus on addressing in therapy how the client practices directing his or her agency in his or her mortal context while at the same time exploring the ends to which agency is directed (the values being created). Many clinical issues that are not the result of biology or social forces—even if these aspects are involved—are related to how clients direct their agency. While an initial assessment is needed to rule out or address the role of both biologically based mental health concerns (such as schizophrenia or endogenous depression) and relational difficulties related specifically to the client's social context (such as racism or group shaming), the work of therapy will most often be focused on how the client directs his or her agency within his or her embodied situated contextuality.

Some of the work of therapy might include: exploring how a client directs his or her agency; encouraging a client to practice directing his or her agency toward particular ends; helping a client learn about the ends to which his or her agency is directed (both in a mortal and spiritual context); helping a client observe the consequences of his or her choices as he or she practices directing his or her agency toward different ends; exploring patterned organizations of meanings that are both healthy and defensive; helping a client explore past ways of organizing experience and its effects on present ways of organizing his or her experience; helping a client experience repressed emotion, modulate "too much" emotional expression, and learn to better integrate emotion with the organizing of meaning both past and future (i.e., emotion regulation skills); addressing spiritual issues when exploring how a client directs his or her agency (e.g., the development of faith, hope, or character); helping a client explore the interaction between agency and context (i.e., learning how to behave depending on specific relationships and contexts in the client's life; working with agency directed toward imagined realities; working with agency directed toward spiritual realities); and helping the client deal with biologically caused emotional suffering or suffering due to how others direct their agency.

Therapists need not abandon the important insights of current therapy approaches, but they must be careful in how they apply them. For example, when using cognitive behavioral therapy techniques, therapists should be careful not to tell clients how to change their core beliefs. While the idea of a core belief fits well with the idea of patterned meaning intended for an end, both imposing the therapist's idea of what a client's core belief is on clients or dictating how a client's beliefs needs to change could limit his or her agency. Instead, the therapist must patiently and humbly explore client material and ask questions that can help clients organize their own experience and take their own pathway in understanding how they have organized their experience in the past, how they will organize their experience going forward, and the reasons for doing so. Respecting client agency means that the therapy process moves more slowly, but because clients' agency is being respected, they can make changes because they are motivated and understand why the changes are being made. In my experience, change is more lasting, and often the therapist is surprised by the direction that clients take. This could not happen if the therapist is quick to impose his or her way of organizing experience on the client. Working with a consideration of the agency of the client is consistent with what writers such as Richards and Bergin (2005) address when they advocate for an explicit minimizing approach to the sharing of therapist values in psychotherapy and caution therapists against imposing their values on clients explicitly or implicitly.

Using the holistic model presented here, once an assessment has clarified the contribution of biology, social forces, and how agency is directed to presenting concerns, therapists begin a process of allowing the client to lead and to bring forth their "stories." Exploration (using basic counseling techniques such as reflection, empathy, and summarizing) and understanding the client's current and past relational and social context is very important so that the therapist does not prematurely intervene and accidently take away the client's agency through making assumptions about the client's experience, or through imposing his or her own way of organizing on the client, or through sharing information that the client is not prepared or ready to hear. A few cues that I check to make sure I am respecting my client's agency and that I am engaging in successful exploration of his or her cognitions include observations about whether or not my client is opening up, sharing more, relaxing, becoming less defensive, and often expressing emotions. Successful emotional exploration should lead to the experience of relief in the client (McCullough et al., 2001).

An agentic perspective creates a spiritual and healing relational context. By modeling a high ethical standard of profound respect for a client's agency by listening and understanding without expecting or needing something from the other, the therapist can offer a very healing experience to clients who have often had their agency limited or distorted. It also creates a space for defensively avoided emotions to be expressed and experienced. This leads to a reorganization of past learning and creates the potential for new learning. The focus of therapy is changed from one where value conflicts arise and the therapist can sometimes take an evaluative role into one in which the therapist is collaborating with clients to help them learn how to better direct their agency. Such a therapeutic environment is crucial for opening clients up to more meaningful experience and to truthful relationships, not only with others, but also with God. A therapist with this holistic perspective, for example, can help clients who feel that God or a faith community has limited their agency to see how family dynamics might be projected onto God and onto faith communities.

When therapists can align with their clients' view of reality, they can facilitate a therapy process focused on helping clients learn more about how they organize experience in their unique mortal conditions and to what ends. There are three aspects to aligning with the client's view of reality and avoiding value conflicts. These are the client's truth (how he or she sees reality), the therapist's response to the client's truth, and the role of the therapist's truth (how he or she sees reality).

The Client's Truth. From an agentic perspective, what the therapist thinks is not irrelevant, but it is not the focus. Rather the focus is on what the client thinks and values, how the client is organizing experience, and how the client has organized experience in the past. Clients feel safe when their therapist truly wants to know and to understand what they value and how they value, and when the therapist celebrates differences and is not threatened by them, even if he or she believes or values something different.

The Therapist's Response to the Client's Truth. The therapist aligns with the client's perspective for the purpose of helping the client learn how to better direct his or her agency, which may include sometimes limiting client agency to help him or her redirect it (e.g., a tangential or overly talkative client or a client who is withdrawn, afraid to be vulnerable, or needing structure). Generally speaking, clients come to therapy with a lot of pain around having had their agency and ability to create restricted or limited in some context in their past or in the present; however, in some families a client was given so much freedom to direct his or her agency that there were no boundaries or no opportunities for him or her to feel shame for behavior that hurt others. It is in these situations that the therapist, with the client's consent, will limit the client's agency to teach the client how to better direct his or her agency with positive consequences in the client's relationships. The therapist's simple observations about how clients organize their experience provides a mirror for clients so they can see their unique patterns of thinking, behaving, regulating emotion, and relating, and to what ends. Defenses are more easily bypassed as the therapist and client work together to help the client change. The client can see that the therapist is on "his or her team" and is continually there to help, guide, and share knowledge when it is asked for, or when an offer to do so is accepted.

The Therapist's Truth. Therapists acknowledge their own inner reactions to their client, but rather than focus on anxiety about potential value conflicts, they instead refocus on the client, using their own subjectivity as a tool to help their client better understand him- or herself. This is something most therapists are trained to do, especially those trained to work with transference and countertransference. The therapist can comment on the client's experience (e.g., "Every time I share something, I notice that you yawn," or "I noticed that you seemed to reject the empathy I gave you," or "I keep yawning, and I wonder if what we are talking about is serving some other purpose"). Therapists are working with clients not to convert clients to their values but to help clients look at how they are valuing, and in the process of valuing how they are creating values; they are helping their clients observe how they pattern and organize experience and to what ends. This approach increases awareness in the client and gives the client new ideas about how to direct his or her agency. Therapists can share information from research or clinical and personal experience when appropriate (see Bergin, 1980, 1985, 1991; Doherty, 1995; Richards & Bergin, 2005). How they use and share their knowledge, however, is informed by an appreciation of needing to respect the client's agency (Hansen and Richards, 2012) and helping the client practice wisely directing his or her agency.

Conclusion

The holistic perspective presented here clarifies responsibility in the therapy relationship. Some psychotherapists, especially less-experienced ones, tend to feel overly responsible for their clients' behavior. They engage more readily in value conflicts, while others, who have slipped into ethical relativism fully wanting to respect their clients' agency, don't recognize the role that they are playing in influencing their clients (Richards & Bergin, 2005). Making agency central to our theorizing makes responsibility clearer. The therapist can explicitly and carefully influence how a client directs his or her agency but cannot make a client act in a particular way. I believe, for example, I would have some responsibility for a client's divorce if my validating his or her anger encouraged his or her divorce. Understanding our agentic nature, however, means that the therapist can always put choice and responsibility back in the client's hands by stating, "I notice that you are pulling for me to validate your anger by becoming defensive when I don't validate it, but when I do so you are leaning towards getting divorced. Is that the direction you want to keep going? Or, could we talk about this pattern you are in?" When the counselor can explain why he or she is intervening and how, clients gains control over their agency and they can better disagree with or guide the counselor in helping them. The counselor and client can become co-workers on the client's problem rather than getting into value conflicts or trying to avoid values by endorsing an ethical relativism.

A holistic approach to clients' psychological nature allows therapists to address the complex causes of emotional suffering (i.e., biological, relational, and spiritual) and provides a framework for the therapeutic work. Not only can the therapist ask questions about how agency is directed, about emotions, cognition (patterned meaning), behavior, biology, and context, but he or she can also ask psychological questions about spiritual matters. For example, what are the spiritual laws, which, if kept, will bring the greatest emotional well-being and happiness? What is the psychological toll for transgressing a spiritual law? What if two spiritual laws are in conflict? How should a person choose? How do emotional problems get in the way of adhering to spiritual laws? How does God use our emotional suffering and woundedness to help others and us?

A different way of thinking is needed in psychology to understand the complexity of our spiritual and temporal nature, one that addresses the eternal and mortal conditions of our nature and their dialectical relationship. From the holistic perspective described here, a theoretical framework that places the moral agent at the center of theorizing and accounts for our embodied, embedded, situated nature, changes how we view the therapeutic endeavor and adds new insights to the work.

References

Bergin, A. E. (1980). Psychotherapy and religious values. *Journal of Consulting and Clinical Psychology, 48*(1), 95–105.

Bergin, A. E. (1985). Proposed values for guiding and evaluating counseling and psychotherapy. *Counseling and Values, 29*, 99–116.

Bergin, A. E. (1991). Values and religious issues in psychotherapy and mental health. *The American Psychologist, 46*(4), 394–403.

Bruner, J. (1990). *Acts of Meaning.* Cambridge Press: Boston.

Christofferson, D. T. (2009, June). Moral agency. *Ensign.*

Doherty, W. J. (1995). *Soul searching: Why psychotherapy must promote moral responsibility.* New York: Basic Books.

Frie, Roger. (2008). The situated nature of psychological agency. In R. Frie (Ed.), *Psychological agency: Theory, practice and culture* (pp. 1–32). Cambridge, MA: MIT Press.

Hansen, K. L., & Richards, P. S. (2012). Ethics of respecting a client's agency and values in treatment: Perspectives from a theistic spiritual view of counseling. *Counseling and Spirituality, 31*(1), 75–93.

Judd, D. K. (2005). Moral Agency. In A. P. Jackson, L. Fischer, & D. Dant (Eds.), *Turning Freud upside down: Gospel perspectives on psychotherapy's fundamental problems* (pp. 98–115).

Martin, J. (2008). Perspectival selves and agents: Agency within sociality. In R. Frie (Ed.). *Psychological agency: Theory, practice and culture* (pp. 97–116). Cambridge, MA: MIT Press.

McCullough, L., Kuhn, N., Andrews, S., Kaplan, A., Wolf, J., & Hurley, C. L. (2003). *Treating affect phobia: A manual for short-term dynamic psychotherapy.* New York: The Guildford Press.

Merleau-Ponty, M. (1966). *Phenomenology and perception.* Trans. C. Smith. London: Routledge and Kegan Paul.

Miller, L. (2015). *The spiritual child.* New York: St. Martin's Press.

Nairne, J. S., Pusen, C., & Widner, R. L., Jr. (1985). Representation of the mental lexicon: Implications for theories of the generation effect. *Memory and Cognition, 13,* 183–191.

Oaks, D. H. (1996, October). Sins and mistakes. *Ensign,* 62–67.

Richards, P. S., & Bergin, A. E. (2005). *A spiritual strategy for counseling and psychotherapy* (2d ed.). Washington, DC: American Psychological Association.

Rychlak, J. F. (1991). *Artificial intelligence and human reason: A teleological critique.* New York: Columbia University Press.

Rychlak, J. F. (1994). *Logical learning theory.* Lincoln: University of Nebraska Press.

Rychlak, J. F. (1997). *In defense of human consciousness.* Washington DC: American Psychological Association.

Sauvayre, P. (2008). Agency as fluid process: Clinical and theoretical considerations. In R. Frie (Ed.). *Psychological agency: Theory, practice, and culture* (pp. 137–153). Cambridge, MA: MIT Press.

Seligman, M. E. P. (2002). *Authentic happiness: Using the new positive psychology to realize your potential for lasting fulfillment.* New York: Free Press.

Slife, B. D. & Reber, J. S. (2005). Comparing the practical implications of secular and Christian truth in psychotherapy. In A. P. Jackson, L. Fischer, & D. Dant (Eds.), *Turning Freud upside down: Gospel perspectives on psychotherapy's fundamental problems* (pp. 160–182). Provo, UT: Brigham Young University Press.

Slife, B. D. & Reber, J. S. (2009). Is there a pervasive implicit bias against theism in psychology? *Journal of Theoretical and Philosophical Psychology, 29*(2), 63.

Slife, B. D. & Williams, R. N. (1995). *What's behind the research? Discovering hidden assumptions in the behavioral sciences.* Thousand Oaks, CA: Sage Publications.

Stern, D. N. (1985). *The interpersonal world of the infant: A view from psychoanalysis and developmental psychology.* New York: Basic Books.

Sugarman, J. (2008). Understanding persons as relational agents: The philosophy of John MacMurray and its implications for psychology. In R. Frie (Ed.), *Psychological agency: theory, practice, and culture* (pp. 73–94). Cambridge, MA: MIT Press.

Warner, C. T. (2001). *Bonds that make us free: Healing our relationships, coming to ourselves.* Salt Lake City, UT: Shadow Mountain.
Williams, R. N. (1992). The human context of agency. *The American Psychologist, 47,* 752–760.
Williams, R. N. (2002). On being for the other: Freedom as investiture. In E. E. Gantt, & R. N. Williams (Eds.), *Psychology for the other: Levinas, ethics and the practice of psychology* (pp. 143–159). Pittsburgh: Duquesne University Press.
Williams, R. N. (2005). Agency: Philosophical and spiritual foundations for applied psychology. In A. P. Jackson, L. Fischer, & D. Dant (Eds.), *Turning Freud upside down: Gospel perspectives on psychotherapy's fundamental problems* (pp. 116–142). Provo, UT: Brigham Young University Press.

Robert L. Gleave

Justice

THE FOUNDATION OF FORGIVENESS

There are those who, by disposition or experience, already have an adequate sense of a personal claim to justice. For them, the needed emphasis is on moving beyond justice to mercy. There are others who, by disposition or experience, have a tendency to erase themselves and to allow themselves to be victimized rather than to claim personal justice. For them, the needed emphasis is on finding the firm foundation of a personal justice claim from which to forgive. This chapter is addressed to this latter group of our friends (brothers and sisters) and to those who want to help them.

Many authors have written about the need for forgiveness (Warner, 1995, 2001; Ferrell, 2004). I want to state from the outset that I support the majority of what they have written. However, I find that these authors have largely overlooked a small but significant and growing portion of the population who do not possess a needed prerequisite to engage the forgiveness processes they describe.

A Philosophical Problem

This oversight, I believe, results from cultural biases toward modernistic assumptions as well as artifacts of the "veil of forgetfulness," which is ubiquitous in the mortal condition. When we mortals attempt to address one topic or another, we tend to separate that topic from other related topics in order to provide a more detailed (atomistic) analysis of the separate parts (reductionism), the assumption being that a "deeper" understanding of the specifics is *the* way to add clarity and additional completeness to our understanding. Therefore, mainstream writers address forgiveness as a stand-alone concept in a discrete and linear time frame. From within this framework, they have done good and valuable work (figure 1).

Figure 1

Other authors have written about the value of justice and its place in relationships (Sherman et al., 2005) with the same stand-alone limitations and deficits (figure 2). Each set of authors recognizes the proximity of the other concept but discounts it in favor of advocacy for their own. The result is an exchange that ignores common ground and interrelatedness.

Figure 2

Attending to justice alone makes the potential errors of holding onto grudges, wasting energy that could be more productively used elsewhere, developing a bitter disposition, or other similar trapping consequences. On the other hand, attending to forgiveness alone makes the potential errors of discounting the personal hurt and damage caused, exhibiting helplessness and passivity, accepting excessive responsibility, or other similar discounting consequences.

It is my purpose to describe a relationship between forgiveness and justice that assumes they are so interrelated that it is impossible to speak adequately of one without the other. I additionally propose to step beyond the veil of forgetfulness, where I find it self-evident that these concepts are eternally and inextricably bound together, and also bound to the Savior (the white strand in figure 3) in an ongoing relatedness, which of necessity transcends the boundaries of mortal conceptions of time.

Figure 3

A Missing Piece

My goal for this chapter is the same goal I perceive in the writings of many others, which is to help people remove themselves from a position of being victimized. I want to help people move into a position where they are "captain of their own ship" and able to act unilaterally for their own best interest. I agree with the growing evidence that forgiveness allows one to abandon the quest for one's own rescue at the hands of another. It also allows one to disengage competitive exchanges regarding who is to blame and, therefore, who is required to offer restitution and recompense. Souls no longer need to be imprisoned, waiting for the offender to gain sufficient insight, strength, and compassion to enable him or her to offer a healing response to the offended.

Commonly articulated arguments and processes are sufficient to inspire and guide the majority of people to this relieving position. I will call attention to a foundational principle that underlies the ability of this majority to take advantage of the mainstream forgiveness processes. Then I will highlight a minority—but growing—population who do not have that ability. Without this foundational ability, these people find the common descriptions of the forgiveness process incomprehensible and inaccessible. I will also attempt to articulate a process by which one might assist this growing minority to move along the path toward forgiveness and the rich rewards that follow. Additionally, there may be some who, while currently able to find a measure of forgiveness, might still benefit from the exposition presented here.

The foundational principle of which I speak is the individual assertion of a justice claim following an offense. I argue that the personal strength required to take independent action as well as the resulting ability to generate compassion and forgiveness are born in the assertion of a justice claim.

First, it is important to note that there are many consequences of being the recipient of an assault, abuse, or offense of some kind. There are those who have, in the process of being offended (at times in severe or chronic circumstances), had their natural processes of living interrupted (e.g., the ability to make a justice claim). The willingness of an offender to take assaultive action without regard for the resulting damage or the pain that others suffer is an assault as well upon the offended person's value as a human being, his or her integrity as an independent self, and his or her value in an eternal sense. Whether as a result of such intense experiences or a dispositional sensitivity, there are those who turn all (or at least most) responsibility inward and lack the ability to hold an outward source (offender) responsible for losses and pain.

Helplessness and Guilt

An examination of the feelings of helplessness that sometimes follow offenses will help us discover a mechanism by which such deficits can occur. Helplessness, or feeling out of control, is an emotion that we as human beings dislike intensely. It is one of the emotions that are most noxious to us and one that we try to avoid most strenuously. We would prefer almost any other emotion over helplessness. It is a natural human reaction, then, to search frantically to find ways to escape from feelings of helplessness after an assault. We want to directly affect the events or the "outcome." We begin to imagine that had we done something differently—if we had simply chosen not to go to that place or if we had said something differently or if we had left the situation more quickly—the outcome would have been different. All of these responses provide a temporary sense of empowerment. We desperately want, and so we generate, a belief that we are in control, that we would have been able to create a different outcome "if only . . . ." The effect is an immediate although short-term reduction of the sense of helplessness.

Still, the implication is usually not lost on us that if we could have, or should have, done something differently—in other words, if we did have power or ability to change the events and we didn't—then we are in some measure guilty or responsible for the event. However, we prefer feeling temporarily empowered, even though we may also feel guilty. Guilt is an emotion with which we are usually more comfortable. It is an emotion that is familiar, one that makes sense in our day-to-day lives, one around which we know how to arrange the rest of our lives. People can, and at times do, embrace guilt continuously, much preferring that experience to even a few moments of intense helplessness. Paradoxically, using guilt to mask helplessness leaves a false sense of well-being that impedes attempts to correct the original disruption, resulting in generalized and longer term helplessness.

Additionally, offenders, whose interest it is to avoid guilt, often reinforce this pattern of turning helplessness into excessive guilt in those they assault by forcefully denying responsibility while simultaneously powerfully asserting that the responsibility lies with the assaulted. Sometimes family systems that are characterized by defensiveness and guilt avoidance can push the guilt onto vulnerable family members. Recipients of such misplaced and yet readily accepted guilt can develop a habit of being overly quick to see their own errors and to accept excessive responsibility for disruptions in relationships generally. Such people grow accustomed to believing all types of offending messages and to internalizing a "one down" position. In such a state of mind, these people may come to believe that conflict in a relationship is their fault universally and unilaterally; therefore, conflict is seen as further evidence of failure and inadequacy. As a result, the victims can develop a generalized avoidance of conflict and "walk on eggshells" in almost all relationships. They begin to believe that anger or strong self-expression of any kind threatens to disrupt relationships. The victims then have a single option: to withdraw from open relationships where feelings are spoken clearly. Ultimately, they are left with only conflict-avoidant relationships that perpetuate the blaming/abusive style.

Offender's Paradigm

One of the more severe psychological effects of being abused is becoming trapped in a paradigm or worldview that has been pounded into a person in the process of assault and victimization. This paradigm has only two positions—offender and victim. All choosing and concept construction flows from the offender to the victim, whose only role is to satisfy the offender, no matter the victim's personal cost. I call this worldview the offender's paradigm since it is generated by the offender and imposed on victims. Victims often internalize the discounting messages the offender sends and construct a lifestyle that is consistent with having little worth or no claim on reciprocity in relationships. The victim begins to also "believe" other related messages such as discomfort is a crisis, conflict destroys relationships, and personal expression reaps rejection.

For victims, this style can lead to a containment of anger with no appropriate outlets; the anger can get old and rotten and then occasionally explode under pressure. These anger explosions often use the name "justice" or "fairness," but they don't originate in either of those concepts and are, in fact, counterfeits. These outbursts become dominating offenses in their own right and victimize those toward whom the explosions are directed. This perpetuates the pattern, and they become momentarily assaultive themselves—returning quickly to feelings of little worth. One purpose of this chapter is to offer an alternative, proactive way to respond to offense that can restore confidence, autonomy, and independent action.

Self-Interest

Before moving on to the specifics of what I will suggest, I will introduce an additional idea that I believe is foundational and counter to the paradigm the offender inflicts on his or her victim. Consider the primal statement about man and his objectives and purposes in 2 Nephi of the Book of Mormon: "Men are, that they might have joy" (2:25). The LDS Church's teachings are crystal clear on this point—our highest goal and foremost priority is to have joy (reach the celestial kingdom and return and live with our Father in Heaven). This is a "self-interested" individual goal that must be pursued first for ourselves and then afterward for others. If we truly value agency, we won't advocate others taking a larger stake in our own salvation than we do. Nor will we advocate that we take a larger stake in their salvation than they do.[1]

It is important here to differentiate between my use of the word *self-interest* and the word *selfish.* For my purposes here, *selfish* is defined as considering only proximate concerns and responding to current impulses. *Self-interest* is defined as prioritizing choices based on long-term desires and advantages. I suggest that establishing the pursuit of one's own best interest as a foundational principle would do much to counter the offender's paradigm. The selfish message offenders send to their victims is that their own short term comfort, their own absence of upset, their own immediate physical satisfactions, etc., are far more important than any deeply felt pain and long term losses of their victims.

An antithetical thought that seems to bring significant power and relief to victims is that each individual has the opportunity, even responsibility, to seek his or her own best interest as the primary

1. The attention to reparative self-interest in this context belongs to the "Spirit" (Moses 6:60) paradigm (Gleave, 2013). I assert that hedonism/altruism are—along with justice/mercy, female/male, etc.—eternally in relation to each other (to mention one is to the bring the other into the conversation) and with the Savior (see figure 3).

motivation in his or her life. One must be careful with this idea. The offender cannot claim vindication because he or she was just seeking his or her "own best interest," and the victim cannot claim a right to retaliation and vengeance as a pursuit of his or her "own best interest." Such interaction clearly has a proximate focus, is contentious, and is obviously in no one's best interest in the long run. Productive expression of seeking one's *self-interest* requires interactive negotiation (dialogue) in a context of mutual respect and compassion.

Making a Justice Claim

One can recover from the helplessness, and thereby escape from the offender's paradigm, by making a justice claim. Luke 17:3 describes the process very well: "Take heed to yourselves: If thy brother trespass against thee, rebuke him; and if he repent, forgive him." Too often we believe the commandment reads only that if we have been offended, forgive. Notice that in the Luke passage, there is significant and time-consuming work to be done prior to the end goal of forgiveness. It is not possible to go directly from the offense to forgiveness. When we try to do so, we find that we cease to hold the offender accountable for the error and return to helplessness and the offender's paradigm. The effect, then, is to essentially erase ourselves—which is capitulation and not forgiveness.

The internal dialogue often consists of phrases such as, "It's okay," "It doesn't matter," "No harm done," and other expressions that discount the significance of the suffering the offended endured. It is as though the offended is saying, "What you did doesn't matter because my pain doesn't matter, and my pain doesn't matter because I don't matter." Asserting a justice claim is one way to assert one's place or value in the universe. One might even ask, "How do we know that we are important without such a justice claim?"

The commandment to forgive is always given to the person who is offended. Since it is not possible to forgive someone for something that they did not do, the very first step of the forgiveness process is to assign responsibility. Assigning responsibility requires an offended person to decide who it was that caused the pain and losses, what was done that was harmful or hurtful, and how he or she was harmed (including depth, breadth, and duration) by the actions of the offender. This assignment of responsibility is the very beginning of the forgiveness process and cannot be skipped.

This rebuke spoken of in Luke can be done regardless of whether or not there is an exchange between the parties. Sometimes sufferers don't become aware of offenses until after a person has died. At other times, they may not begin to make a justice claim until many years after the fact, when they've lost track of the location of the offender. In some cases, they may make several attempts to receive a satisfactory response only to be met repeatedly with strong resistance and even further offense. The critical part of the rebuke is that the individuals who are offended be very clear about who the offender was, what the offense was, and how they were harmed by the offense.

However, if there is a desire for improvement in a current or ongoing relationship, then the rebuke is best done face-to-face, where the victim can openly express the hurt that he or she received and gently hold the offender responsible. In an ongoing relationship, we can expect that a rebuke will lead to an awareness of and sorrow for the offense on the part of the offender. A soulful outcry that is received with compassion by the offender can validate and legitimize the significance of the offense so that the offended might more readily reject the messages of worthlessness that resulted from the offense. The repentant response of the offender is part of and significantly contributes to a deepening in the relationship.

Notice in the passage in Luke that repentance is a condition for forgiveness: "and *if* he repent, forgive him" (17:3, emphasis added). If a person accepts the responsibility that the person who has been hurt assigns, if he or she acknowledges that his or her action has hurt the offended party and expresses deep regret and sorrow for the suffering he or she has caused—to the extent that he or she is willing to make reparative efforts and change his or her life so that such offenses do not occur again to this person or to anyone else—then moving on and letting go—in short, forgiveness—can occur with relative ease. Since we all make errors, it is relatively easy to allow others to move past their offenses toward us after they accept responsibility, validate our hurt and suffering, make up losses to the degree possible, and make the change to move in a different direction.

Justice demands this work of repentance prior to the offering of forgiveness. Yet such interactions are not always so responsive. One is left to ask, Can I really forgive if the offender is not repentant? What if the person refuses to do the required work or denies responsibility for the hurt that they have caused? The offender may express disdain for the offended and not care at all about the impact of sorrow and loss felt by that person, offering no recompense. What if no attempt whatsoever is made to make changes? Can one still forgive? I assert that it is impossible to forgive at this point without returning to the previous problem—the offended feeling that his or her pain does not matter, and erasing themselves. There must be a response to the pain that has been caused; the person who has been hurt must have an immutable claim (Gleave & Belisle, 2003). The outcry of the sorrow and suffering is significant and eternal and cannot be swept aside by the offender's unwillingness to acknowledge it.

Justice

Forgiveness in these cases cannot be offered directly. Another mechanism must be employed. Doctrine and Covenants 64:10–11 tells us what course we can pursue. We read verse 10 often, but we don't read verse 11 often enough. Verse 10 says, "I, the Lord, will forgive whom I will forgive, but of you it is required to forgive all men." This verse, when standing alone, is often misinterpreted to mean that we must set aside our hurt and personal suffering as of no consequence in the service of providing relief and rescue to the offender. Must we forgive even when the person is not repentant, dismissing ourselves in the process and denying the immutable outcry of one who has been harmed?

Verse 11 gives us an answer by telling us how to forgive when we do not receive a repentant response: "And ye ought to say in your hearts—let God judge between me and thee, and reward thee according to thy deeds." The invitation here is to take your dilemma to the Lord and express your awareness of who the offender was, what the offense was, and how you were harmed by the offense. Let him know of your dilemma, that you know and clearly see the nature of the offense, and that you can't get a repentant response. Acknowledge your attempts to make the rebuke, whether done directly or whether there were circumstances that made it impossible or unhelpful to do so directly. Ask the Lord to put this offense on the list for this person for judgment day. Acknowledge your need to be responded to and to receive a repentant response from the offender or to receive an awareness of his or her punishment for the offense.

This ability to assign deficits or error to another is one of the very processes that are undermined during intense and ongoing assaults. At times much effort must be spent on this step, specifically to break the pattern of turning helplessness into guilt and to begin to more clearly see the nature of the offense. Part of this time might necessarily be spent in reestablishing the pursuit of one's own best interest, which is also a frequent casualty of intense or chronic offense. With the reestablishment of a sense of self-care and with the ability to assign responsibility to others, one can begin the process of rebuke.

We are asked to let the Lord know that we would like to forgive this person as soon as he or she repents. We can ask him to forgive the person quickly when he or she acknowledges our pain and makes attempts to change his or her life, but we can also ask that if the offender doesn't repent, that their feet be held to the fire, so to speak. Some form of punishment is required so they understand that the suffering they inflicted was significant and that it matters. The Lord then can agree that he loves us to the point that he will accept this responsibility from us and that he, as Mediator, will take on our worry and concern about this particular event. He has a wonderful memory, and he will not forget. He counts our pain as significant. He also loves the offender and sees it as in the offender's best interest to be presented with the consequences of his or her actions. He will assure that the person either makes a repentant response or receives justified punishment.

In Doctrine and Covenants 121:1–25, we find a description of this process. Following a soulful outcry, the Lord is clear with Joseph Smith that he will take on his cause and respond in his own way and in his own time. With this assurance, Joseph could act unilaterally and confidently to forgive in the present circumstance. Former victims can also believe the Lord and trust that he will handle offending events appropriately—that the right amount of forgiveness will be offered and that the right amount of punishment will be meted out. They too can say, "Lord, if thou wilt take that for me, I will put it into thy hands and I will go on with my life."

Notice in this response that there is a preservation of the inherent value and worth of each soul. The outcry of an injured individual carries immense weight and is responded to without being diminished in any way. One can proceed forward without any feeling of being devalued, dismissed, or erased. The pain was significant, but a compassionate, eternal response allows the sufferer to let go of the proximate burden. The offering of forgiveness at that point is from a position of strength, not a position of helplessness. It is not an abdication of the legitimacy of the justice claim but rather a confident gift of charity from one who has been eternally validated and wishes to proactively offer benevolence and goodwill.

I believe that it is the misunderstanding of the nature of forgiveness that contributes much toward feelings of helplessness. Not knowing how to make this kind of justice claim can leave us with few options in the face of chronic offenses or overpowering abuses. When we do not see the option of making a justice claim, the inevitability of helplessness looms large, and it is an understandable turn that we often make toward the guilt and illusion of control spoken of earlier.

Outcry

Once conceptual structures are in place, an efficient way to begin the process of helping clients make a justice claim is to first encourage them to allow the feeling of helplessness to be part of the offense. The beginning of the rebuke process is to experience the depth of the pain, sorrow, discounting, devaluing, etc., that the offense caused. It is in allowing these deeply felt emotions that the beginning of an outcry is formed. The groaning of a suffering soul rumbles deeply and profoundly and rises until the yearnings of an eternal soul are put into words and clarifying constructs as the voice carries an outcry to the heavens about the damage, sorrow, and loss that have been experienced. Whether this process takes moments, hours, days, or years, it is essential that the deep stirrings of an eternal soul speak to the heavens about its losses and sufferings.

This honest, open, and free expression of the pain of the soul is extremely helpful in clarifying the role of each party. Not only is the role of the offender clarified but so is the role of the sufferer, in that he or she is also able to acknowledge any personal contribution to the situation. In the heartfelt outcry, there is no need for one or the other party to bear full responsibility in an all or nothing way. Should the offended find that some element of self-correction is needed, it does not diminish the offense, and neither does the clarity with which the other's offense is seen override or eliminate personal responsibility. One does not simply become the pawn of the offender by identifying the actions of the offender as hurtful. The offended can still maintain autonomy and recognize personal choices in the matter, but recognizing those choices does not mitigate the offender's choices and wrongdoing.

As an example, suppose you leave your keys in an unlocked car and someone then steals the car. It is clear that the person who stole the car made choices worthy of being arrested and punished by the legal system. While you can acknowledge your behavior as being unwise and take steps to correct future incidents, you are not subject to arrest or prosecution under the law. The deep outcry of the soul allows for this kind of clarity and assigning of responsibility.

One of many emotions that can come as part of this kind of clarity and assigning of responsibility is anger. Anger is a very important emotion. I believe a loving Father expects us to use our assertive anger to bring us the clarity and energy of soul required to overcome obstacles that block our progress. It is important for me to not be misunderstood here. The anger I refer to must be differentiated as a feeling, not as an expression or behavior. I use the word *anger* here to validate the internal experience of emotion that some self-define as anger—the setting of clear personal boundaries that one will not allow others to cross without a self-validating response of rejection and outcry.

Some may be more comfortable with assertiveness as a label for the self-defined feelings of anger. However, it is essential to include, and not stifle, the feelings of anger inherent in a soulful outcry. Joseph Smith wrote an exceptional outcry, following the Saints being driven from the state of Missouri, as recorded in Doctrine and Covenants 123. Notice that, while not advocating angry actions or anything that might be seen as aggressive, he uses strong language as fueled by angry feelings. It is very clear that his response could never be described as passive or dismissive.

The reality is that uncaring offenders can overpower and overrun boundaries, but an assertive response can always follow—fueled by angry feelings. With the energy of this anger, we can firmly resolve, with sufficient emotion to aid our memory, that we will not back away from our justice claim. It is in this outcry—this holding responsible, this deeply heartfelt emotional response—that we can find the value and benefit of a justice claim.

Purposes and Benefits of a Justice Claim

I would like to be clear that such a justice claim has no bearing whatsoever on the events that will occur in the future or on the environment, which may or may not change. The purpose for advocating the justice claim here is purely personal and for the offended's benefit; it is to provide an option other than helplessness in the face of being assaulted; it is a relationship between a person and the Lord that may or may not make a difference in the observable world. Thieves may go unpunished. Molesters may never be confronted in this life. Unfair business practices may never come to light in this world. However, those who suffer at the hands of those who have done such acts need not remain helpless. Moving beyond helplessness does not necessarily mean that the world will understand who is "right," because a justice claim is not intended to set public opinion in one direction or another. No punitive action can be justified on the basis of a justice claim; a justice claim provides perspective, understanding, and grounding only. It cannot be used as rationale for retaliation or vengeance, for taking a larger share of the goods available in life, or for diminishing a responsibility or required effort.

The benefits of a justice claim to an individual, however, are manifold and priceless. Standing firmly on the foundation of a justice claim, we need not diminish ourselves. We need not be excessively self-critical. We can see our own errors in perspective and also rejoice in our righteous choices, even in the face of strong opposition. We need not jump to the conclusion that we have no value just because we have been defined as being without value by another. We can tenaciously assert our own value and be confident that the self matters, that the pain we experienced matters—not more than another's but as much as another's. We can make the offensive event a singular one and not a definitional one. Rather than shrink and retire from public view and social interaction, we can move on to further confident interactions, no longer excessively fearful of future offenses. Our sense of self can become grounded in eternal principle.

Through a justice claim, we feel deeply connected to, indebted to, and loved by the Savior. He becomes the rock upon which we build. "Building upon the rock" is an active process; the energy of a soulful outcry anchors our house to the rock with a firm attachment. We can know wherein our strength lies and the ultimate triumph of the Savior's judgment and love. The resulting confidence and energy—and sense of ability to impact our own future—creates a context from which ongoing righteous action can continue in the face of the experienced assault. With this kind of clarity of thought, we do not need to distract from the pain caused by the injury. We do not need to hide from the implications of possible unworthiness. Rather, we can move forward with optimism, purpose, and benevolence. We have reason to maintain grounding in having value and loving ourselves, which then opens possibilities of loving "thy neighbour as thyself" (Gal. 5:14).

Forgiveness

Forgiveness also is an active process—one that requires significant strength of soul. To forgive is not to submit to the will, actions, or definitions of an offender but rather to actively reject the offender's assertions. It is a powerful statement of commitment that says the offended will not allow the incident to create significant interruptions in his or her chosen goals and course of life. It demands awareness that the sum of existence is greater than the current circumstance and that the offended has the available resources necessary to move forward with purpose, confidence, and hope. That movement toward the future may be more complicated or difficult as a result of the offense, but the offended will "come off conqueror" (D&C 10:5).

Forgiveness from this mindset is offered as a free gift to the self, the offender, and the Savior. It is an active manifestation of a soul that wants to take up part of the Savior's cross and bring significant benevolence into the world. Such forgiveness frees the soul to offer love toward enemies and metabolize the poisons of this mortal world. Offering healing in the face of harm and light in a darkened situation can be counted a blessed opportunity to contribute to self, others, and the divine. In short, as others have written, forgiveness is an active gift.

Conclusion

From this grounded position of a justice claim followed by forgiveness, one can enter interpersonal interactions from a vastly different perspective. One no longer expects a response from the other to restore functioning or losses. The losses are swallowed up in the hope of the Savior. The reason for interaction is to move forward, to make the future more agreeable and full of more benevolence, and to enhance relationships. Giving up the demand for the other party to set things right removes major obstacles in any conflict negotiation process. Unilateral movement toward peace and the absorption of loss and damage are possible in the service of better ongoing relations. One no longer needs to drain one's energy by dwelling on the past, but knowing what one wants for the future can be the reason for decision making. Interpersonal interaction that has no expectation to restore the past but has only a desire to move toward more satisfying relationships in the future has a much better chance for success.

This exposition has been long and detailed to give a foundation for helping people for whom this process is not yet complete or automatic. With practice or training, the suggested response to offenses can be made early and quickly and may involve lower levels of emotion than those described here.

I once more assert that the personal strength required to take independent action, as well as the resulting ability to generate compassion and forgiveness, are born in the assertion of a justice claim. When either is overemphasized at the expense of the other, or when the necessity of the relationship between them is ignored, the result cannot be optimal.

The powerful Old Testament story of Abigail, who represents a type of the Savior as she mediates between David and her husband, Nabal, has no meaning and would never have been written had David not drawn his sword in a righteous justice claim (1 Sam. 25:13; Ferrell, 2004). We can be equally assured that the story would not have been included had David not used the strength of his justice claim to forgive.

References

Ferrell, J. L. (2004). *The peacegiver: How Christ offers to heal our hearts and homes.* Salt Lake City, UT: Deseret Book.

Gleave, Robert L. (2013). Paradigms. In *Common ground, different opinions: Latter-day Saints and contemporary issues.* White, J. F., & Faulconer, J. E., Eds. Draper, Utah: Greg Kofford Books.

Gleave, R. L., & Belisle, R. H. (2003). The mediator: Justice and mercy as a type for bringing unity out of conflict. *Journal of the Association of Mormon Counselors and Psychotherapists, 28,* 67–72.

Sherman, L. W., Strang, H., Angel, C., Woods, D., Barnes, G. C., Bennett, S., & Inkpen, N. (2005). Effects of face-to-face restorative justice on victims of crime in four randomized, controlled trials. *Journal of Experimental Criminology, 1*(3), 367–395.

Warner, C. T. (1995). *Bonds of anguish, bonds of love.* Salt Lake City, UT: The Arbinger Company.

Warner, C. T. (2001). *Bonds that make us free: Healing our relationships, coming to ourselves.* Salt Lake City, UT: Shadow Mountain.

AARON P. JACKSON

Truth and Values in Counseling

BEYOND POSITIVISM, RELATIVISM, VALUES CLASHES, AND CRYPTO-PROSELYTIZING

Applied psychology has always been plagued by the question of its morality. For most of its history, the profession has tried to avoid this question by framing psychotherapy as an objective endeavor aimed at improving health. It has avoided questions about what is "good" or "true" and has focused on questions of what is "empirically supported" and "healthy." And while empirical evidence is useful and health is a laudable goal, it has become increasingly obvious that objectivity is impossible and that psychotherapy is about more than just improving health (Fowers, 2005). In this chapter, I will try to directly address the question of psychology's morality and hopefully deepen the conversation about truth and values in psychotherapy.

Periodically, issues arise in professional psychology that bring the question of what is good or true or valuable to the fore. These tend to be hot-button social issues like abortion or sexual orientation (see Mintz et al., 2009). While these issues highlight values clashes in psychotherapy and bring brief attention to the moral nature of psychotherapy, they do not seem to sufficiently illuminate the fact that all psychotherapeutic interactions involve some degree of values conflict (see Richardson, Fowers, & Guignon, 1999). It seems to me that the very premise of psychotherapy is a values conflict of sorts; a situation in which, by definition, we have two people with different and, to some degree, competing values. Clients come to psychotherapy because they don't know what is best to do, or how best to be, and hope the counselor will be able to help them determine what is best. The counselor has a theory or philosophy that he or she applies to the presenting problems. This theory or philosophy is, at some level of abstraction, a set of values—a set of assumptions about what is good or true. So, therapy is a contest, or at least a confluence, of the counselor's values and those of the client—an attempt to come to a new and better truth for the sake of the client.

Truth and Values

Truth is almost a taboo construct in psychology. As Slife and Reber (2005) pointed out in the initial volume of this series, discussions of truth—or any constructs that hint of goodness or badness, rightness or wrongness—are religiously avoided in mainstream psychology. Interestingly, psychology is much more comfortable with the term "value," despite the fact that the terms are fairly synonymous.

The *Dictionary of Psychology* defines a value as "a moral, social, or aesthetic principle accepted by an individual or society as a guide to what is good, desirable, or important" (VandenBos, 2015, p. 1129). The Merriam-Webster Dictionary defines truth as a "belief; a statement of belief, a creed" (Truth, n.d.).

A comparison of these definitions suggests that truth and value are roughly parallel terms that are getting at the same notion—the idea that human beings hold ideas and assumptions that they believe are good (i.e., valuable or true). For example, a cognitive therapist might value rational thought. The truth or value is that rational cognitions are better than irrational cognitions. Psychodynamic therapists value insight—a truth or value in this approach. Tjeltveit (1999) summarizes this notion: "Any therapeutic goal held by therapists, clients, or third parties (e.g., insurance companies or government funding sources) represents a commitment (implicit or explicit, limited or extensive) to some value(s) and some working ethical theory" (p. 6). In other words, all theoretical notions are also ethical and moral notions.

Human values (truths) vary from the rather mundane (e.g., valuing natural foods over processed foods) to the divisive (e.g., valuing sexual abstinence outside of marriage). In either case, however, one is asserting a good. One either thinks it is better (truer, more valuable) to abstain from sex outside of marriage, or one doesn't. Psychotherapists sometimes couch their values in terms of health, or functioning, or flourishing. However, these are purely semantic differences. To say that clients should think more rationally, or be more insightful, or be more congruent because to do so is functional or healthy, is no different than saying it is better, or truer, or more valuable. Accordingly, I will use the terms value and truth and good somewhat interchangeably—in part, to break down the artificial distinctions among these terms.

Positivism and Relativism

Avoidance of the question of truth in psychology is based in two seemingly different philosophical camps, positivism and relativism. I will argue that while these are putatively opposing perspectives on truth, they are similar in that they both essentially preclude any sincere dialogue about values and truth. One might argue that they preclude any sincere dialogue at all. That is because both positivism and relativism propose that truth can be known only from certain privileged positions.

Positivism. Historically, psychology tried to pattern itself after the positivistic/objectivistic model of traditional nonhuman sciences. This model proposes that scientists and practitioners can be objective and value-neutral. It proposes that science (or the scientific method) can transcend values and questions of good and evil and be simply pragmatic or utilitarian—as if those weren't values in themselves. Positivism "recognize[es] only observable phenomena and empirically verifiable scientific facts and laws, and reject[s] inquiry into ultimate causes or origins as belonging to outmoded metaphysical or theological stages of thought" (Positivism, n.d.). In other words, positivism privileges certain kinds of experience and certain kinds of knowledge as more valuable and more true than other kinds of experience and knowledge. Ironically, it assumes an "ultimate" or universal truth that transcends interpretation. The truthfulness or value of knowledge is dependent on its adherence to the assumptions and values inherent in the traditional (i.e. positivistic) scientific method.

Critics of positivism have called many of its assumptions into question—including the assumption that one can transcend values. While a comprehensive review of these critiques is beyond the scope of this chapter, I will touch on some major points. Positivism doesn't really allow for the notion of values or truths as most people think of them. From a positivistic perspective, values are really based in more fundamental "desires" (Appiah, 2006, p. 21) or instincts or responses (in the Skinnerian sense). That is, people prefer things or believe they are valuable or true because of *real* things (in the positivistic sense) such as brain structures, drives, neurotransmitters, and reinforcement histories. The notion that people have values and some moral agency to determine those values is simply epiphenomenal from the positivistic perspective. Accordingly, positivism doesn't really allow for pluralism—because it necessitates either a universalism or (ironically) a solipsistic relativism. You have only two ways to understand truth within a positivistic perspective. Either there are fundamental, universal realities that are true and everything that varies from them is a distortion, or there are fundamentally different *individual* truths that are determined by the underlying realities (e.g., brain structures, reinforcement contingencies, cultural norms) and are therefore unknowable across those realities. The universalistic perspective allows for only a singular truth—a universal set of values. The individualistic positivistic perspective privileges the underlying realities but allows that they might be relative to a person's particular context. However, because each of us is bound up in a particular context, we can't really understand or relate across these different contexts—a particular form of relativism sometimes called solipsism.

Very few psychotherapists would say they subscribe to a purely universalistic perspective on values. Such a perspective would set the psychologist up as a guru of *the* true set of values—a seemingly objective helper who is in fact proselytizing a particular perspective (Meehl, 1959). Universalism would also imply that only one approach to psychotherapy can be true (or most true and therefore most helpful). Some approaches to psychotherapy, especially those that espouse a traditional positivistic paradigm, do seem to establish a singular, unitary dogma that can be applied across contexts. Such approaches, true to their roots, have a formula, or set of principles—in other words, a fundamental universal truth that leads to better psychological health. However, devout positivists would balk at the notion that such principles are in fact values. Nonetheless, that is what I contend they are. And I believe in order to become more ethical as a profession, we must begin to identify them as such.

Relativism. Psychotherapists in general seem much more comfortable with relativistic perspectives on values than with universalistic perspectives. Relativism is "a name given to theories or doctrines that truth, morality, etc., are relative to situations and are not absolute" (Relativism, n.d.). From both the positivist/universalist/objectivist perspective and the relativistic perspective, the question of truths or values becomes somewhat moot. For the objectivists, it is moot because truth has been circumscribed to include only one kind of knowledge—that purports to come from a valueless source. For the relativists, the question of truth is moot because any perspective is as valuable or truthful as another. In the social sciences, the term values has been used rather than truth—because it is easier to talk about values being relative than it is to talk about truth being relative. However, the difference is purely semantic. Relativists, whether they use the term truth or value, believe that the definitive source of what is good is the individual.

Recently, scholars from several quarters have called into question the assumptions of relativism (Appiah, 2006; Haraway, 1988; Mintz et al., 2009). They suggest that relativism has some of the same inherent problems as positivism. A major problem for relativists is their positing the source of truth in the individual. Granted, some relativistic perspectives argue that truth is socially constructed and essentially a process of consensus. But even most consensual models grant that the individual is the fundamental reality and that communal or cultural values are based in collections of those individual perspectives (see Gergen, 2009).

Ultimately, as was discussed above, a fundamental problem for relativists is one of privilege. The question is, what privileges one to know the truth or to establish a value as legitimate or good? For positivists, the privilege is given to a certain kind of knowledge or a certain way of knowing. For most relativists, the privilege is given to each individual (Haraway, 1988). Each individual is entitled to be the source and legitimizer of their own truth or good. Accordingly, no one can challenge the values or truth of another and no one can really understand the truth or values of another, unless they are willing to adopt the other person's perspective and give up their own. This individualistic version of relativism essentially precludes the possibility of interpersonal knowledge or genuine empathy. It gives up on the question of values clashes—other than to suggest that people can persuade each other to adopt their position and hope for consensus. As with positivism, it doesn't really allow for pluralism in any meaningful sense. While it does allow for multiple perspectives, it does not provide a way to understand how diverse perspectives can be reconciled or appreciated. Nor does it provide a means for diverse perspectives to coexist—other than under threat of being subsumed or annihilated (see Gergen, 2009).

Values in Psychotherapy

While applied psychology has generally ignored the issue of values in counseling, religious psychologists have had a particularly vested interest in advancing our thinking on these issues. Religious psychotherapists, particularly LDS psychotherapists, typically have a worldview in which truth and values are very salient. For LDS psychotherapists, one question might be, How do I reconcile my religious beliefs with my professional beliefs? Another question might be, How do, and how should, my values play out in my counseling practice? The former question has been, and will continue to be, the focus of the *Turning Freud Upside Down* series. The latter question, the question of how values are a part of psychotherapy, is another focus of this chapter.

Despite the articulated value of "improv[ing] the condition of individuals, organizations, and society," the American Psychological Association is rather mute on the question of truths and values that would lead to such improvement (APA, 2002, preamble). While the APA Ethics Code does articulate some values, such as justice and respect for autonomy, it does not provide a comprehensive guide as to what ought to be valued by psychologists. This is likely due to the diversity of opinions among psychologists about what should be valued in psychotherapy and related professional work. However, the fact that professional organizations are reluctant to articulate values does not mean that values are somehow avoidable or insignificant in actual clinical practice. All approaches to psychotherapy are based in a set of values—whether they are articulated or not (Slife, Smith, & Burchfield, 2003). At a superficial level, we can see that some psychotherapists place a high value on the reduction of symptoms as defined by the client. Others value the acquisition of insights. Still others value the improvement of relationships or other social systems. Even at this level we can see that the values inherent in various theories may be at odds with one another. For example, if I primarily value symptom reduction I might encourage a client to get out of a marriage relationship that seems to exacerbate symptoms and be painful to the client. On the other hand, if I primarily value commitment and stability in relationships, I might encourage the client to stay in the relationship—despite the risk of some symptoms.

As we deepen the level at which we analyze psychotherapists' assumptions and the values inherent in them (sometimes called an *axiological* analysis), the starkness of these values clashes becomes more apparent. If we use the above example, the therapist who is valuing symptom reduction may have a more basic value of hedonism—the notion that pain *should* be minimized and pleasure *should* be maximized (see Gantt, 2005). At this level, the idea that symptoms should be reduced is not just a desirable option, but it becomes a moral imperative. It becomes *the good* toward which the psychotherapist and client are working. The therapist who values relationships and thinks that committed relationships should be maintained may value fidelity or commitment. That is, the therapist may believe that fidelity or commitment in relationships should be maintained even if it results in less pleasure or some pain for one or both partners. We begin to see that therapists' values—as informed by philosophy and theory—can be radically different and can lead to radically different interventions. However, many psychotherapists try to take comfort in the notion that they can somehow avoid having their values impact the client. Both the empirical and philosophical literature argue against the idea that the psychotherapist's values can somehow be bracketed, suspended, or otherwise transcend the psychotherapeutic encounter. I will briefly review the empirical and philosophical literature before continuing to discuss how to address dilemmas raised by the unavoidable presence of values in psychotherapy.

The empirical literature on values in psychotherapy demonstrates the need for greater attention to the issue of values. A review of this literature—from Rosenthal's (1955) classic studies, through Beutler's (1979, 1981) studies of values convergence, to the work of Kelly and Strupp (1992)—shows two important empirical findings (see Kelly, 1990; Slife et al., 2003; Tjeltveit, 1986). First, psychotherapists' and clients' values tend to converge over the course of therapy. That is, they tend to become more similar in what they value as therapy progresses. As you might imagine, clients' values tend to shift much more toward those of the therapist than vice versa. Second, therapists tend to evaluate client improvement in terms of how much clients' values become like their own. In other words, successful psychotherapy is defined, to some degree, as the client "converting" (Tjeltveit, 1986, p. 516) to the therapist's values. Meehl's (1959) anticipation of this phenomenon led him to coin the term "crypto-missionaries" (p. 257) in describing how therapists might be seen to be covertly proselytizing their clients toward a particular set of values. Though this literature has defined and measured values in many different ways, in general "all sorts of values seem to be important to perceived client improvement—professional values, moral values, and in many studies religious values" (Slife et al., 2003, p. 63).

The research on values in psychotherapy highlights the importance of psychotherapists better understanding their values. If clients adopt a set of values, or modify their existing values, as part of the change process in therapy, then we as a discipline have a profound ethical responsibility to insure that the values inherent in our therapy models, as well as the values of psychotherapists themselves, are viable for our diverse clientele and ultimately good for our society. Likewise, if the change process in therapy involves clients adopting the values of their therapists, we have a responsibility to develop the philosophical sophistication that will enable us to examine our values in light of professional standards and to develop a psychotherapeutic values system that is internally coherent and valid in communities in which we practice.

Gospel Perspectives on Truth and Values

Although the empirical research clearly establishes the value-laden nature of psychotherapy, most ethical and theoretical writings in psychology seem to have skirted the issue of values by appealing to positivism and its corollary objective models or some form of relativism (Anderson, 2007; Slife et al., 2003). The objectivist stance is that one can take a position independent of one's values. The relativist position is that any position is legitimate because each individual has a right to his or her own legitimate values. There are clearly problems with both of these stances from both a philosophical perspective and from the perspective of the restored gospel.

Objectivism. Objectivism is "the belief that certain things (esp. moral truths) exist independently of human knowledge or perception of them" (Objectivism, n.d.). Accordingly, objectivism requires that there be one true set of universal values or truths. At first blush this seems attractive to many Latter-day Saints and other religious individuals. The notion that there is an objective truth "out there" that we are trying to access seems consistent with a God who is "the same yesterday, today, and forever" (Morm. 9:9). However, a closer look at truth in the restored gospel helps to highlight the inherent shortcomings of an objectivist perspective on truth and values. First, it is clear that while God is in fact "the same yesterday, today, and forever" (2 Ne. 29:9), gospel truths are, to some degree at least, contextual (see D&C 93:30). That is, they seem to vary somewhat depending on the situation. Perhaps the most poignant example of this in LDS theology is the practice of polygamy. The Lord states that, in general, polygamy is "abominable before me" (Jacob 2:24). However, he also grants that "if I will . . . raise up seed unto me, I will command my people [to live polygamy], otherwise they shall hearken unto these things [i.e. the prohibition on polygamy]" (Jacob 2:30). It seems clear that practicing polygamy can be true in certain contexts but is generally false. A similar example is when Christ encourages his disciples to gather grain on the Sabbath (Mark 2:23–28). While some would suggest that he is merely appealing to a higher objective law—a better explanation may be that the truth of "keeping the sabbath day holy" is contextual rather than objective and universal.

Describing truths as contextual may make some believers nervous. They may confuse contextual truth with relativistic truth. Many faithful people quickly reject the notion of relativism because they recognize that it dismisses the notion of general truths—such as the existence of God and the reality of enduring commandments and revelations. The following section will attempt to distinguish relativism from contextualism.

Relativism vs. Contextualism. The challenge that emerges from the examples outlined above is that seeing polygamy or Sabbath observance as contextual truths can easily be confused with being relativistic. Understanding the distinction between contextualism (as I will use the term) and relativism requires a finer analysis of relativism and its corollary assumptions. Generally, when we talk about relativism we are talking about individual relativism. That is, we are saying that "truth" for a given individual at a given time is relative to that individual. This notion has even made its way into our clinical conversations. Psychotherapists may encourage a client to "be true to himself" or suggest that "only she can know what is best for her." Such statements may reflect a value of individual relativism. In this form of relativism, the individual is the ontological reality and the ultimate source of truth. One key difference between relativism and contextualism, as I use the terms, is the ontological assumptions in each. Relativism assumes an individual ontology, whereas contextualism relies on a relational ontology—a primary assumption that relationships are the fundamental reality (see Gergen, 2009). I will expand on the notion of relationism a bit more below.

While many religious people reject relativism because of its antitheistic implications, others reject relativism for its philosophical and social inadequacies. For example, postmodern feminists (see Haraway, 1988; Haraway, 1990) and others (Appiah, 2006) have criticized relativism for perpetuating privileged perspectives that undermine genuine dialogue and democracy. Ironically, relativists in their response to the authoritarian implications of objectivism have established their own privileged system that, like objectivism, marginalizes all other views besides the privileged one. Appiah (2006) has summed up the problem nicely: "People often recommend relativism because they think it will lead to tolerance. But if we cannot learn from one another what is right to think and feel and do, then conversation between us will be pointless. Relativism of that sort isn't a way to encourage conversations; it's just a reason to fall silent" (p. 31).

Psychotherapists, particularly religious psychotherapists, have the same dilemma. If they are objectivists, then they subscribe to a set of universal rules that they in turn impart to their clients. This too sets the stage for irreconcilable value conflicts in psychotherapy. Basically, the client would be expected to adopt the psychotherapists' values for therapy to be successful. This again suggests that psychotherapy is really crypto-proselytizing or, from an LDS perspective, priestcraft (2 Ne. 26:29). On the other hand, if psychotherapists take a relativistic position, then they would have to abandon the notion of all values except that of relativism. That is, in order to adopt a truly relativistic perspective, relativism has to be one's only value. One would have to adopt an ontology that is ultimately individualistic and solipsistic. Such a perspective not only undermines the premises of religious faith, but it also undermines the entire premise of psychotherapy—that there is something valuable or true in dialogue. And, as Appiah (2006) noted above, relativism implies that "conversations between us will be pointless" and is ultimately only a "reason to fall silent" (p. 31). It appears to me that religious psychotherapists encounter what they perceive to be a dichotomy between crypto-proselytizing and falling silent about the value clashes and the questions of truth they encounter in psychotherapy. I believe that a relational contextual perspective allows for a less polarizing alternative.

A primary distinction between relativism and contextualism centers on the issue of dialogue. Relativism posits that truth is found in the individual (or in an individual culture). Contextualism allows for truth to be found in conversations, in dialogue, and in relationships. I suggest that this is the inherent value in psychotherapy. It is a context in which clients and counselors come together to determine truth. If counselors are not in the business of coming to truth with their clients—learning "what is right to think and feel and do" (Appiah, 2006, p. 31)—then it's hard for me to imagine what purpose the counseling enterprise has at all. On the other hand, if psychotherapy is focused on helping clients know "what is right to think and feel and do," then psychotherapists may need to radically reconceptualize their understanding of values and how they are a part of psychotherapy.

Beyond Objectivism and Relativism

As discussed above, there are multiple problems with both relativistic and objective paradigms, in terms of their abilities to provide a meaningful understanding of how values are a part of psychotherapy. According to most definitions of values, objectivism and relativism are themselves value stances. Furthermore, they epitomize the privileged notion that a perspective is justified simply by its position or status (see Haraway, 1990). Objectivists assert power based in being above values and biases. The implied argument of objectivism is that by transcending values it establishes itself as the ultimate authority. Relativists assert power in their individuality and thereby avoid responsibility to others. Importantly, then, these philosophies inevitably leave those with value differences either in a power struggle or at a solipsistic impasse in the question of which values are most tenable. Within an objectivist philosophy, when there is a clash of values, the most powerful entity's value will "win" simply because of the power differential. Likewise, in a relativist philosophy, any individual's perspective is *de facto* a privileged one (i.e., immune from critique) because all perspectives are equal. So, appealing to objective models or relativism really does little to help address the issue of values in counseling—they each inhibit dialogue in their own way. Instead, psychotherapists will need to explore and articulate philosophical perspectives that provide alternatives to traditional objectivist or relativistic philosophies. Religious psychotherapists in particular, with their inherent interest in truth and values, should be at the forefront of understanding and defining ethical means to address the reality that values are inherent in the psychotherapeutic process.

Though a comprehensive review of alternatives to objectivism and relativism is beyond the scope of this chapter, ideas from a few postmodern philosophies that hold particular promise will be discussed.

Cosmopolitanism. Appiah's (2006) philosophy of cosmopolitanism is a recent attempt to go beyond positivistic and relativistic models. He proposes that most cultures share a set of universal values. However, his universalism is nonpositivistic in that it does not assume that such values are transcendent or inherent. "Cosmopolitans suppose that all cultures have enough overlap in their vocabulary of values to begin a conversation. But they don't suppose, like some universalists, that we could all come to agreement if we only had the same vocabulary" (Appiah, 2006, p. 57).

Appiah proposed three beliefs that undergird this benign universalism. The first is "that every human being has obligations to every other. Everybody matters" (p. 144). Second is a commitment to pluralism. "Cosmopolitans think that there are many values worth living by and that you cannot live by all of them" (p. 144). The third belief is fallibilism, "the sense that our knowledge is imperfect, provisional, subject to revision" (p. 144). Cosmopolitanism also assumes that the values that are not shared can be understood and appreciated where they come into conflict. This capacity for genuine empathy is inherent in the relational philosophy implied by Appiah's other propositions.

Postmodern Feminism. The ideas of postmodern feminist philosophers such as Donna Haraway are particularly relevant to the discussion of values regarding diversity in counseling. Pointing out the problems and biases inherent in both the objectivist and relativist positions, Haraway (1988, 1990) proposed an alternative epistemology in which the knower is not absolved by an appeal to either universal values or individual ones. She and others have argued that there is no privileged perspective from which one can know or see values. Instead "our epistemic situation as characterized by a permanent plurality of perspectives, none of which can claim objectivity—that is transcendence of situatedness" (Anderson, 2007, p. 2). In other words, feminist postmodernism

> rejects both objectivism and relativism for the ways they let knowers escape responsibility for the representations they construct. To claim objectivity for a representation is to claim that "the world made me represent things this way." To claim relativism is to claim that "my identity (my situation) made me represent things this way." (Anderson, 2007, p. 3)

In the feminist postmodern alternative, our values—personal or professional—are never final or fixed, nor can they escape critical dialogue. We are each situated or located in a value-laden context that is inextricably intertwined with others and their contexts. Accordingly, values and other types of knowing are always under construction—never knowable in any absolute or complete sense. At the same time, these inextricable connections allow us to come to some social agreements—or disagreements—about what we value. Individuals, cultures, and groups can construct values that are responsible to each other and viable across relationships, cultures, and groups. We are always left with a certain amount of tentativeness and humility in these constructions—given our incomplete and ever-evolving understanding. Anderson (2007), summarizing postmodern feminist philosophy, makes two recommendations that flow from this perspective. First, one must accept responsibility by acknowledging the situatedness involved in the construction of one's representations (e.g., values). Second, responsible practice in one's approach to values involves adopting an attitude of "world traveling" or "mobile positioning"—trying to see the world from many other perspectives (p. 2).

Hermeneutic Interpretation. A third attempt at an alternative to objectivism and relativism can be found in the hermeneutic tradition. Hermeneutic philosophy assumes that dialogue is fundamental and that we are "dialogical selves" (Richardson et al., 1999, p. 263). Hermeneutic interpretation is based in dialogue that "aims at reaching a shared agreement about the truth of what is being discussed—not a merging of subjectivities but a 'fusion of horizons'" (Richardson et al., 1999, p. 251). So, the truth is neither an external objectivity nor an individual relativity. Rather, it is found in the interfaces between us as we engage in sincere dialogue. Accordingly, truth and values are radically contextual. Gadamer (2004) argued that human biases are inherent and inescapable. However, he also argued that one's historicity and biases are inextricably part of the process of coming to truth. In response to objectivists, he said that "a person who does not admit that he is dominated by prejudices will fail to see what manifests itself by their light" (Gadamer, 2004, p. 354). So, open engagement with others, or dialogue, is key to the process of refining our biases and merging our horizons.

Gadamer (2004) described the art of hermeneutic dialogue as follows.

> What characterizes a dialogue . . . is precisely this: that in dialogue spoken language—in the process of question and answer, giving and taking, talking at cross purposes and seeing each other's point—performs the communication of meaning that, with respect to the written tradition, is the task of hermeneutics. (p. 361)

Gadamer (2004) proposed that this process leads us to truth—via hermeneutic interpretation. "What emerges in its truth is the logos, which is neither mine nor yours and hence so far transcends the interlocutors' subjective opinions that even the person leading the conversation knows that he does not know" (p. 361).

Levinas's Ethical Ontology. A final perspective, the relational philosophy of Kelly Oliver (2001)—her interpretation of Immanuel Levinas's writings—has profound implications for addressing the diversity of values in counseling practice. One of Oliver's fundamental proposals is that knowledge—particularly knowledge about others and ourselves—is based in a relational ontology rather than an individual one. In other words, she proposed that the fundamental reality and the source of knowledge and understanding are in relationships—as opposed to in one's mind, as is commonly assumed in Western philosophies. She argued that the shift, from seeing oneself as an individual who must be recognized to seeing oneself as a member of a dyad, group, or community, is a key in avoiding the inevitably antagonistic nature of individualistic ontologies. In other words, if we are able to see ourselves as responsible to others, and others as inextricable aspects of ourselves, we will be able to reconcile, or at least appreciate, the value differences we encounter.

Oliver (2001) suggested, "Only if we imagine ourselves forever cut off from others and the world around us do we need to create elaborate schemes for bridging the gap. We create an impossible problem for ourselves by presuming to be separated in the first place" (p. 12). She further outlined the tenets of her philosophy. "If we are selves, subjects, and have subjectivity and agency by virtue of our dialogic relationships with others, then we are not opposed to others. We *are* by virtue of others" (p. 18, emphasis added). The implications of her philosophy for practice—particularly for the task of addressing value differences—are straightforward. Specifically, she proposed two applications of her ideas. First, she suggested witnessing as a means to understanding and truth. She suggested that the process of witnessing—telling one's story—is the means by which people can come together and reconcile seeming differences. Second, she argued that an ethic of love is essential in order for relational learning and growth to take place. Quoting Hooks, she stated, "Without an ethic of love shaping the direction of our political vision and our radical aspiration, we are often seduced, in one way or the other, into continued allegiance to systems of domination—imperialism, sexism, racism, classism" (as cited in Oliver, 2001, p. 218). One implication of Oliver's work is that individualism (and its corollaries of positivism and relativism) inevitably leads to and perpetuates these dangerous "isms."

A Hybrid Philosophy

Distilling from the above-mentioned ideas, we can generate several common themes. These might serve as a foundation for a counseling philosophy that avoids both universalism and relativism. First is the suggestion of an alternative ontology—a relational ontology. This is a more radical notion than it may seem on the surface. A radical relationism implies that we are not fundamentally individual selves. Rather, our self—our *subjectivity*, as philosophers call it—is secondary to our relationships (see Gergen, 2009; Levinas, 2002). As Levinas (2002) argues, the fundamental reality, prior to all others, is our ethical and moral obligation to others. This ontology has implications for other aspects of the philosophy. If truth and values are not found in our individual minds but rather in our relationships, then the importance of dialogue is elevated. We can come to know truth and construct values only in dialogue. Likewise, a relational ontology requires a radically different way of viewing others. Rather than seeing ourselves and others as independent beings whom we either love or not, we must consider our fundamental obligation and connection to others—as part of everything we do and are. The primal reality then is my obligation to the other (or others)—and what I will do about it. Love not only becomes a part of our theorizing and our practice—it becomes a necessary part. Love becomes the inherent question in every human interaction. By requiring love in our philosophy, we allow for a genuine pluralism. By considering our inescapable and obligated connection to others, we are able to appreciate and value others and their perspectives on truth in a qualitatively different way than is possible in individualistic philosophies. Accordingly, pluralism becomes a genuine possibility.

These four interrelated concepts—relationism, dialogue, love, and pluralism—provide a basis for a radically different philosophy of psychotherapy. It redefines what might be seen as the outcomes of psychotherapy. Rather than focusing primarily on symptoms, the client's engagement in relationships and their depth and quality become the barometers of health—or, more accurately, the barometers of the degree to which the client is living truthfully. Likewise, a client's capacity to engage a pluralistic world with love and tolerance could be seen as appropriate and desired outcomes. Symptom relief would typically accompany such outcomes. There is ample research to suggest that meaningful relationships and accepting attitudes are related to fewer physical symptoms (Cohen, 2004; Frech & Williams, 2007; Holt-Lunstad, Smith, & Layton, 2010; Kiecolt-Glaser & Newton, 2001; Uchino, Caciopo, & Kiecolt-Glaser, 1996).

Relational Perspectives and the Restored Gospel. My reading of the restored gospel finds consistency with the themes mentioned above. For example, consider Nephi's dialogue with the Spirit in 1 Nephi 11:11. Nephi characterizes this dialogue as one where "one man speaketh with another." Initially, Nephi wanted to see the things his father dreamed (v. 3). The Spirit grants that request but goes on to deepen the conversation, repeating a previous query, "What desirest thou?" (vv. 3, 10). Nephi then asks about the interpretation of the dream (v. 11). As the conversation continues to deepen, the Spirit asks Nephi to "look" at him. Nephi "looked as if to look upon him" and "saw him not; for he had gone from before [Nephi's] presence" (1 Ne. 11:12). Nephi then sees Mary and the context of the Savior's birth. An angel then appears and asks Nephi, "Knowest thou the condescension of God?" (v. 16). Nephi replies that he does not, other than his knowledge that "[God] loveth his children" (v. 17). The angel then proceeds to show Nephi the Savior's birth, life, and death—and their relation to Lehi's dream. This remarkable vision is described in chapters 12–14 of 1 Nephi.

It is interesting to consider the process of the dialogue. Nephi's initial query to see his father's dream becomes a deeper query about its meaning—and ultimately a window to an apocalyptic vision. Through the process of dialogue and in the context of this relationship, the participants come to truths far beyond those anticipated in the initial question. This process is similar to what Gadamer (2004) describes as hermeneutic interpretation. Nephi's vision is really a vision within a vision. That is, his conversation with the Spirit becomes a means to him seeing the vision. In this case, Nephi is able to see the "condescension of God" by literally looking through the personage of the Spirit. In contrast to Western notions of ideas coming to one's individual mind, Nephi is only able to see the truth by looking through the Other—in this case the Spirit. The message for the reader seems to be that revelations come in conversations in which we see through (or with) the other. In this case that is literally true.

The relational approach also allows for important Christian values such as moral agency and altruism, without requiring adherence to any particular religious belief. Rather than trying to maintain different philosophical positions for their personal, religious, and professional lives—psychotherapists could potentially reconcile their values to be consistent across their various identities. A relational perspective also provides a significantly stronger philosophical foundation for the act of psychotherapy—the loving engagement of another in dialogue, in service of truthful living. A relational philosophy argues that relationships are fundamental to all aspects of human beings. Indeed, there is no such thing as a human being independent of relationships. So, relationships, such as the counseling relationship, are not just one of many means for helping clients define themselves and their values; they are the fundamental and primary means for doing so. From a relational perspective, intervening at a relational level (psychotherapy) isn't just a way to help people: it is a true way to help people.

References

American Psychological Association. (2002). *Ethical principles of psychologists and code of conduct.* Retrieved from http://www.apa.org/ethics/code/index.aspx.

Anderson, E. (2007). Feminist epistemology and philosophy of science. In E. N. Zalta (Ed.), *The Stanford encyclopedia of philosophy, Spring 2007.* Retrieved March 28, 2007, from http://plato.stanford.edu/archives/spr2007/entries/feminism-epistemology/.

Appiah, K. A. (2006). *Cosmopolitanism: Ethics in a world of strangers.* New York: Norton.

Beutler, L. E. (1979). Values, beliefs, religion and the persuasive influence of psychotherapy. *Psychotherapy: Theory, Research, and Practice, 16*(4), 432–440.

Beutler, L. E. (1981). Convergence in counseling and psychotherapy: A current look. *Clinical Psychology Review, 1*(1), 79–101.

Cohen, S. (2004). Social relationships and health. *The American Psychologist, 59*(8), 676–684. doi:10.1037/0003-066X.59.8.676.

Fowers, B. J. (2005). *Virtue and psychology: Pursuing excellence in ordinary practices.* Washington, DC: American Psychological Association.

Frech, A., & Williams, K. (2007). Depression and the psychological benefits of entering marriage. *Journal of Health and Social Behavior, 48*, 149–163.

Gadamer, H. G. (2004). *Truth and method* (2nd ed.). New York: Continuum.

Gantt, E. E. (2005). Hedonism, suffering, and redemption. In A. Jackson & L. Fischer (Eds.), *Turning Freud upside down: Gospel perspectives on psychotherapy's fundamental problems* (pp. 52–79). Provo, UT: Brigham Young University Press.

Gergen, K. J. (2009). *Relational being: Beyond self and community.* New York: Oxford University Press.

Haraway, D. (1988). Situated knowledges: The science question in feminism and the privilege of partial perspective. *Feminist Studies, 14*(3), 575–599.

Haraway, D. (1990). A manifesto for cyborgs: Science, technology, and socialist feminism in the 1980s. In L. J. Nicholson (Ed.), *Feminism/postmodernism* (pp. 190–233). New York: Routledge.

Holt-Lunstad, J., Smith T. B., & Layton J. B. (2010). Social relationships and mortality risk: A meta-analytic review. *PLOS Medicine, 7*(7), 1–21. doi:10.1371/journal.pmed.1000316.

Kelly, T. A. (1990). The role of values in psychotherapy: A critical review of process and outcome effects. *Clinical Psychology Review, 10*(2), 171–186.

Kiecolt-Glaser, J. K., & Newton, T. L. (2001). Marriage and health: His and hers. *Psychological Bulletin, 127*(4), 472–503. doi:10.1037/0033-2909.127.4.472.
Levinas, E. (2002). *Otherwise than being: Or beyond essence.* (A. Lingis, Trans.). Pittsburgh: Duquesne University Press.
Meehl, P. E. (1959). Religious factors and values in counseling: A symposium. *Journal of Counseling Psychology, 6*(4), 255–259.
Mintz, L. B., Jackson, A. P., Neville, H. A., Illfelder-Kaye, J., Winterowd, C. L., & Loewy, M. I. (2009). The need for a counseling psychology model training values statement addressing diversity. *The Counseling Psychologist, 37*(5), 644–675.
Objectivism. (n.d.). In *Oxford English dictionary online.* Retrieved from http://www.oed.com.
Oliver, K. (2001). *Witnessing: Beyond recognition.* Minneapolis, MN: University of Minnesota Press.
Positivism. (n.d.). In *Oxford English dictionary online.* Retrieved from http://www.oed.com.
Relativism. (n.d.). In *Oxford English dictionary online.* Retrieved from http://www.oed.com.
Richardson, F. C., Fowers, B. J., & Guignon, C. B. (1999). *Re-envisioning psychology: Moral dimensions of theory and practice.* San Francisco: Jossey-Bass.
Rosenthal, D. (1955). Changes in some moral values following psychotherapy. *Journal of Consulting Psychology, 19*(6), 431–436.
Slife, B. D., Smith, A. M., & Burchfield, C. (2003). Psychotherapists as crypto-missionaries: An exemplar on the crossroads of history, theory, and philosophy. In D. B. Hill & M. J. Kral (Eds.), *About psychology: Essays at the crossroads of history, theory, and philosophy* (pp. 55–72). Albany, NY: SUNY Press.
Slife, B. D., & Reber, J. S. (2005). Comparing the practical implications of secular and Christian truth in psychotherapy. In A. P. Jackson & L. Fischer (Eds.), *Turning freud upside down: Gospel perspectives on psychotherapy's fundamental problems* (pp. 160–182). Provo, UT: Brigham Young University Press.
Strupp, H. H. (1992). Overview: Psychotherapy research. In D. K. Freedheim (Ed.), *History of Psychotherapy: A century of change* (pp. 307–308). Washington, DC: American Psychological Association.
Tjeltveit, A. C. (1986). The ethics of value conversion in psychotherapy: Appropriate and inappropriate therapist influences on client values. *Clinical Psychology Review, 6*(6), 515–537.
Tjeltveit, A. C. (1999). *Ethics and values in psychotherapy.* New York: Routledge.
Truth. (n.d.). In *Merriam-Websters online dictionary.* Retrieved from http://www.merriam-webster.com.
Uchino, B. N., Cacioppo, J. T., & Kiecolt-Glaser, J. K. (1996). The relationship between social support and physiological processes: A review with emphasis on underlying mechanisms and implications for health. *Psychological Bulletin, 119*(3), 488–531. doi: 10.1037/0033-2909.119.3.488.
VandenBos, G. R. (2015). *APA dictionary of psychology* (2nd ed.). Washington, DC: American Psychological Association.

Edwin E. Gantt
and
Stan J. Knapp

Contracts, Covenants, and the Meaning of Marriage

Few areas of counseling and psychotherapy have received as much sustained scholarly attention in recent decades or enjoyed as much general public interest as marriage and family relations. The scientific pronouncements of marriage researchers are not only enthusiastically reported in the popular media, but are also seriously considered by those who make important policy decisions at local, national, and international levels. Likewise, the sagelike recommendations of professional marriage therapists and family counselors routinely find their way onto the nation's bestseller lists, then onto the afternoon talk shows, and finally, into the conventional wisdom of our everyday lives. Even a brief examination of the current scholarly literature on marriage reveals a flourishing field of theorizing and research dedicated to assessing marital satisfaction, measuring relational distress, and identifying the predictors of both marital success and failure (see, e.g., Bengtson, Acock, Allen, Dilworth-Anderson, & Klein, 2005; Hahlweg & Richter, 2010; Lamanna & Riedmann, 2012; Litzinger & Gordon, 2005; Rogge, Bradbury, Hahlweg, Engl, & Thurmaier, 2006; Twenge, Campbell, & Foster, 2003). When one's survey is expanded to include not only the hundreds of titles on the shelves of the psychology and self-help sections of the local bookstore, but also the continually growing number of internet websites, it is difficult *not* to be impressed by the staggering amount of time and energy being devoted to the issues of marital success, divorce prevention, and healthy family relations.

Of course, given the undeniably central role that marriage has played and continues to play in both individual and cultural life throughout the world, such an expenditure of intellectual and cultural resources should come as no surprise. Neither should it be surprising that—given the doctrinal significance attached to marriage and family—Latter-day Saints, social scientists, and therapists are deeply interested in and influenced by this more general cultural and intellectual concern with the nature and meaning of marriage and family. Indeed, a number of prominent LDS researchers and practitioners have made noteworthy and valuable contributions to this burgeoning literature (see, e.g., Burr, Marks, & Day, 2012; Carroll, Hymowitz, Wilcox, & Kaye, 2013; Gantt, Williams, & Reynolds, 2014; Hawkins, 2007; Holmes, Dunn, Harper, Dyer, & Day, 2013; Lambert & Dollahite, 2008; Marks, Dollahite, & Baumgartner, 2010).

However, a growing number of researchers and theorists have begun to question the role that contemporary social science theories of marriage and family may be playing in perpetuating the very problems they seek to address (Doherty, 2002; Doherty & Beaton, 2000; Fowers, 1998, 2000; Wachtel & Wachtel, 1986). Indeed, marriage and family therapists and other family scholars may be, as Richardson, Fowers, and Guignon (1999) suggest, "in the awkward position of perpetuating a potent ideology that seems to bear some of the responsibility for the very distress that family therapists seek to remedy" (p. 73). We believe that LDS therapists and counselors need to make a careful and critical reexamination of the conceptual framework that underlies much of contemporary research and theorizing about marriage. We will argue that because most mainstream theories of marriage are grounded in an assumption of fundamental egoism, they are inherently incapable of conceiving of marriage as anything other than simply one of many ways individual egos seek out and obtain individual gratification. The underlying commitment to egoism—characteristic of so many psychological theories—can be seen in the literature's almost obsessive concern with increasing effective communication, identifying individual needs, and achieving higher levels of personal satisfaction through effectively managed marital relationships. We will argue that such theories and consequent practices are not only incapable of providing an adequate base to articulate the inherently moral nature of marriage and family, but that they are also fundamentally incompatible with the covenant-based understanding of marriage common to the teachings of latter-day prophets and holy scripture.

Marriage as Contractual: The Egoistic Perspective

Commenting on changes in both our common everyday as well as professional understandings of marriage and family, Porter (1995) suggests that the most significant change of all has been "a change from shared community values to an absorption of the cultural emphasis on *individualism*" (p. 14; italics in the original). She further defines individualism as "an egocentrism where an individual regards most aspects of life only in relation to him/herself. Individualism ranks self-interest and self-preference as the highest priorities"

(p. 14). Marriage has thus come to be understood, Porter argues, as a contractual arrangement between two independent, and presumably equal, parties seeking to maximize individual benefit through a mutually rewarding but ultimately economic or instrumental relationship (see, e.g., Bellah, Madsen, Sullivan, Swidler, & Tipton, 1985). As Popenoe (1993) has similarly pointed out, "Today marriage is understood mainly as a path to self-fulfillment. One's own self-development is seen to require a significant other, and marital partners are picked primarily to be personal companions" (p. 533).

A chief concern of many marriage and family researchers has been identifying the essential characteristics of and conditions for "the good marriage" (Wallerstein & Blakeslee, 1995). The good marriage is commonly understood (both professionally and popularly) as one in which individual partners are able to achieve a high degree of individual fulfillment or personal satisfaction by experiencing understanding, acceptance, love, affection, nurturance, support, and open and honest communication (see, e.g., Barich & Bielby, 1996; Markman, Stanley, & Blumberg, 1994; Wallerstein & Blakeslee, 1995). The good (i.e., optimally satisfying) marriage, in such an account, is one in which both spouses negotiate (and continually renegotiate) their relational roles, requirements, and expectations so as to foster a climate wherein each can derive maximal individual benefit from the relationship (see, e. g., Harley, 1986; Notarius & Markman, 1993). Through effective communication and relational negotiation, spouses can work to develop a healthy "marital coalition" in which they work together to "develop a sense of their own individuality and self-worth in addition to a joint identity as a couple" (Glick, Berman, Clarkin, & Rait, 2000, p. 68).

The egoistic vision of marriage emphasizes the self as the foundation of all human relationships. The self is understood essentially as the source of value, and the individual's preferences and desires direct particular courses of action in the formation of human relationships. This assumption is common to social exchange and rational choice perspectives on marriage (e.g., Grossbard-Shechtman, 1993; Moe, 2003) but also informs marital research in general through a focus on marital satisfaction as the most critical and defining feature of a good or successful marriage (Gottman 1994a; Notarius & Markman,

1993; Wallerstein, & Blakeslee, 1995). In this view, the value of a marriage for an individual is determined by the level of satisfaction that it provides that individual. The dominance of this perspective on marriage is revealed by an overwhelming emphasis on marital satisfaction as the variable of choice to define a "successful marriage" (Gottman, 1994a; 1994b).

This focus on the self as the foundation for marriage might seem in many ways to be self-evident and unproblematic. "Of course a good marriage is one in which each spouse is happy and satisfied," we might be inclined to say. For most of us, the incongruence of the following statement is readily apparent: "We have a good marriage, but I'm not very happy with it." This is the case because we tend to view the two statements, "We have a good marriage" and "I'm really happy with my marriage," as essentially identical. The goodness of marriage is determined by its evaluation by the self and how well it as a relational source of gratification meets the particular needs of the self.

Effective Communication and the Good Marriage

A particularly significant implication of the assumption that marriage is primarily a contractual relationship between two independent egos seeking maximization of personal satisfaction is reflected in the emphasis most marriage researchers and therapists place on the importance of effective communication, identification of individual needs, and relational negotiation. For example, as one popular Marriage and Family Therapy textbook teaches about courtship and early marriage: "It is important in this early state for couples to understand what marriage is about. It is not simply about establishing a family, finding the right person, or being chosen by the right person. It is about providing a setting for personal growth" (Glick et al., 2000, p. 67). Likewise, this same textbook speaks of the centrality of developing a healthy "marital coalition" in which spouses work together to "develop a sense of their own individuality and self-worth in addition to a joint identity as a couple" (p. 68). The authors, although never explicitly using the word "contract," discuss the nature of the marital coalition in terms that make its contractual and individualistic nature quite apparent. For example:

> The process of working out a satisfactory marital relationship involves tacit, shared agreements between the two people involved. These agreements may consist of explicit rules, implicit rules (rules that the couple adhere to without discussing), and rules that an observer would note but that the couple themselves probably would deny. Seen this way, conflicts in marriage arise when there are disagreements about the rules of living together, about who is to set the rules, and about who is to enforce those rules that are mutually incompatible. (Glick et at., 2000, p. 68)

What is being arranged in this conceptual scheme is an equitable distribution of satisfaction between husband and wife, fundamentally understood as independent egos driven by their nature to seek individual gratification.

If the marriage relationship is understood as one whose value is determined by its congruence with the needs and wants of its participants, then a critical element in the foundation of a good marriage would be for each spouse to first know and accept themselves. Each spouse must know what his or her real wants and needs are. Failure to adequately know oneself cannot only result in actions that are detrimental to one's well-being, but can also preclude the ability of an actor to successfully communicate individual wants and needs to the spouse. While some theoretical approaches adopt the view that the needs and wants of the actor are transparent (e.g., social exchange and rational choice theory) and others adopt a view in which self-knowledge is more problematic (e.g., psychoanalytic and attachment theories), they all agree that adequate self-knowledge is a necessary condition for the creation of a good marriage. This perspective is perhaps most commonly expressed as the requirement that you must first learn to love yourself before you can learn to love others.

Given the often significant obstacles likely to be encountered in trying not only to clarify one's own needs but also in trying to find ways to effectively communicate those needs to one's spouse, the importance of obtaining some sort of expert intervention by a trained marriage and family therapist is clear. Such therapists are uniquely situated to provide couples with scientifically based instruction in effective communication techniques and rational problem resolution. As Glick et al. (2000) put it, "The therapist is by training an expert in communication and thus can help family members express their thoughts and feelings more clearly to one another" (p. 246). Learning how to teach married couples important interpersonal skills such as nondefensive listening, self-disclosure, editing, feeling awareness, and needs clarification constitutes a major component of almost all professional training in marital therapy (see, e.g., Brock & Barnard, 1999; Fowers, 1998; Glick et al., 2000; Gottman, 1994b; Markman et al., 1994). Furthermore, because most marriage therapists value this sort of skills training so highly, "in the typical case, a great deal of therapy time is devoted to the acquisition of communication and conflict resolution skills" (Holtzworth-Munroe & Jacobson, 1991; p. 110). The ultimate goal of such therapy is "the improved functioning of the family as an interlocking system and network of individuals" (Glick et al. 2000, p. 21).

The driving force behind much of this concern for teaching and developing effective communication skills in both therapists and married couples seems to be the (typically unexamined) assumption that human beings are first and foremost individual egos composed of varying sorts of needs requiring fulfillment and that, as such, they are naturally driven to seek out the gratification of those needs as best they can. On this model, then, marriage is just one of the many ways we human beings have found over the centuries to obtain some significant measure of satisfaction of our individual, social, sexual, and economic needs (among, no doubt, many others). Of course, this does not mean that marriage is unique in its ability to provide such forms of gratification, since there are an almost infinite number of activities and relationships in which one can find pleasure. Rather, marriage is unique in respect to the sorts of gratifications it can provide, as well as in terms of the potential intensity and endurance of those gratifications. Ultimately, from this egoistic perspective, marriage serves a primarily instrumental function in the achievement of fundamentally individual ends and, therefore, is thought by many in the discipline to be worthy of our best professional efforts to ensure its continuance and success. In other words, the real significance of marriage is the way in which it provides us with an arena wherein we can pursue greater degrees of personal satisfaction and fulfillment than might otherwise be available to us.

Marriage as Contract and the Problem of Meaning

One of the most problematic implications of this sort of egoistic perspective is, however, that it reduces the meaning of all human relationships and interactions to the level of mere instrumental or utilitarian function. Likewise, all human beings other than the self are reduced to the status of mere objects—peculiar objects, to be sure, but ultimately nothing more than sources of either frustration or gratification. The meaning and value of one's marital and family relations are, in this egoistic perspective, directly tied to the degree of individual benefit such relations happen to provide—whether calculated in terms of immediate benefit or in terms of delayed gratification. One's spouse is a sort of "consumable good" whose particular behavioral characteristics, psychological qualities, and physical features provide the means of satisfying some sort of lack in or need of the self.[1] Effective communication becomes a principle way in which I learn what conditions my spouse is going to place on my obtaining what I need from her (e.g., time, recognition, affection, support, or independence) to assuage my own desires and further my own purposes. Likewise, by employing the therapeutic techniques of self-disclosure and feeling awareness, I am able to detail for my spouse my own conditions for providing her with that of mine which she happens to desire. As Holtzworth-Munroe and Jacobson (1991) state, "The direct communication of each person's desires is an important skill in maintaining a satisfying relationship" (p. 115).

The aim of all this contract-style negotiation in marriage is to see that, if possible, both parties can achieve what they happen to individually desire or feel that they need for themselves. Being willing to engage in a relationship of reasonable give-and-take is the order of the day so long as both parties come away from the therapy having agreed to a more equitable and satisfying distribution of interpersonal, economic, psychological, and sexual goods. As Fowers (2000) points out, "The most widely used scientific theory of marriage is

1. Doherty (2001) has coined the term "consumer marriage" to reflect this common understanding of the nature of the marriage relation and has tied it the rise of individualism and consumerism in Western culture generally.

called *social exchange theory,* which tells us that a relationship is nothing more than a series of exchanges: we give our time and energy in various ways to our spouses, and we expect benefits in return" (p. 92). This theory, which draws its inspiration from behaviorist psychology and certain economic models of thought, "portrays spouses as hard-nosed comparison shoppers who restlessly evaluate whether they are getting the best relationship deal that the market can offer" (Fowers, 2000, p. 92). Thus, if one's marital relationship seems to stack up well against competing alternatives in terms of perceived personal benefits, then one is likely to remain involved and committed to the marriage. If, on the other hand, one's marital relationship does not seem quite as attractive as other possible alternatives, and the barriers to ending it are weak, then one is likely to end the relationship and seek gratification elsewhere.

From within the contractual model, the marriage and family professional becomes not just a psychological or emotional facilitator, but is, even more fundamentally, the very representative of enlightened rationality itself. Indeed, by virtue of his or her expert status and scientific credentials, the marriage professional occupies a powerful position from which to advance a vision of human rationality that is grounded firmly (but often inexplicitly) in the philosophy of egoism. Armed with metaphors such as the "love bank" (Harley, 1986), the "relationship bank account" (Notarius & Markman, 1993), "self-disclosure" (Holtzworth-Munroe & Jacobson, 1991), "starter marriages" (Paul, 2002), and the "marital coalition" (Glick et al., 2000), as well as a technical language derived from social exchange theory and behavioral theory, the marriage professional can present a very compelling case for fundamental egoism to the unsuspecting couple seeking help in reviving their love and resolving their differences. The tragic irony of this approach, however, is that because it encourages "individuals to operate from self-interest and from concern with maximizing their personal fulfillment bottom line" (Fowers, 2000, p. 93), it may well be contributing to the very fragility of marital relation it was developed to address. By inviting couples to view marriage as essentially an economic relationship between individuals seeking the satisfaction of personal needs and by encouraging spouses to view one another as either objects of frustration or gratification, the egoistic approach to marriage destroys the possibility for a genuinely social and moral understanding of the marriage relation either by professionals or by the lay public seeking assistance.

Marriage and Covenant

In light of the many problematic conceptual and moral consequences that accompany an egoistic or contractual model of marriage, we urge LDS counselors and therapists to carefully reflect on the assumptions informing their approach to dealing with marital and family problems. Do our theories and practices take sufficient account of the divinely appointed moral context of the marital relation? As the entry on "Marriage: Social and Behavioral Perspectives" in the *Encyclopedia of Mormonism* points out: "Marriage is more than a matter of social convention or individual need fulfillment in Latter-day Saint society and lifestyle; it is central to the exaltation of the individual person" (Ludlow, 1995, p. 300). Likewise, the Proclamation on the Family solemnly states that "marriage between a man and a woman is ordained of God and that the family is central to the Creator's plan for the eternal destiny of His children" and that "children are entitled to birth within the bonds of matrimony, and to be reared by a father and a mother who honor marital vows with complete fidelity" (Family, 1995). Furthermore, this divinely-inspired document teaches that "successful marriages and families are established and maintained on principles of faith, prayer, repentance, forgiveness, respect, love, compassion, work, and wholesome recreational activities." Such declarations seem to require an understanding of the marriage relationship that is at odds with the instrumentalist and egoistic conceptions so prevalent in mainstream theories of marriage and family today.

In contrast to egoistic and contractual understandings of marriage, we argue that the nature and meaning of marriage can be more fruitfully understood in terms of covenant, an approach that acknowledges the spiritual foundations and moral obligations of the marriage relationship. We suggest that understanding how the concept of covenant lies at the heart of Latter-day Saint teachings about the nature and meaning of marriage, both temporal and eternal, will also assist family scholars in developing approaches designed to heal relational discord in marriages and families and the myriad forms of suffering such discord entails. In short, we argue that only when marriage therapists and family counselors abandon approaches grounded in the problematic assumption of instrumental egoism in favor of the fundamentally alterocentric (lit., "other-centered") orientation of covenant will they be able to offer the couples and families who seek them out the possibility of genuinely healing.

The Covenant Concept

The original meaning of the concept of covenant has in many ways been lost to the modern world. The Oxford English Dictionary (OED) notes, for example, that the term is "no longer in ordinary use except when coloured by legal or theological associations" (Covenant, n.d.). Today, outside theological circles, the term *covenant* is most often invoked as a synonym for contract and taken to refer to a two-way promise between mutually interested and more or less equal parties. Indeed, in light of its limited modern usage, the OED defines covenant as: "A mutual agreement between two or more persons to do or refrain from doing certain acts; a compact, contract, bargain" (Covenant, n.d.).[2] This definition is all but indistinguishable from the one for contract: "A mutual agreement between two or more parties that something shall be done or forborne by one or both; a compact, covenant, bargain" (Contract, n.d.).

The modern tendency to equate covenant and contract obscures the fact that covenant has historically been used to refer to a relationship with God that cannot be understood as a mere contract. According to Boston University theologian Bernard Anderson (1993), writing in *The Oxford Companion to the Bible,* "Covenant expresses a novel element of the religion of ancient Israel: the people are bound in relationship to the one God, Yahweh, who makes an exclusive ('jealous') claim upon their loyalty in worship and social life" (p. 138). In ancient biblical times, the concept of covenant was "the foundation of social order and social relations, and it was particularly the foundation for an understanding of humanity's relationship with God" (Richards, 1991, pp. 193–194).

2. Even some biblical dictionaries fail to adequately distinguish between contract and covenant, employing the more modern sense of the term and defining it as "an agreement between two or more parties outlining mutual rights and responsibilities" (Myers, 1996, p. 240).

Interestingly, "The Hebrew word for covenant is 'b'rît'" and "seems to have the root meaning bond, fetter, indicating a binding relationship" (Anderson, 1993, p. 138; see also Brinig, 2000). As Hugenberger (1994) states, "The predominant sense of covenant in Biblical Hebrew is an elected, as opposed to natural, relationship of obligation established under divine sanction" (p. 171). Likewise, in discussing this Hebrew concept of covenant, Rabbi Telushkin (1991) notes that the first "commandment" of the Ten Commandments, the Mosaic covenant, is actually not a commandment at all, but rather "a statement of what God has done for the Israelites. His accomplishments on their behalf entitles Him to make demands of them" (p. 54). In their covenant relation with God, the ancient Israelites found themselves always already obligated and indebted to God, even before they themselves had acknowledged or recognized their indebtedness to him. Thus, they were bound to their God by sacred obligation and were responsible for a debt (i.e., their freedom from bondage in Egypt) they could never possibly repay. In this sense, the obligation the ancient Israelites discovered in their covenant relation with God was an infinite and asymmetrical one. After all, how can one ever possibly repay the author of one's identity, the unanticipated liberator who provides freedom itself—a freedom to which one has no inherent right? Yahweh accomplished for Israel that which they could not do for themselves, and, indeed, could never have done, and, thereby, they became continuously accountable to him for the identity and the freedom he had given them.

This notion of covenant obligation and profound indebtedness can be seen in the powerful sermon that King Benjamin delivered to his people gathered at the temple in the city of Zarahemla:

> I say unto you that if ye should serve him who has created you from the beginning, and is preserving you from day to day, by lending you breath, that ye may live and move and do according to your own will, and even supporting you from one moment to another—I say, if ye should serve him with all your whole souls yet ye would be unprofitable servants. And behold, all that he requires of you is to keep his commandments; and he has promised you that if ye would keep his commandments ye should prosper in the land; and he never doth vary from that which he hath said; therefore, if ye do keep his commandments he doth bless you and prosper you. And now, in the first place, he hath

> created you, and granted unto you your lives, for which ye are indebted unto him. And secondly, he doth require that ye should do as he hath commanded you; for which if ye do, he doth immediately bless you; and therefore he hath paid you. And ye are still indebted unto him, and are, and will be, forever and ever; therefore, of what have ye to boast? (Mosiah 2:21–24)

As Stephen D. Ricks (1999) and others have shown, King Benjamin's oration and assemblage of his people at the temple represents a centuries-old "Covenant Renewal Ceremony" (pp. 189–194). Throughout his address, King Benjamin continually exhorts his people to "always retain in remembrance" (Mosiah 4:11) the nature of their covenant relationship with God, and humbly "submit to all things which the Lord seeth fit to inflict . . . , even as a child doth submit to his father" (Mosiah 3:19). The assurance is that the love of the Father is such that he will always succor his children in their need and as they obey his commands, but that there is nothing they can do to earn such favor and nothing that they have done to deserve such love.

There are many such passages in both ancient and modern scripture that help to illuminate this asymmetrical and obligatory nature of a covenant relationship. Perhaps one of the most moving and profound explications of the nature of a covenant relationship is found in Exodus 19:3–8:

> And Moses went up unto God, and the Lord called unto him out of the mountain, saying, Thus shalt thou say to the house of Jacob, and tell the children of Israel; Ye have seen what I did unto the Egyptians, and how I bare you on eagles' wings, and brought you unto myself. Now therefore, if ye will obey my voice indeed, and keep my covenant, then ye shall be a peculiar treasure unto me above all people: for all the earth is mine: And ye shall be unto me a kingdom of priests, and an holy nation. These are the words which thou shalt speak unto the children of Israel. And Moses came and called for the elders of the people, and laid before their faces all these words which the Lord commanded him. And all the people answered together, and said, All that the Lord hath spoken we will do. And Moses returned the words of the people unto the Lord.

In this passage, we learn a number of important things about the nature of the covenant relationship as delineated in scripture. First, for example, we learn that a covenant is not in essence a two-way promise entered into by two roughly equal parties. Rather, the Lord reminds the children of Israel of his love and mercy and his efforts on their behalf. He reminds them that he has brought them to the position they find themselves in. Their freedom has been constituted through him. He then offers them the opportunity to enter into a covenant relationship with him. The Lord asks only whether or not the children of Israel are willing to accept the covenant relation he has offered them—if they are willing to accept being his people and promise to "obey my voice" and to "keep my covenant." The Lord promises that should they continue as his people, they will become a "peculiar treasure unto me above all people . . . a kingdom of priests, and an holy nation"—although the specifics of that blessing, like the specifics of what it will mean to "keep my covenant" are quite vague at this point. Indeed, the details of the covenant and its keeping are not to be revealed in their fullness to the Israelites until after they return an affirmative answer to the Lord via his prophet and spokesman, Moses.

At this early stage of the game, the central issue confronting the children of Israel seems to be whether they will answer "yes" or "no" to an invitation from the Lord to receive his having already elected them to be his people and to continue to be his people by promising to obey his voice and do his will. The rub here is, of course, that they do not yet know exactly what it is they will be asked to do for their God. They have not yet had revealed to them the details of what "obey[ing] my voice" will mean. The consequences and the details of their response will follow after the fact. Further, it is important to note that those consequences and details will not be open for negotiation by the children of Israel. Rather, once the Israelites have agreed to be the Lord's Chosen people, they will have thereby chosen to do whatever it is the Lord should command them—whether they happen to fully understand his will, agree or disagree with its provisions, or take a personal liking to it or not. The essence of the covenant relationship here seems to be that the children of Israel are being asked to trust fully in the Lord and to give themselves over to him by receiving what he has already done for them, all the while knowing only that he will care for them in his own way and manner. As such, the covenant is, in essence, an invitation to be reborn through receiving the great things the Lord has done to save us and constitute our self anew (cf. 2 Ne. 1:1–6). To receive the covenant is to recognize that we have become his and accept the Lord's declaration: "I [have] brought you unto myself."

Thus we see that covenant opposes egoism not with a call to self-denial or even self-sacrifice but with a call to receive a more truthful understanding of our relation to God. This understanding requires recognition of what "great things the Lord [has] done for [us]" (2 Ne. 1:1). Without such a recognition, we cannot receive the covenant, for the covenant is to be his people. If we fail to realize how the Lord has already made us his, then we cannot enter into the covenant with him for such recognition and remembrance is constitutive of the covenant relation.

Understanding how a covenant remakes who we are can also help us understand why covenant relations almost always require some kind of ritual practice to effectuate or bring into being the recognition of the covenant relation. As Anderson (1993) indicates, a covenant "relationship is usually sealed by a rite—for example, an oath, sacred meal, blood sacrifice, invocation of blessings and curses—which makes it binding" (p. 138). Building on the recognition of how covenant relations with God are entered through ritual, we can also see the importance of marital rituals that can serve to both constitute the marital relation and also to perhaps renew it. Weddings (even nonsectarian and civil ones), for example, typically involve elaborate ritual performances involving the exchange of oaths, special commemorative meals, and the invocations of various blessings on the couple. Likewise, marriage is held in most cultures to be a special, often divinely appointed relationship between two people based on promises and obligations reflective of a special commitment to one another, the larger community, and to deity, and which, it is at least hoped, will prove to be durable and reliable. It would appear that ancient biblical and other religious traditions' emphasis on the ritual constitution of a covenant relation would also indicate the need for the continuation and perhaps invention of cultural rituals that can help establish similar understandings of marriage today.

Marriage as Covenant

It is interesting to note that in the context of the restored gospel of Jesus Christ and temple worship, there are only two beings with whom we enter into formal covenant relationship: God the Father and our chosen spouse. In the temples of the Most High, we stand in holy places and kneel at holy altars to answer either "yes" or "no" in response to the question of our willingness to enter into sacred covenant with our Father in Heaven and with the husband or wife to whom we will be legally and lawfully wed. Again, as the *Encyclopedia of Mormonism* states, "Through this ordinance of eternal marriage, men and women commit themselves in pure love to remain true to each other and to God through all eternity" (Ludlow, 1995, p. 306). This is to say that, while I have many special obligations and responsibilities to my children, to my friends and neighbors, and even to strangers, widows, and orphans (see, e.g., Deut. 16:11–14; Jer. 22:3; Zech. 7:10), I am fully in covenant relation—with all of its attendant responsibilities and blessings—with only my God and my spouse. What, though, might all of this mean for us as LDS marriage counselors and family therapists, especially in light of the fact that many couples with whom we may work will not have been married in an LDS temple and will not have entered into such a formal covenant relationship as part of their marriage?

We believe that the concept of covenant is one that can have a profound impact on not only our professional understanding of the nature and meaning of the marriage relationship as LDS therapists, counselors, and theorists, but also on the personal understanding of marriage embraced by our clients, their spouses, and families—whether LDS or not. Perhaps the most important feature of the concept of marriage as a covenant relationship is the notion that covenants involve fundamentally changing how we understand ourselves. Although there are no doubt significant differences in the meaning and expression of the covenant relationship we have with our Heavenly Father and that we have with our spouse, central to both covenant relationships is the recognition that we now belong to the other and are bound to them in ways that cannot be fully specified. By entering into a covenant relation, we have become willing to abide by its conditions, namely, we have become willing to live for the other.

This should not be taken to mean, of course, that in a covenant relationship we are simply to be a doormat upon which our spouse can wipe his or her feet. Accepting marriage as a covenant relationship in which I am first and foremost concerned with the welfare of my spouse does not mean that it is appropriate for me to passively submit to abuse, betrayal, or deceit. In covenant, I am called to be more than an occasion for my spouse to sin. A central obligation of the marriage covenant is complete fidelity, which entails far more than the mere refusal of adultery. Complete fidelity in marriage is to willingly shoulder the burden of being truthful to one's spouse by refusing to participate in the lies and self-deceptions that are part and parcel of unrighteous dominion. Genuine covenantal fidelity in marriage demands that we always and in all ways seek that which is best for our spouse in a spirit of loving compassion and self-forgetfulness.

In covenant, the other to whom I have promised my whole soul and to whom I have dedicated my will is not an object whose instrumentality is defined by the degree of frustration or gratification he or she can provide me in the course of our relationship. Further, my spouse and I are not independent contractors cunningly negotiating particular goods and services in a market of hard bargains, estimated risks, and skillful communication whose ultimate goal is always to achieve the best (i.e., most personally gratifying) deal possible. Rather, on the covenant model of marriage, the one with whom I have entered into covenant is fully other in his or her own right, worthy as such of my deepest respect and reverence, a divine other to whom I am obligated and for whom I am responsible—before and beyond myself. Indeed, it is this divine other before whom and in whom I find the very foundations of my own humanity as I take upon myself to share his or her burdens, struggles, joys, pains, fears, failures, and triumphs. President Kimball clearly understood the essence of marriage as a call to responsibility and obligation when he taught:

> We have come to realize that the mere performance of a ceremony does not bring happiness and a successful marriage. Happiness does not come by pressing a button, as does the electric light; happiness is a state of mind and comes from within. It must be earned. It cannot be purchased with money; it cannot be taken for nothing. Some think of happiness as a glamorous life of ease, luxury, and constant thrills; but true marriage is based on a happiness which is more than that, one which comes

> from giving, serving, sharing, sacrificing, and selflessness. Two people coming from different backgrounds learn soon after the ceremony is performed that stark reality must be faced. There is no longer a life of fantasy or of make-believe; we must come out of the clouds and put our feet firmly on the earth. Responsibility must be assumed and new duties must be accepted. Some personal freedoms must be relinquished, and many adjustments, unselfish adjustments, must be made. (Kimball, 2002, p. 40)

Thus, marriage is a relationship that by its very nature summons us and calls upon us to keep our responsibilities for our spouse and to receive the invitation to live for the life of another.

At the heart of marriage and family, in this perspective, is the concept that the marriage relationship is a covenant relationship, and that as such it involves a total giving of oneself to one's spouse with "complete fidelity" (*Proclamation on the Family*) and concern for his or her emotional, physical, intellectual, and spiritual welfare above all else. As President Howard W. Hunter explained:

> The Lord has defined marriage for us. He said, "For this cause shall a man leave father and mother, and shall cleave to his wife: and they twain shall be one flesh" (Matthew 19:5). Surely the happiest marriages are those where your hurt is my hurt, my pain is your pain, my victory, your victory, my concerns, your concerns. The oneness of heart, of soul, of flesh seems to be more of a challenge than ever before in the world in which the question seems to be: "What is there in this for me?" Far too many marriage partners have become merely an ornament on the sleeve rather than a part of the heart. (Hunter, 1997, p. 137)

Clearly, the Lord's commandment that husbands and wives become "one flesh" implies a great deal more than just the sharing of sexual intimacies. A marriage covenant unites us as it brings us to be for our spouse even as Christ is for us: "Husbands [and wives], love your wives [and husbands], even as Christ also loved the church, and gave himself for it" (Eph. 5:25).

Even if a particular marriage has not been formalized at sacred altars in holy temples, the concept of marriage as covenant can still be relevant for and vital to helping couples understand the opportunities their marital relationship offers them. Helping struggling couples and families to find their way out of resentment, jealousy, fear, and the abiding pain of betrayal can, we believe, most fully come about as they learn to see one another in the light of a covenant love and experience the healing power of other-focused service and compassionate care. As the language of therapy shifts away from the conceptually problematic and alienating vocabulary of individual needs and wants, with its attendant strategies of communication and negotiation, and instead moves toward a liberating vocabulary of compassionate service and forgiveness, the problems and struggles of making a marriage start to radically change as new and often unimagined possibilities begin to open up.

This does not mean, however, that quality communication in marriage is unimportant or unnecessary and should not be a concern in marriage counseling. Rather, what is of primary concern here is the purpose and meaning of communication in the marital relationship. In other words, are we as therapists and counselors instructing our clients in the varied techniques of effective communication such that they might achieve greater success in the pursuit of certain fundamentally individualistic goals that may well be ultimately toxic to the vibrancy and depth of a genuinely intimate and compassionate marriage relationship? Attentive and sensitive listening is truly an important part of a loving marital relation, but only when motivated out of genuine concern for the welfare of one's spouse and one's family and not merely as a useful tool for negotiating more personally satisfying outcomes.

The concepts of selfless giving and complete fidelity are, of course, not the sole province of religion and religious understanding, though that is most certainly where such concepts originate and find their fullest context of expression. Thus, it is conceivable that the language of marriage as covenant will resonate with even those who might not yet be ready to embrace other, more overt religious ideas or practices. Nonetheless, we firmly believe that as marriage therapists make space for their clients to engage their spouse, their marriage, and their family in the transformative light of covenant relations rather than in terms of instrumental egoism, then perhaps we can all begin to genuinely and fully invite the Lord himself into the consulting room where he can begin to speak peace to the souls of those who stand most in need of his loving perspective and healing presence.

References

Anderson, B. (1993). Covenant. In B. M. Metzger & M. D. Coogan (Eds.), *The Oxford companion to the Bible* (pp. 138–139). New York: Oxford University Press.
Barich, R. R., & Bielby, D. D. (1996). Rethinking marriage: Change and stability in expectations, 1967–1994. *Journal of Family Issues, 17*(2), 139–169.
Bellah, R. N., Madsen, R., Sullivan, W. M., Swidler, A., & Tiption, S. M. (1985). *Habits of the heart: Individualism and commitment in American life*. New York: Harper & Row.
Bengtson, V. L., Acock, A. C., Allen, K. R., Dilworth-Anderson, P., & Klein, D. M. (Eds.) (2005). *Sourcebook of family therapy and research*. Thousand Oaks, CA: Sage Publications.
Brinig, M. F. (2000). *From contract to covenant: Beyond the law and economics of the family*. Cambridge, MA: Harvard University Press.
Brock, G. W., & Barnard, C. P. (1999). *Procedures in marriage and family therapy* (3rd edition). Boston: Allyn & Bacon.
Burr, W. R., Marks, L. D., & Day, R. (2012). *Sacred matters: Religion and spirituality in families*. New York: Routledge.
Carroll, J. S., Hymowitz, K., Wilcox, W. B., & Kaye, K. (2013). *Knot yet: The benefits and costs of delayed marriage in America*. A commissioned report sponsored by the National Campaign to Prevent Teen and Unplanned Pregnancy, the RELATE Institute, and the National Marriage Project.
Contract. (n.d.). In *Merriam-Webster's online dictionary*. Retrieved from http://www.merriam-webster.com.
Covenant. (n.d.). In *Merriam-Webster's online dictionary*. Retrieved from http://www.merriam-webster.com.
Doherty, W. J. (2001). *Take back your marriage: Sticking together in a world that pulls us apart*. New York: The Guilford Press.
Doherty, W. J. (2002). How therapists harm marriages and what we can do about it. *Journal of Couple and Relationship Therapy: Innovations in Clinical and Educational Interventions, 1*(2), 1–17.
Doherty, W. J., & Beaton, J. M. (2000). Family therapists, community, and civic renewal. *Family Process, 39*(2), 149–161.
Family: A proclamation to the world. (1995, November). *Ensign*. Retrieved from https://www.lds.org/ensign/1995/11/the-family-a-proclamation-to-the-world?lang=eng.
Fowers, B. J. (1998). Psychology and the good marriage: Social theory as practice. *American Behavioral Scientist, 41*(4), 516–541.
Fowers, B. J. (2000). *Beyond the myth of marital happiness: How embracing the virtues of loyalty, generosity, justice, and courage can strengthen your relationship*. San Francisco: Jossey-Bass Publishers.
Gantt, E. E., Williams, R. N., & Reynolds, E. M. (2014). Meaning and ontology in family science: It's persons all the way down. *Family in America, 28*(3), 263–280.
Glick, I. D., Berman, E. M., Clarkin, J. F., & Rait, D. S. (2000). *Marital and family therapy* (4th Edition). Washington, DC: American Psychiatric Press, Inc.
Gottman, J. M. (1994a). *Why marriages succeed or fail: And how you can make yours last*. New York: Simon and Schuster.
Gottman, J. M. (1994b). *What predicts divorce: The relationship between marital processes and marital outcomes*. Hillsdale, NJ: Lawrence Erlbaum.

Grossbard-Shechtman, S. (1993). *On the economics of marriage: A theory of marriage, labor, and divorce*. Boulder, CO: Westview Press.

Hahlweg, K., & Richter, D. (2010). Prevention of marital instability and distress. Results of an 11-year longitudinal follow-up study. *Behavior Research and Therapy, 48*(5), 377–383.

Harley, W. F. (1986). *His needs, her needs*. Tarrytown, NY: Fleming H. Revell Company.

Hawkins, A. J. (2007). Will legislation to encourage premarital education strengthen marriage and reduce divorce? *Journal of Law and Family Studies, 9*(1), 79–99.

Holmes, E. K., Dunn, K. C., Harper, J. M., Dyer, W. J., & Day, R. D. (2013). Mother knows best? Inhibitory maternal gatekeeping, psychological control, and the mother-adolescent relationship. *Journal of Adolescence, 36*(1), 91–101.

Holtzworth-Munroe, A., & Jacobson, N. S. (1991). Behavioral marital therapy. In A. S. Gurman & D. P. Kniskern (Eds.), *Handbook of family therapy* (vol. 2, pp. 96–133). New York: Brunner/Mazel.

Hugenberger, G. P. (1994). *Marriage as a covenant: A study of biblical law and ethics governing marriage developed from the perspective of Malachi*. New York: E. J. Brill.

Hunter, H. W. (1997). *The teachings of Howard W. Hunter*. C. J. Williams (Ed.). Salt Lake City: Bookcraft.

Kimball, S. W. (2002, October). Oneness in marriage. *Ensign*. Retrieved from https://www.lds.org/ensign/2002/10/oneness-in-marriage?lang=eng.

Lamanna, M. A., & Riedmann, A. C. (2012). *Marriages, families, and relationships: Making choices in a diverse society*. Belmont, CA: Wadsworth.

Lambert, N. M., & Dollahite, D. C. (2008). The threefold cord: Marital commitment in religious couples. *Journal of Family Issues, 29*(5), 592–614.

Litzinger, S., & Gordon, K. C. (2005). Exploring relationships among communication, sexual satisfaction, and marital satisfaction. *Journal of Sex and Marital Therapy, 31*(5), 409–424.

Ludlow, D. H. (Ed.). (1995). *The church and society: Selections from the Encyclopedia of Mormonism*. Salt Lake City: Deseret Book Company.

Markman, H., Stanley, S., & Blumberg, S. L. (1994). *Fighting for your marriage: Positive steps for preventing divorce and preserving a lasting love*. San Francisco: Jossey-Bass Publishers.

Marks, L. D., Dollahite, D. C., & Baumgartner, J. (2010). In God we trust: Qualitative findings on finances, family, and faith from a diverse sample of U.S. families. *Family Relations, 59*(4), 439–452.

Moe, K. S. (Ed.). (2003). *Women, family, and work: Writings in the economics of gender*. Oxford, UK: Basil Blackwell Publishers.

Myers, A. C. (Ed.). (1996). *The Eerdmans Bible dictionary* (paperback edition). Grand Rapids, MI: William B. Eerdmans Publishing Company.

Notarius, C., & Markman, H. (1993). *We can work it out: Making sense of marital conflict*. New York: G. P. Putnam's Sons.

Paul, P. (2002). *The starter marriage and the future of matrimony*. New York: Villard Books.

Popenoe, D. (1993). American family decline, 1960–1990: A review and appraisal. *Journal of Marriage and Family, 55*(3), 527–555.

Porter, E. J. (1995). *Building good families in a changing world*. Carlton, Australia: Melbourne University Press.

Richards, L. O. (1991). *New international encyclopedia of Bible words.* Grand Rapids, MI: Zondervan Publishing House.

Richardson, F. C., Fowers, B. J., & Guignon, C. B. (1999). *Re-envisioning psychology: Moral dimensions of theory and practice.* San Francisco: Jossey-Bass Publications.

Ricks, S. D. (1999). Kingship, coronation, and covenant in Mosiah 1–6. In J. W. Welch and S. D. Ricks (Eds.), *King Benjamin's speech made simple* (pp. 175–200). Provo, UT: Foundation for Ancient Research and Mormon Studies.

Rogge, R. D., Bradbury, T. N., Hahlweg, K., Engl, J., & Thurmaier, F. (2006). Predicting marital distress and dissolution: Refining the two-factor hypothesis. *Journal of Family Psychology, 20*(1), 156–159.

Telushkin, J. (1991). *Jewish literacy: The most important things to know about the Jewish religion, its people, and its history.* New York: William Morrow and Company, Inc.

Twenge, J. M., Campbell, W. K., & Foster, C. A. (2003). Parenthood and marital satisfaction: A meta-analytic review. *Journal of Marriage and Family, 65*(3), 574–583.

Wachtel, E., & Wachtel, P. (1986). *Family dynamics in individual psychotherapy.* New York: The Guilford Press.

Wallerstein, J., & Blakeslee, S. (1995). *The good marriage: How and why love lasts.* Boston: Houghton Mifflin.

JEFFREY S. REBER

A Gospel Challenge to Psychology's Culture of Suspicion

ASSUMPTIONS, ALTERNATIVES, AND PSYCHOTHERAPEUTIC IMPLICATIONS

According to renowned psychoanalyst Jacques Lacan (1968), Sigmund Freud along with Karl Marx and Frederick Nietzsche ushered in an era of mistrust of bourgeois society, morals, and consciousness. While this mistrust was initially focused on the middle class, it inevitably had a much broader and more profound impact. In psychology, for example, this societal mistrust may have contributed to a culture of suspicion within the discipline. The noted philosopher and ethicist Alasdair MacIntyre (1985) has identified a psychology that mistrusts the face-value accounts of persons with an overinterpretative mode of life. Speaking of Freud's contribution to overinterpretation specifically, MacIntyre has asserted that Freud "made available the thought of the unacknowledged motive as an all-pervasive presence, so that each of us is encouraged to try and look behind the overt simplicities of the behavior of others to what is actually moving them and equally encouraged to respond to that hidden reality rather than to the surface appearance of the other" (p. 899). Psychologist and historian Thomas Leahey (2001) agrees with MacIntrye. He asserts that when psychologists work "within the overinterpretative mode of life, nothing can be believed; every statement, every action, requires an interpretative gloss. . . . What Freud and the Party of Suspicion have bequeathed us," he asserts, "is paranoia" (p. 145–146).

Among Freud's many contributions to the culture of suspicion, none is more significant or influential than his belief that there are underlying causal mechanisms that explain psychological phenomena and conscious experience. For Freud, it was the psychodynamic tension between the id, ego, and superego that constituted the most important explanatory causal mechanism of human thoughts, feelings, and behavior. This mechanism is the "hidden reality" (MacIntyre, 1985, p. 899) behind the façade of consciousness, and it is this hidden reality that Freud believed ought to be the psychoanalyst's primary focus in therapy.

Many psychologists and psychotherapists are not interested in Freud's conception of the unconscious today, but they have certainly maintained his focus on the causal mechanisms that lie behind our everyday experiences and behaviors (Hedström & Ylikoski, 2010). As Elster (1989) has noted, in contemporary social science, "citing an earlier event as the cause of the event we want to explain . . . is not enough:

the causal mechanism must also be provided, or at least suggested" (pp. 3–4). In a post-Freud psychology, an adequate explanation of a psychological phenomenon must include the postulation of underlying causal mechanisms. Conscious phenomena, experiences, and their meanings cannot count as proper explanations in and of themselves (cf., Gantt, Reber, & Hyde, 2013). This discounting of psychological phenomena and conscious experience as having no real explanatory value is the chief manifestation of a psychological culture of suspicion.

This legacy of Freud's conception of an unconscious causal mechanism for contemporary psychology and psychotherapeutic practice entails a number of potential implications for human thought, emotion, and behavior, including: (1) a mistrust of the conscious mind, (2) a suspicion of apparent altruistic or nonhedonistic motivations, (3) a conception of the self that is atomistic (i.e., the real reasons behind our actions are self-contained within the unconscious mind), and (4) an epistemological and moral relativism that negates the possibility of universal truth.

This chapter asserts that for psychologists, counselors, and therapists whose worldview is informed and enhanced by the gospel of Jesus Christ it is imperative that theories of psychology that breed suspicion of client motives and invite us to look beyond the mark of conscious experience be recognized, critically evaluated, and challenged. In what follows, the importance of such a challenge will be illustrated by comparing and contrasting the four implications of the assumption of unconscious causal mechanisms that were just described with four alternatives that arise out of the perspective of the gospel of Jesus Christ. These alternatives support: (1) the agency and meaning of the conscious mind, (2) the possibility of genuinely nonhedonistic motivations, (3) the fundamentality of relationships among persons, and (4) the universality of a truth that is embodied in the living Christ and experienced through our relationship to him.

The format for critically examining each contrasting implication pair will proceed in the following manner. First, the implication of an unconscious causal mechanism will be explicated through the exemplar of Freud's classic psychodynamic theory. Second, several contemporary examples of the implication will be outlined to demonstrate the pervasiveness of the implication in psychology today. Third, an alternative implication that follows from the restored gospel of Jesus Christ will be described and contrasted with the conventional implication. Finally, the therapeutic applications that logically follow from the contrasting implications will be compared.

Implication #1: Mistrust of the Conscious Mind

Freudian Exemplar: Unconscious Determinism. A basic premise of Freud's psychodynamic theory is that "there are purposes in people which can become operative without their knowing about them" (Freud, 1917, p. 74). For Freud, this means that the rational thinking mind—that people are aware of and think of as constituting their self—is merely one component of the human psyche, and not the most fundamental one at that. The most basic psychic entity is the id: the primitive, bestial, and fully unconscious source of human motivations, drives, and desires. The id always operates according to the pleasure principle and seeks only immediate gratification and minimization of pain. While the ego may direct the drives of the id toward realistic and socially acceptable goals, it cannot stop or ultimately control the id's desires. At the end of the day, the ego is subject to the id's wishes and can only direct or deflect those wishes in light of the realities of the physical and social world and within the constraints of the superego or conscience.

Because the id ultimately determines human actions and because the id is wholly unconscious, the ego's conscious experience of human agency or free will cannot be trusted. That is, although the conscious mind appears to make genuine choices—even choices that sometimes seem to work against individual pleasure or satisfaction—for Freud, it ultimately does not. The ego may delay the id's need for gratification for a time or sublimate it in socially acceptable ways, but at the end of the day, the ego's "choice" is determined by the id and the pleasure it demands. Consequently, a person's conscious experience of agency is an epiphenomenon, a byproduct of defense mechanisms that facilitate repression of the id and its primal impulses by deceiving the ego into thinking it is in control. Paradoxically, then, the ego's experience of agency actually helps preserve the id's covert and wholly deterministic pursuit of satisfaction. The ego never sees a need to question the legitimacy of its conscious motives because, in its self-deceived experience of free will, the ego falsely believes that it is making genuine choices. But alas, it is not.

In the same way that the ego experiences itself making choices that are not really free, so too is the conscious meaning the ego assigns to its choices epiphenomenal. The meaning the ego assigns to its choices and actions is typically that which satisfies the superego's demand for social appropriateness. In this way, the id successfully avoids the guilt and shame the superego would impose on any actions that manifested the reality of the id's primal drive toward immediate pleasure. For example, a husband may bring flowers home to his wife as a demonstration of what he believes is a consciously chosen and meaningfully experienced expression of his gratitude for her love and support. For Freud, in actuality, his act is a socially acceptable means of gratifying id wishes for pleasure without incurring the painful guilt and shame that would emerge if he tried a more directly gratifying approach. His meaning, like his experience of agency, is a self-deception.

Moreover, his false sense of agency and the façade of meaning accompanying it is not only a deception to himself, but also to his wife. If she also believes he has given her flowers freely and meaningfully, then she too has been deceived by the conscious reasons he gives for his actions. For Freud, these conscious reasons are not the real reasons behind his actions. One significant upshot of Freud's theory of the unconscious, then, is that people cannot really trust themselves or each other as to the choices they think they make and the meaning they think they share.

Unconscious Determinism in Contemporary Psychology. The majority of today's psychologists, counselors, and therapists are not practitioners of classical Freudian psychoanalysis and therefore do not endorse Freud's particular conception of the unconscious. However, many do postulate causal mechanisms for human behavior that are often unconscious and unobservable. Consider, as one fairly obvious and increasingly popular example, evolutionary psychological theories that distinguish the conscious experience of love and choice in mate selection from the evolutionarily developed and wholly unconscious drive for genetic proliferation. Though the controlling elements are somewhat different from Freud's (e.g., numerous domain-specific cognitive computational modules replace Freud's three intrapsychic forces), the process is virtually the same. People are determined by some underlying causal mechanism, which is not directly experienced or understood, that explains and may ultimately explain away the conscious experience of agency and meaning.

From the perspective of evolutionary psychology, the husband who brings flowers home to his wife could experience meaning and affection like that of a Shakespearean sonnet when he considers his love for his wife. However, beneath his conscious experience, at the more fundamental evolutionary level, he is unknowingly acting out a computational script that facilitated the adaptive advantage of his ancestors living in "the environment of evolutionary adaptation (EEA)" (Samuels, 1998, p. 577) millions of years ago. His wife satisfies the computational algorithm in that she is an adequate reproductive target with the proper youthfulness, fertility, and waist-to-hip ratio for the propagation of his DNA into the next generation (Fisher, 2004). A distinctly female computational module will determine her response to his gesture as well. As with Freud, and in a manner that is fully consistent with the materialistic predilection of a psychological science, it is the more bodily based unconscious side of the experience that evolutionary psychologists take to be primary and therefore determinative of the actions of the person. The conscious mind—that part of the person that experiences the agency and meaning of love and is not necessarily material—is rendered little more than an adaptive byproduct of the human species' naturally selected method of genetic proliferation.

Even strict behaviorists, who held sway over American psychology through much of the twentieth century and adamantly oppose the use of mental concepts to explain human behavior, benefit from Freud's mistrust of the conscious mind. For behaviorists, the mind, whether conscious or not, is irrelevant to the learning process. Consequently, it does not matter what the organism believes are the reasons for its actions. Its behaviors are, at the end of the day, fully determined by the reinforcement contingencies that act upon the organism over time. In this sense, the entirety of the mind is secondary to the mechanistic processes of conditioning and, therefore, cannot be trusted as the origin of human action or meaning.

A husband who brings flowers home to his wife, then, is simply enacting a behavior that has been reinforced in the past. If that behavior continues to be reinforced, it will take place again in the future. All of this is determined to occur, for the behaviorist, regardless of the meaning and value that the husband might append to the behavior. The wife's response to the gesture is similarly conditioned by her reinforcement history, not by a choice or the meaning she assigns to it.

Perhaps more surprisingly, some approaches to humanistic psychology, such as those that postulate a bodily based self-actualizing potential (e.g., Rogers, 1951) or biologically seated instinctoids (e.g., Maslow, 1954), endorse a causal mechanism for human action that can lead to suspicion of the conscious mind. The form of causation may be more teleological in these cases, but the true self is still the material, less-conscious side of the person. The conscious self, which tends to conform to social norms and the expectations of others, is often viewed as inauthentic and incongruent with the individual's innate biologically based potential. In this sense, a husband who gets his wife flowers (especially on Valentine's Day or their anniversary) will be suspected of conforming to the sociocultural expectations for male romantic behaviors in his society rather than acting in congruence with his true bodily based self.

Given that many of the dominant theories in psychology parallel key features of Freud's conception of an unconscious causal mechanism, it should come as little surprise that many therapists too, often regardless of orientation, are trained to mistrust the conscious mind of the client and to focus on unconscious, often bodily based processes. The most obvious and prominent example of this is manifested by therapists whose diagnoses and treatments assume a primary biological cause. These therapists assume that "the brain is the master control center of everything we say and do" (Morris & Maisto, 2005, p. 47). If the brain is the causal mechanism underlying all behavior, then its biological processes and structures ultimately explain client symptoms. Indeed, it is not only therapists, but as Valenstein (1998) makes clear, "It is widely believed by most authorities and the public alike that the cause [of mental disorder] is a chemical imbalance in the brain. . . . Brain chemistry is believed to be not only the cause of mental disorders, but also the explanation of normal variations in personality and behavior" (p. 1).

Of course, clients are not conscious of their "chemical imbalances." They have no direct awareness of serotonin or dopamine levels. These biological processes and activities operate beneath the threshold of their awareness and are also unobservable to the therapist. And because they are not directly observable or consciously experienced, the therapist, much like Freud, must rely on indirect methods of diagnosis to try to discern the causal mechanism behind the client's experienced symptoms, including interviews, questionnaires, and the reports of others who have observed the client for extended periods of time. As with Freud's psychodynamic theory, the underlying causal mechanism is the proper target for treatment. While the client's experiences, feelings, and thoughts may exacerbate or lessen the effects of this mechanism, it is the biologically based causal mechanism that is taken to be primarily responsible for the disorder.

A friend of mine experienced one consequence of this approach to therapy several years ago. He was feeling very depressed and suicidal and knew he needed help. My friend researched therapists throughout the entire state in which he lived until he found the one with the highest credentials, a psychiatrist working in the largest city in the state. My friend made an appointment, and when he arrived he was escorted in to a large office. He sat in the chair across from the therapist sitting at his desk.

My friend recalled that the therapist made no eye contact and didn't greet him. Instead, he reached into a desk drawer and pulled out a questionnaire (probably the Beck Depression Inventory) and asked my friend a series of questions, making marks on the paper after each response. Then he opened another desk drawer and took out a prescription tablet. He wrote down a prescription for an antidepressant medication for my friend and dismissed him. The whole session lasted less than ten minutes. No client history was taken, and no other potential contributing factors were assessed. This may be a very unusual experience. I certainly hope it is. But it does illustrate in the most extreme of ways how a therapist's focus on an underlying biological causal mechanism can lead him or her to disregard the client's conscious feelings and thoughts.

Space will not permit a thorough review of all the psychological theories and therapeutic practices that have been similarly influenced by Freud's assumption of an underlying causal mechanism. Suffice it to say that there is a precedent in psychological theorizing and practice for a mistrust of the conscious mind. This mistrust is often based on the assumption that an underlying causal mechanism, however defined, determines thoughts, feelings, and actions. This unconscious, deterministic implication suggests that conscious experiences, including experiences of agency and meaning, are epiphenomenal or at least secondary to more basic, often bodily based mechanistic processes.

An LDS Alternative: Agency and Meaning. By contrast, an LDS perspective does not view people as bifurcated into a conscious mind that is under the governance of an underlying causal mechanism or process. An LDS perspective also does not consider the conscious experience of agency and meaning to be merely epiphenomenal or secondary. On the contrary, an LDS perspective follows revealed scripture concerning the nature of man. In Doctrine and Covenants 88:15, it was revealed to the Prophet Joseph Smith that "the spirit and the body are the soul of man." Also, in D&C 93:33 we read that "spirit and element, inseparably connected, receive a fullness of joy." Granted, this perspective does understand the human soul to be made up of two parts, spirit and body, but it does not suggest that one part of the person is the cause of the other or is deceived by the other. It certainly does not indicate that one part of a person is depraved and bestial. Recall that for Freud, the bodily based id is the more carnal aspect of the psyche and the super-ego is the morally socialized part of the mind, with the ego stuck somewhere in the middle. The LDS perspective, on the other hand, sees the spirit and body as equally good and worthy or as equally carnal and corrupt, depending upon the person's obedience to the commandments and repentance. Consequently, one cannot blame the body or the spirit for one's actions because both parts share equally in the quality of one's soul.

As regards underlying causal mechanisms, there surely are aspects of bodies and spirits outside conscious awareness that limit our possibilities for action. However, from an LDS perspective, these constraints cannot operate on people in such a way that agency is altogether lost, because agency is of critical importance to God and is an essential component of his plan for his children. While it is true that people are not directly aware of many of the biological processes that limit their possibilities (e.g., people are not conscious of their neurons firing and the hormones released into their bloodstream when they experience a loving feeling toward someone else), there is no reason to assume that these processes determine human behaviors.

It may be that a person needs firing neurons in the brain and hormones in the blood if they are to function and if they are to love. However, to say that bodily structures and processes like these are necessary to a person's thoughts, feelings, and behaviors does not mean they are sufficient to explain that functioning or that they are the cause of the actions, thoughts, and feelings. In other words, to say that I cannot experience love without neuronal firing and hormone release does not mean I love because of those biological activities (see Reber & Beyers, 2000, for a review). Such an argument commits the classical logical fallacy of inferring causation from correlation. A more proper LDS perspective would view the body as a necessary constraint upon human thought, feeling, and action that must be included in any comprehensive account of agency, but not to the extent that the body becomes viewed as the sufficient cause and agency is lost.

Similarly, from the LDS perspective there are aspects of the human spirit that are beneath conscious awareness. But these aspects also are insufficient to explain or determine human actions in a way that would negate human agency. We know, for example, from revealed scripture that our spirits lived before this earth life. We are not conscious of this pre-earth life because of the veil of forgetfulness. The veil of forgetfulness preserves our agency by ensuring that the spirit has no pre-earthly upper hand on the body, no secretive knowledge, and no directing influence from beneath the surface of awareness. Rather, united with the body, the spirit comes on the scene of earthly existence enveloped in a soul that is bodily and spiritually unaware of what went on before and what awaits it in the future.

The little we do know about pre-earth life comes to us from prophetic revelation, such as Abraham's vision in which he observed that "there were many of the noble and great ones" (Abr. 3:22) there. Such revelations often act to correct any false or imbalanced attributions to the body or spirit. In this case, Abraham's vision reveals that if we are to question the nature of our unconscious at all—which hardly seems necessary given the veil that undoes any preadvantage our spirits may have upon us—we should question the Freudian notion that the unconscious aspects of persons are depraved and bestial. Quite the contrary, it is possible that the spiritual part of us that we cannot directly access (and whose memories are forgotten to us) may actually be noble and great. Thus, the unconscious features of neither the spirit nor the body are necessarily predisposed toward evil and sin.

With regard to agency, then, it is precisely because the spirit and body are united into the soul of a person, with neither side being *a priori* determined toward good or evil, that genuine agency is possible. A person is not controlled or caused by some unconscious part of their soul, but as the prophet Lehi makes clear in 2 Nephi 2, God's children have the agentic capacity to act without being acted upon. Thus, neither the body nor the spirit compels a person to act; rather, each of us is capable of making genuine choices within the constraints of the soul (body and spirit) and the limitations of the broader physical, social, and spiritual context in which we find ourselves (D&C 93:30; also see Slife & Williams, 1995, for a discussion of embodiment and contextual agency). Because our conscious choices are genuine albeit constrained choices, so too is the meaning that accompanies them. Thus, if a husband chooses to bring flowers home to his wife as a conscious and intentional expression of his love and gratitude, that conscious experience could be the proper explanation of his action.

Implications for Psychotherapy. The understanding of human consciousness, agency, and meaning that the restored gospel provides supports LDS counselors and psychotherapists who approach their clients and their therapeutic practice without the presumption of a deterministic underlying causal mechanism. Certainly, many LDS counselors and therapists already recognize to some extent the problematic implications of an underlying causal mechanism for their clients' agency and meaning. The purpose of this chapter is to bolster therapists' theoretical and theological confidence in those practices that support the meaning-filled, consciously chosen thoughts, feelings, and behaviors of their clients. Space will not permit a fully detailed comparison of the implications that follow from the presumption of an underlying causal mechanism and the implications that ensue from a gospel-based perspective. However, the table below highlights some of the key differences between the two perspectives that counselors and therapists can consider and evaluate as they relate them to their own practice.

Table 1

Consciousness: Contrasting Implications for Psychotherapy

Culture of Suspicion	Gospel-based Perspective
Unconscious determinism	Conscious agency (within constraints)
Reject clients' face-value accounts	Open to clients' face-value accounts
Abstract analysis of unconscious causes	Concrete presence to conscious meaning and agency
Facilitate insight and coping	Empower client agency and facilitate genuine change
Client meaning and values are secondary	Client meaning and values are primary
Treat the underlying cause (e.g., psychic tension, genes, biological process)	Treat the soul of the person (body and spirit)
Therapist as expert	Client as expert

Implication #2: Hedonism

Freudian Exemplar: Motivation Is Ultimately Hedonistic. A second assumption stemming from Freud's concept of the unconscious is a widely accepted belief in the fundamentally hedonistic motivation of human beings. Hedonism is the idea that we are either determined to pursue pleasure and minimize pain or that we ought to do so because it is good and right. For Freud, there can be no question about how thoroughgoing his commitment to the deterministic form of hedonistic motivation was, because for him "our total mental activity is directed towards pleasure and avoiding unpleasure" (1917, p. 356). He believed that humans, like other animal species, are driven by a bodily based instinct, a pleasure principle, which seeks immediate gratification while also avoiding pain and suffering.

Indeed, Freud's dedication to hedonism is so all-encompassing that he also assumes its activity in the ego and superego, albeit indirectly. The ego, Freud says, "obeys the reality principle, which also at bottom seeks to obtain pleasure, but pleasure which is assured through taking account of reality, even though it is pleasure postponed and diminished" (1963, p. 357). The superego too operates according to hedonism as it exerts its influence on the ego by imposing the very pain (usually through guilt and shame) that the id seeks to avoid. In this sense, all our actions, thoughts, and feelings are driven by pleasure and pain in a hedonistic, homeostatic psychic dynamic.

For Freud, one can never really act in a way that disregards pleasure and pain, and certainly not in a manner that genuinely and ultimately pursues pain and avoids pleasure. Such activities would be decidedly unnatural, irrational, and disordered. Consequently, there can be no genuinely nonhedonistic reasons for healthy human activities. For Freud, it is also impossible, or at least psychologically unsound, to perform a truly altruistic or self-sacrificing act. This is why Freud asserted that "all who wish to be more noble-minded than their constitution allows fall victims to neurosis" (as cited in Wallach & Wallach, 1983, p. 44). A person whose actions risk great personal discomfort, injury, or even death must be either acting for the sake of some unconscious pleasure that outweighs potential suffering or to avoid psychological pain (e.g., guilt) that exceeds potential hurt. If not, that person is acting in some disordered way and cannot be described as a psychologically healthy individual.

Hedonistic Motivation in Contemporary Psychology. As with the unconscious, Freud's contribution to psychology with regard to hedonism is not that psychology has adopted his specific conception of it. Instead, his legacy is a pervasive focus on an underlying causal mechanism that operates in a primarily hedonistic way (Wallach & Wallach, 1983). In behaviorism, for example, it is not a psychic pleasure principle that drives learning. Instead, the hedonistic mechanisms of reward, satisfaction, reinforcement, and punishment developed by Skinner and Thorndike, among others, clearly base learning on the pleasurable and painful consequences that follow a response (Hergenhahn & Olson, 2000). Actions that are not followed by a reward or punishment do not result in learning, and actions that seem to go against rewards and punishments never really do so. The rewards and punishments are just less obvious.

Even some less overtly hedonistic theories of psychology implicate pleasure and pain as primary motivations for action. In humanistic psychology, for instance, becoming a fully functioning person depends on receiving pleasurable unconditional positive regard and reducing the painful conditional positive regard received from the significant people in one's life (Rogers, 1961). Some forms of existential psychotherapy seek to relieve the painful angst that accompanies facing the inevitability of one's own death, the meaninglessness of life, and the suffering of an inescapable freedom and responsibility for one's own being (Yalom, 1980).

Regardless of the form it takes, hedonism plays a significant role in many psychologists' understanding of humans and their behaviors. Consequently, for psychologists who practice therapy, helping a client almost always includes a primary focus on relieving the client's suffering or promoting the person's pleasurable feelings in some way (Richardson, 2005). Indeed, therapists often mark the well-being of their clients and measure the successful outcomes of therapy in hedonistic terms. Successful therapy typically includes increased happiness and satisfaction with themselves, their relationships, and their life pursuits, and decreased depression, anxiety, and distress (Richardson, Fowers & Guignon, 1999).

Therapists too may assess the quality of their therapeutic work hedonistically. A therapist may need to find some pleasure in his or her work in order to continue in it and to avoid burnout. As hard as the work may be, it probably has to be ultimately hedonically satisfying to some degree for both clients and therapists to continue in therapy. It is important to point out here that pleasure and pain are not necessarily bad things. On the contrary, finding pleasure in one's work or gaining relief from pain through therapeutic treatment are important and useful things.

The concern of this chapter is the overweighting of hedonistic causal mechanisms that make pleasure and pain the primary or only motives of human behavior. If other, nonhedonistic motives are omitted or considered secondary to the motives of pleasure and pain, there will be a tendency to frame all experiences solely or primarily in terms of the proximal or ultimate pleasure and pain involved.

The social exchange theory of marital satisfaction (Bagarozzi, 1993) provides one illustration of this implication. According to this theory, a husband and wife will have a satisfying and enduring marriage if their respective benefits (i.e., reinforcements) from and contributions (i.e., punishments) to the marriage are equitable. If one spouse has to put more effort into the marriage but gets more pleasure out of it, while the other partner puts less work into the marriage and gets less satisfaction from it, then the marriage may not be equal, but it is equitable and both parties should be satisfied. If it is not equitable, then one or both spouses will be unsatisfied and may terminate the marriage so they can pursue a different relationship that is more balanced in the rewards and punishments it entails.

All social exchange theories of parenting, therapy, business, and other relationships are based on the economic assumption of exchange. Exchange is the idea that it is rational to enter into and remain in relationships only insofar as the reciprocal exchanges in that relationship mutually maximize individual pleasures and reduce individual pains. Participation in relationships that do not provide maximal benefits and minimize costs—or, even worse, those that increase pain and reduce pleasure—is thought to be irrational. This hedonistic social theory derived from economics may capture one important aspect of a marriage and other relationships, but its narrow focus on pleasure and pain omits other potentially important and even primary motives for staying in a marriage and finding it worthwhile. Similar to Freud's view on the matter, it also renders any other motives irrational.

An LDS Alternative: Nonhedonistic Motivations. From the perspective of an LDS faith, this narrow focus on hedonism as the sole or primary motivation of human beings is very problematic. An LDS perspective surely acknowledges the importance of pain and pleasure and other oppositional motives to human existence and agency. It also recognizes hedonic motivation as being possible and often important. However, it would not regard these important aspects of human experience as the only motives for action or even the most fundamental motives for behavior. The scriptures are replete with examples of hedonistic motivation, especially in the Old Testament, where the threat of God's punishment hangs over the heads of the disobedient and the promise of prosperity awaits the righteous (e.g., Mal. 3). However, we also find other motives for human action described in scripture, like experience, love, knowledge, a personal relationship with God, and doing what is right ("let the consequence follow").

As regards the motivation of experience, consider the words of the Lord to Joseph Smith in Liberty Jail. In response to Joseph's complaints of his own and the Saints' suffering and agony, the Lord stated, "Know thou, my son, that all these things shall give thee experience, and shall be for thy good" (D&C 122:7). Note that the Lord did not say that the experiences would be for Joseph's pleasure or even for his happiness, but rather for his good, a good that is not described hedonistically at all. The Lord is similarly nonhedonistic in John 14:15 when he asks his disciples to keep his commandments because they love him, not because it will make them feel good or ease their suffering. Granted, he does promise the peace and calm of the Comforter to those who keep the commandments, but that is what he describes as ensuing from obedience motivated by love. It is not what he asks his disciples to pursue. It is because they love him that they should obey him.

In John 17:3, the Savior emphasizes nonhedonistic motives again in his statement concerning eternal life, defining it in terms of knowing God and Jesus Christ, rather than in terms of reward and pleasure. Here again, we may find that pleasure and happiness follow from an intimate relationship with our Father in Heaven and the Savior. However, the Lord does not define eternal life in those hedonistic terms, nor does he ask that we seek eternal life or to know him and God so we can ultimately achieve those hedonistic outcomes. Instead, he simply provides an alternative, nonhedonistic motive for our actions—that we might know him and the Father.

As a final example of the possibility of nonhedonistic motivation, consider the words of Victor Frankl. Frankl suffered through the horrors of Auschwitz and fully understood the limitations of hedonistic motivation in a manner that is consistent with the LDS perspective. In the preface of his best-known text, *Man's Search for Meaning,* Frankl (1984) offers two nonhedonistic motivations for action that he clearly sees as superior to pleasure and pain. He states:

> Don't aim at success—the more you aim at it and make it a target, the more you are going to miss it. For success, like happiness, cannot be pursued; it must ensue, and it only does so as the unintended side-effect of one's *personal dedication to a cause greater than oneself* or as the by-product of one's *surrender to a person other than oneself.* Happiness must happen, and the same

> holds for success: you have to let it happen by not caring about it. I want you to listen to what your conscience commands you to do and go on to carry it out to the best of your knowledge. Then you will live to see that in the long run—in the long run, I say!—success will follow you precisely because you had forgotten to think of it. (p. xx, italics added)

As Frankl makes clear in this quote and throughout his text, alternative, nonhedonistic motivations for action are always available to us, though they may not always be easily noticed. Moreover, they are typically regarded by the Lord and by others (e.g., those being helped) as more preferable than those motives based in fear, guilt, and reward. Importantly, these alternative motives also capture the experience and meaning of marriages and other relationships that are often based on much more than mere equity between individual rewards and punishments.

Rather than deny the meaning of nonhedonistically motivated relationships and actions by labeling them irrational, an LDS perspective allows for the genuinely meaningful conscious experience of a choice motivated by nonhedonistic desires. Moreover, it affirms our faith that God gave his Only Begotten Son as a sacrifice for our sins because he loves us (John 3:16), not because it satisfied his ultimately hedonistic drives. It also means that Christ's willingness to take our sins and infirmities upon himself was not an irrational, disordered act. Christ, like his Father, acted on a different, nonhedonistic motive, which was his love for us. Finally, an LDS perspective on motivation bolsters our confidence that we too can enter into and maintain relationships with others because of a genuine love for them, or because it will help us know our God, or because it will give us experience. And because an LDS perspective asserts that we are not compelled to act by a bodily based hedonistic causal mechanism, we can accept the conscious meaning of our nonhedonistic actions. Moreover, we can trust that it is possible that the people who relate to us can do so in genuine, rational, and healthy nonhedonistic ways.

Implications for Psychotherapy. In light of the contrast between psychologies that assume a hedonistic causal mechanism as our primary or only motivation and an LDS perspective that allows for the possibility of nonhedonistic motives, a number of different psychotherapeutic implications emerge. As the table below indicates, a therapist who does not take hedonism for granted as an underlying motive is in a position to rethink the purposes and practices of therapy, including a reconsideration of the clients' suffering and well-being, therapeutic goals, and the value of nonhedonistic motives.

Table 2

Motivation: Contrasting Implications for Psychotherapy

Culture of Suspicion	Gospel-based Perspective
Pain and suffering work against our hedonistic nature and need to be relieved	Rethink the role of suffering in light of clients achieving potentially non-hedonistic therapeutic goals
Happiness is pursued	Happiness ensues
Client motives and goals are and should be fundamentally hedonistic	Clients are capable of nonhedonistic motives and goals and may be encouraged to pursue them
Nonhedonistic motives are either impossible or irrational and work against the well-being of the client	Nonhedonistic motives are possible, rational, and potentially desirable for clients
Effective therapeutic outcomes center on relief from suffering and increased individual satisfaction	Effective therapeutic outcomes could include wisdom gained from experiences, greater love of others, and closer, more meaningful relationships

Implication #3: Atomism

Freudian Exemplar: The Intrapsychic Relationship. Another consequence of the culture of suspicion that Freud's theories have helped originate and reinforce is that of atomism. Atomism is the idea that the properties of a thing are self-contained. For Freud, the individual psyche contains the psychological properties of a person. Consequently, the intrapsychic relationship between id, ego, and superego is the only relationship that really needs analysis. While it is true that the ego and superego must take some account of the external social world, people ultimately internalize the most important aspects of that sociality by around age six.

From then on, the dynamic that operates upon individuals and determines their actions is almost wholly self-contained within the individual psyche. This interiority led Freud and his followers to assert that "humans are anti-social by instinct and driven principally by intrapsychic forces" (Kohn, 1994, p. 249). Because only the intrapsychic relationship contained within the individual really mattered, Freud was just as content to analyze dreams as conscious experience. In fact, he could learn more from dreams than interpersonal relationships because dreams more clearly manifested the symbolized desires and issues of the unconscious mind than did waking life (Freud, 1900). Thus, for Freud it did not ultimately matter if the person being analyzed described an interaction with actual others or with dreamed others. Both descriptions revealed the intrapsychic reality of the individual through the projections of the unconscious id in its tensional relationship with the superego and ego.

One consequence of Freud's psychodynamic atomism is that we are never directly relating to others, but only to our projections of others as constituted by and filtered through intrapsychic conflicts and desires. In this sense, another person is reduced to an internalized object, such as an object of the id's wish fulfillment, as in the case of an unresolved oedipal issue relating to one's mother. The other could also be an internalized object of guilt projected by the superego, as in an authoritative father figure. God, for Freud, would be just such a psychic object—a projected father figure who imposes guilt and shame for wrongdoing rather than an actual being with whom genuine relationship is possible. In any case, the relationship of significance for Freud is not really the interpersonal relationship. Rather it is the intrapersonal relationship with the psychic object that ultimately satisfies a person's hedonistic desires.

Because the psyche only relates to its projections and not to another person directly, and because a majority of the psyche is unconscious, we can never really know ourselves or others. The self is essentially locked in to its own mind just as the other person is locked into his or hers, and consequently people can have no direct access to each other's feelings or thoughts. This promotes an inevitable egocentrism. Even empathy, which is often considered the most intimate form of connection with another person, cannot achieve more than identification with one's own self or some aspect of the self that is projected onto another person. Furthermore, this egocentrism, coupled with the hedonism described in the previous section, results in a strong deterministic form of egoism. The individual is ultimately driven by the unconscious id to satisfy his or her individual needs by maximizing intrapsychic pleasure and minimizing intrapsychic pain.

Atomism in Contemporary Psychology. Atomism has always been a pervasive assumption of Western philosophy and natural science, but with the support of Freud's notion of a self-contained psyche, it has become a common assumption of many psychological theories as well. The noted social commentator Alfie Kohn (1994) describes the pervasiveness of atomism in psychology in terms of individualism:

> Now that psychology has emerged as a discipline in its own right, we find that almost every branch, school, specialty, and theory within it is premised on individualism. . . . For behaviorists, the laws of learning pertain to the individual organism as it responds to the contingencies of its environment. For humanists, the *summum bonum* is self-actualization with the human potential movement undertaking the deification of the isolated self. Developmental psychologists generally equate maturity and health with autonomy and individuation; theories of achievement and motivation focus almost exclusively on the individual. (pp. 248–249)

Therapy too, is primarily an individualistic enterprise. Frank Richardson (2005) has shown that therapy tends to pursue atomistic goals of self-sufficiency and autonomous well-being, even at the expense of communal goals and needs. In his cultural analysis of the discipline, Edward Sampson (1977) similarly concluded that the entire discipline of psychology "plays an important role in reinforcing an individualistic, self-contained perspective" (p. 780).

This emphasis on the self-contained individual combined with the assumption of a hedonistic causal mechanism has resulted in a predominantly egoistic psychology. Indeed, when psychology came into disciplinary existence as a social science, ethical egoism was already so dominant an assumption in philosophy, biology, and other social sciences (e.g., economics) that egoism was seen not only as the right way to live one's life but as the natural way of life. Kohn (1994) has cogently argued this point, stating that "ethical egoism, in short, begets psychological egoism. That is, a common belief that we should restrict ourselves to self-interest, however that belief manifests itself, will ultimately incline us to see this exclusive devotion to self as a fact of life" (p. 196). The consequence of this tradition is a psychology that almost without exception, and generally without question, assumes that people are naturally selfish. Indeed, the assumption of egoism is so ubiquitous in psychology that Wallach and Wallach (1983) have concluded that "psychological theories of motivation are, almost without exception, fundamentally egoistic" (p. 204).

An LDS Alternative: Eternal Relationality. The LDS alternative begins with a very different assumption, which is that relationships with others are fundamental to our being and can be genuinely achieved. Indeed, revealed scripture teaches that our relationships are an essential part of this life and the next life (D&C 130:2). In the premortal world, there was a great council, "God stood among those that were spirits" (Abr. 3:23), and those spirits spoke and interacted with each other to some extent. We continue our relationships with each other and with God the Father and his Son in this life through the light of Christ (D&C 88:7–13) and the power and gift of the Holy Ghost (John 15:26). Finally, we know that our relationships, including our relationship with the Savior, the Father, and our family can be sealed to endure beyond death and into the next life (D&C 132:19). So important are relationships to the LDS perspective that the relationship itself must be sealed by priesthood authority if we are to achieve exaltation.

Clearly, from a gospel-based perspective, genuine relationships are not only possible, but they are absolutely essential to our existence. Consequently, LDS psychologists must take into account the interpersonal dynamic taking place between and among real persons. This includes our interpersonal relationship with God. We are taught in D&C 130:22 that God is not merely a projection of an unconscious authority figure generated by the superego—a fiction of the mind. On the contrary, he is a real person with whom a genuine relationship is possible and necessary to our being. The Jewish theologian and philosopher Martin Buber (1958) describes our relationship with God in this way: "God enters into a direct relation with us men in creative, revealing, and redeeming acts, and thus makes it possible for us to enter into a direct relation with him. This ground and meaning of our existence constitutes a mutuality, arising again and again, such as can subsist only between persons" (p. 135).

Because our relationship with God is a real interpersonal relationship, we can really and truly be enticed by God, the person, to do good, just as Satan, the person, can tempt us to do evil. Moreover, we can make genuine choices with real relational consequences (e.g., drawing closer to or farther from God), rather than being compelled by components of an internal psychic causal mechanism that projects God and Satan as nothing more than symbols of unconscious superego impulses. It is also possible to have genuine dialogue with others, to truly listen to and understand them, and to empathize with them. Prayer, from this perspective, is not an internal monologue. It is a genuine conversation between a person and God, just as repentance and forgiveness constitute a genuine reconciliation to God through the Atonement of Jesus Christ. We really can come unto the Savior and become yoked together with him as coparticipants in our salvation.

From an LDS perspective, we are always and already in relation to the Savior, our Father in Heaven, and others. Because we are dependent upon others for our existence in this life and our exaltation in the next, we are not inherently self-contained, egoistic beings. We are familial beings, sealed to each other and bound together to our brother, the Savior, and God, our Father. We can also become fully communal beings with, as Alma put it, our "hearts knit together in unity and in love one towards another" (Mosiah 18:21) through covenants like baptism and our promise to mourn with those that mourn and comfort those needing comfort.

Finally, we are not egocentric by nature, and we are not locked into our own intrapsychic dynamic. We can have other motives for our actions than atomistic, hedonistic motives, and we are not basically and deterministically selfish. We can choose to be selfish to be sure, but we are not compelled to be selfish by an unconscious, atomistic, and hedonistic causal mechanism.

Implications for Psychotherapy. As we compare the relational emphasis of the LDS perspective to the implicit atomism of the many psychologies influenced by the culture of suspicion, a number of contrasting therapeutic implications become salient. Table 3 provides a brief sketch of some of these key differences in emphasis, including: (1) the extent to which therapists emphasize intrapsychic and interpersonal client issues; (2) the degree to which therapists focus on individualistic, relational, familial, and communal goals; and (3) the likelihood that therapists will include more interpersonal therapies in their practice.

The comparison of atomistic and relational psychotherapies raises an especially noteworthy contrast regarding religiosity and spiritual experiences. On the atomistic side, spiritual experiences are typically considered to be properties of the individual and religious practices are examined in terms of their usefulness for healthy individual functioning and well-being (Helminiak, 2001). For the Latter-day Saint relational therapist, on the other hand, spiritual phenomena are shared among persons, including divine persons (D&C 50:13–22). Moreover, religious practices are as important for relational, familial, and communal well-being as they are for individuals. Put another way, it matters a great deal if a therapist approaches something like forgiveness with a theistic client as a psychotherapeutic technique designed to release psychic tensions between and among the id, ego, and superego, or whether forgiveness is understood as a relational activity that actually requires the participation of a divine being whose atoning sacrifice for sin makes repentance and forgiveness possible.

Table 3

Personhood: Contrasting Implications for Psychotherapy

Culture of Suspicion	Gospel-based Perspective
Analyze the intrapersonal dynamic	Analyze the interpersonal dynamic
Emphasize individualistic goals (e.g., autonomy, individual happiness)	Emphasize relational, familial, and communal goals (e.g., intimacy, friendship, service)
Treat the person	Treat the relationship
Individual therapy predominates	A balance of individual, couples, family, and group therapies
Religion and spirituality treated as intrapersonal phenomena	Religion and spirituality treated as interpersonal phenomena

Implication #4: Epistemological and Moral Relativism

Freudian Exemplar: Suspicion of Universal Truth. A final and enduring concern of contemporary culture to which Freud's postulation of an intrapsychic causal mechanism has made a noteworthy contribution is a suspicion of universal truth and morality. If, as Freud argued, we cannot trust our conscious mind due to ego defense mechanisms that keep us from facing the real truth of our unconscious desires and drives, then how can we trust the collective truths we consciously share? Would not our collective conscious truths be just as much a deception as our individual conscious truths are? For Freud, what we together have constructed as truth is ultimately an accumulation of the self-deceived beliefs of our individual egos, making it possible that claims of universal truth are nothing more than shared delusions.

For Freud, religion would be one example of this shared delusion. In religions, large groups of people come together, apparently with similar intrapsychic conflicts and projections (e.g., God), and form a religious belief system and culture to support their delusion and satisfy their unconscious hedonistic desires. Although in their conscious minds the truth they espouse is given by God and is therefore universal and good, they are all deceived. The real truth is housed in each of their individual psyches in the form of unconscious hedonistic id wishes. This means that truth is individualistic, not universal, and all people carry their own truth within themselves from context to context, though they are almost completely unaware of their truth. Similarly, they carry their own morality around within themselves, in the form of their unconscious superegos, each of which is formed uniquely by the individual's developmental experiences.

Relativistic Truth and Morality in Contemporary Psychology. One significant consequence of this mistrust of collectively held conscious truths and shared morality is epistemological and moral relativism. A number of postmodern psychologies share a suspicion of universal truth claims. Many postmodernists see the grand narratives of truth and ethics that have sustained modern culture (e.g., religion, science, democracy) as hegemonies that unfairly treated Western local truths as if they were absolute. In the place of these imperialistic claims of absolute truths, many postmodernists assert that the particular forms of knowledge a culture develops are only "true" for that culture. Consequently, "we should not assume that *our* ways of understanding are necessarily better, in terms of being any nearer the truth, than other ways" (Burr, 1995, p. 4). "We have to accept the historical and cultural relativism of all forms of knowledge" (p. 6), Burr contends, from which "it follows that the notion of 'truth' becomes problematic" (p. 6).

With regard to truth's problems in psychology, Ken Gergen (1996) has argued that "discourses of truth . . . [have] cease[d] to be commanding rhetorics" (p. 14), largely because the "constructionist critique challenged . . . truth beyond a culture standpoint" (p. 14). In Gergen's view, constructionism has demonstrated "how claims to the true and the good are born of historical tradition" (p. 15), such that "theories cannot, in effect, 'tell the truth'" (p. 13). From this perspective, psychological theories do not provide universal truths but are more like stories that are true only for those psychologists who adhere to the theory. Consequently, it is impossible to judge any cultural worldview, philosophical premise, or psychological theory as being more truthful than any other, because they cannot be compared or universalized.

The epistemological and moral relativism that follows from this critique of universal or absolute truth reinforces two current developments in psychology: fragmentation and eclecticism. Fragmentation speaks to the ever-growing separation and proliferation of psychological subdisciplines and theoretical enclaves. From the postmodern perspective, each subdiscipline can be viewed as a kind of culture with its own local truths, theoretical assumptions, and practical applications. In some cases, subdisciplines even speak different languages (e.g., neuropsychologists and humanists). This diversity and plurality shows sensitivity to the complexity of the subject matter and can be very useful in illuminating different features of psychology. Specialization surely has its advantages.

However, it is not specialization or diversity that is of concern in a fragmented psychology. The problem with fragmentation is, as Yanchar and Slife (1997) have described it, that "psychology offers no univocal definition of what its phenomena are . . . and no univocal corpus of psychological knowledge. . . . On the whole psychology appears to be a congeries of loosely related study areas than a coherent, unified, evolving science" (p. 235). Given their loose relationship, psychology subdisciplines really answer only to their indigenous epistemological and philosophical assumptions. This contributes to an epistemological relativism where the standards for what counts as scientific evidence are somewhat unique to each subdisciplinary culture and its "evidence" cannot be evaluated by other subdisciplines. The ultimate result is that psychology contains no unified and coherent body of knowledge.

A second outcome of the epistemological and moral relativism that is fueled by the mistrust of universal truth claims is eclecticism. Eclecticism is a dominant psychotherapeutic and counseling orientation (Poznanski & McLennan, 1995, Bergin & Garfield, 1994). This orientation stems from the postmodern-minded belief that no one theory can fully account for the variety of clients and presenting problems a therapist will face (Lazarus, Beutler, & Norcross, 1992). In keeping with the relativism of many forms of postmodern thought, the eclectic therapist acknowledges the unique history and culture of each client as well as the epistemological limitations of psychological theories. In response, the eclectic therapist tries to tailor his or her therapeutic approach to the individual needs of the client.

This tailoring approach may involve some form of theoretical integration, even when the theories may have contradictory assumptions (e.g., behaviorism and psychoanalysis). Other eclectics endorse a type of technical eclecticism, which typically relies on empirical studies to determine the efficacy of the techniques developed within traditional theoretical orientations, including psychodynamic, behavioral, cognitive, and so on (see Lazarus, 1995, for a review of these and other types of eclecticism). A key problem for technical eclecticism, from the postmodern perspective, is that it tends to rely on the scientific method to measure the effectiveness of techniques. For many postmodern psychologists and philosophers, the scientific method, like other modern grand narratives of truth, is a "one size fits all" theory that works against the epistemological relativism that heralded the need for eclectic psychotherapy in the first place. (For a thorough review of these and other problematic issues raised by eclectic psychotherapy, see Slife & Reber, 2001.)

As significant as these two outcomes may be for psychology and therapeutic practice, they do not trace the full implication of Freud's contribution to the culture of suspicion on this point far enough. Indeed, if we take Freud's assumption of intrapsychic truth and morality to its logical conclusion, then even cultural, subdisciplinary, or technical truths cannot be trusted. Any truth that is asserted and shared at any conscious level, be it individual, group, community, culture, or nation, must be looked upon with suspicion, given every person's inevitable ignorance of the unconscious drives and desires that determine their conscious thoughts, feelings, and behaviors. Thus, for Freud, and for the postmodern epistemological and moral relativism his ideas continue to support, the truth ultimately resides within self-contained individuals. Individuals are, for the most part, not fully aware of their truths, but those truths are nevertheless theirs alone. Because the truths are theirs alone, they cannot be judged and evaluated by others.

An LDS Alternative—Christian Truth. From the perspective of the restored gospel, there is a reliable truth that transcends historical and cultural contexts and can be consciously accessed and followed. This truth is not founded upon a theory or method, nor does it come in the primary form of universal laws or principles. This truth, as we learn from John 14:6, which reads, "I am the way, the truth, and the life," comes primarily and foundationally in the living embodied Savior, who is Jesus Christ (Slife & Reber, 2005). The universality of this truth is found in Christ's all-encompassing relationship to the world and all things in it, including human beings. Doctrine and Covenants 88 teaches that Christ

> ascended up on high, as also he descended below all things, in that he comprehended all things, that he might be in all and through all things, the light of truth; which truth shineth. This is the light of Christ. . . . And the light which shineth, which giveth you light, is through him who enlighteneth your eyes, which is the same light that quickeneth your understandings; which light proceedeth forth from the presence of God to fill the immensity of space—the light which is in all things, which giveth life to all things, which is the law by which all things are governed, even the power of God who sitteth upon his throne, who is in the bosom of eternity, who is in the midst of all things..(vv. 6–13)

Thus, it is through the light of Christ as well as through the gift and power of the Holy Ghost that each of us can consciously access a living, embodied truth that is universally available to all people.

Christian truth is embodied in a being who knows each of us personally and who understands the challenges and issues of human life that each of us face. As such, Christ can enter into our unique contexts and circumstances through his light or Holy Spirit and provide knowledge and direction that is relative to our situation and need. Consider the examples of Nephi, the son of Lehi, and Peter the Apostle. Both Nephi and Peter were devout followers of the law of Moses, a law that was given by Christ to the Israelites to prepare them for his coming, his teachings, and his atoning sacrifice. Yet when each of them was commanded by the Lord to violate a teaching of that law, they each knew it was more important to obey the lawgiver than the law.

Both Nephi and Peter obeyed because the Lord, as the living truth who was present with them in their context, knew exactly what needed to be done in that moment. Consequently, Nephi killed Laban and retrieved the brass plates that were necessary for the spiritual faith of his family and a great nation. And Peter taught and baptized Cornelius and other Gentiles and opened the door to what would become a truly worldwide religion.

In this sense, a gospel-based truth is both universal and relative, or more properly put, it is relational. As the prophet Mormon has taught, "the spirit of Christ is given to every man" (Moro. 7:16), so that each of us is in relationship with a divine being whose knowledge, light, and spirit is universally available. At the same time, because Christ descended below all things and suffered both body and spirit, he can also enter into and fully understand the historical, cultural, and embodied contexts of our individual and collective lives. He can communicate with us, guide us, and give us the truth and knowledge we need. As such, the living truth of the embodied Christ is also available to therapists and clients in the unique context of their therapy (see Slife & Reber, 2005, for a more detailed treatment of this concept).

Of course, the receptivity of any given therapist or client to the living truth will be constrained by their unique limitations of body, mind, environment, socialization, and so on. For example, it will likely be much more difficult for a client actively suffering from hallucinations associated with schizophrenia to discern spiritual promptings. Similarly, a therapist whose theoretical assumptions and training tend to lock him or her into stereotypical interpretations of client symptoms, diagnostic labels, and treatment methods (e.g., Rosenhahn, 1973) may struggle to attend to and appreciate divine inklings to the contrary. For this reason, there must be open and regular dialog between client and therapist with both parties checking in with one another (and, as needed and appropriate, with extended members of the therapist's and client's respective communities) for help in accurately discerning the truth and removing any obstacles to that discernment. In those conversations, clients and therapists would pay attention not only to what is being said, but to what is being felt and might be an inkling from a divine origin, and would discuss those potential promptings together. None of this entails a necessary change of therapeutic orientation or practice. LDS therapists of any stripe can adopt a posture of intentional receptivity to the living truth and can make any promptings they or the client experience an explicit part of the therapy process.

Implications for Psychotherapy. These contrasting perspectives on truth suggest very different therapeutic emphases and goals. If truth is thought to be unconscious, relativistic, and self-contained, then an individual psychoanalytic approach makes a lot of sense. In such a case, clients should be encouraged to seek truth by looking inward into their psyche for insight. On the other hand, if truth is the embodied Christ, whom therapist and client can encounter together through the Spirit in therapy, then a more relational form of therapy is implicated. From this perspective, clients and therapists are encouraged to engage one another (and, if needed, relevant others) in open dialog about potential promptings from the living truth that may be present with them in the therapy session. Table 4 outlines these and other implications that differ between the two views.

Table 4

Truth: Contrasting Implications for Psychotherapy

Culture of Suspicion	Gospel-based Perspective
Mistrust and deny individual and collectively held conscious truths and moralities	Make conscious truth and morality an explicit focus of therapy
Focus on the underlying, unconscious truth of the self-contained psyche	Focus on the embodied, living truth of Christ and clients' relationship to him
Rely on therapeutic knowledge and expertise	Rely on revelation in the therapeutic context
Teach clients to identify and cope with intrapsychic conflict	Teach clients to discern and follow revealed truth in their everyday life

Conclusion

Today, psychology does not identify itself with Freudian psychoanalysis, and few counselors and psychotherapists would label themselves psychodynamic in the classical sense. Still, it would be a mistake to underestimate the impact of Freud's ideas on the discipline of psychology, therapeutic practice, and culture at large. Freud may not have anticipated or even desired some of the implications that followed from his ideas (e.g., the relativism of truth). Nevertheless, his ideas have contributed to a psychological culture that favors explanations in terms of underlying causal mechanisms over conscious face-value experiences and accounts.

This chapter endeavored to show that it is not necessary to take these mechanisms and their implications for granted. On the contrary, LDS psychologists and counselors are in a unique position to critically examine psychology's culture of suspicion from the perspective of the restored gospel of Jesus Christ. An LDS perspective provides an alternative understanding of the human mind, motivation, and relationships. LDS psychologists and therapists may find this alternative more congruent with their faith and their experiences with clients. The critical analysis of the few assumptions addressed in this chapter may also encourage LDS psychologists and counselors to examine other taken-for-granted ideas that follow from Freud or other theorists who have contributed to the culture of suspicion. Ultimately, an LDS perspective could replace a culture that discounts clients' conscious experiences, choices, and meanings with a culture that takes seriously the agency and meaning that clients consciously experience.

References

Bagarozzi, D. A. (1993). Clinical uses of social exchange principles. In P. Boss, W. Doherty, R. LaRossa, W. Schumm, & S. Steinmetz (Eds.), *Sourcebook of family theories and methods: A contextual approach* (pp. 412–417). New York: Plenum.

Bergin, A. E., & Garfield, S. L. (Eds.). (1994). *Handbook of psychotherapy and behavior change*. New York: J. Wiley and Sons.

Buber, M. (1958). *I and thou*. New York: Scribner and Sons.

Burr, V. (1995). *An introduction to social constructionism*. New York: Routledge.

Elster, J. (1989). *Nuts and bolts for the social sciences*. Cambridge: Cambridge University Press.

Fisher, H. E. (2004). *Why we love: The nature and chemistry of romantic love.* New York: Henry Holt and Company.
Frankl, V. E. (1984). *Man's search for meaning: An introduction to logotherapy.* New York: Touchstone Books.
Freud, S. (1917). General introduction to psychoanalysis. In *The standard edition of the complete psychological works of Sigmund Freud* (vol. 15). (J. Strachey, Trans.). London: Hogarth Press, 74.
Freud, S. (1963). *The standard edition of the complete psychological works of Sigmund Freud* (vol. 15) (J. Strachey, Trans.). London: Hogarth Press.
Freud, S. (1968). *The interpretation of dreams.* New York: Avon.
Gantt, E. E., Reber, J. S., & Hyde, J. (2013). The psychology of altruism and the problems of mechanism, egoism, and determinism. In H. Koppel (Ed.), *Psychology of altruism.* New York: Nova Science Publishers.
Gergen, K. J. (1996). Theory under threat: Social construction and identity politics. In C.W. Tolman, F. Cherry, R. Hezewijk, & I. Lubek (Eds.) *Problems of theoretical psychology*. (pp. 13–23) North York, Ontario: Captus University.
Hedström, P., & Ylikoski, P. (2010). Causal mechanisms in the social sciences. *Annual Review of Sociology, 36,* 49–67.
Helminiak, D. A. (2001). Treating spiritual issues in secular psychotherapy. *Counseling and Values, 45*(3), 163–189.
Hergenhahn, B. R. & Olson, M. H. (2000). *An introduction to theories of learning* (6th ed.). Upper Saddle River, NJ: Prentice Hall.
Kohn, A. (1994). *The brighter side of human nature: Altruism and empathy in everyday life.* New York: Basic Books.
Lacan, J. (1968). *The language of the self: The function of language in psychoanalysis* (A. Wilden, Trans.). Baltimore: Johns Hopkins University.
Lazarus, A. A. (1995). Different types of eclecticism and integration: Let's be aware of the dangers. *Journal of Psychotherapy Integration, 5*(1), 27–39.
Lazarus, A. A., Beutler, L. E., & Norcross, J. C. (1992). The future of technical eclecticism. *Psychotherapy: Theory, Research, and Practice, 29*(1), 11–20.
Leahey, T. H. (2001). *A history of modern psychology* (3rd ed.). Upper Saddle River, NJ: Prentice-Hall.
MacIntyre, A. (1985). How psychology makes itself true—or false. In S. Koch & D. Leary (Eds.), *A century of psychology as science.* New York: McGraw-Hill.
Maslow, A. H. (1954). The instinctoid nature of basic needs. *Journal of Personality, 22*(3), 326–347.
Morris, C. G., & Maisto, A. A. (2005). *Psychology: An introduction* (10th ed.). Upper Saddle River, NJ: Prentice-Hall.
Poznanski, J. J., & McLennan, J. (1995). Conceptualizing and measuring counselors' theoretical orientation. *Journal of Counseling Psychology, 42*(4), 411–422.
Reber, J. S., & Beyers, M. S. (2000). Love is not an evolutionarily derived mechanism. In B. D. Slife (Ed.), *Taking sides: Clashing views on controversial psychological issues* (11th ed.). Guilford, CT: Dushkin Publications.
Richardson, F. C. (2005). Psychotherapy and modern dilemmas. In B. D. Slife, J. S. Reber, & F. C. Richardson (Eds.), *Critical thinking about psychology: Hidden assumptions and plausible alternatives* (pp. 17–38). Washington, DC: APA Books.
Richardson, F. C., Fowers, B. J., & Guignon, C. B. (1999). *Re-envisioning psychology: Moral dimensions of theory and practice.* San Francisco: Jossey-Bass.

Rogers, C. R. (1951). *Client-centered therapy: Its current practice, implications and theory*. London: Constable.

Rogers, C. R. (1961). *On becoming a person: A therapist's view of psychotherapy.* New York: Houghton-Mifflin.

Rosenhahn, D. L. (1973). On being sane in insane places. *Science, 179,* 250–258.

Sampson, E. E. (1977). Psychology and the American ideal. *Journal of Personality and Social Psychology, 35*(11), 767–782.

Samuels, R. (1998). Evolutionary psychology and the massive modularity hypothesis. *British Journal for the Philosophy of Science, 49*(4), 575–602.

Slife, B. D., & Reber, J. S. (2001). Eclecticism in psychotherapy: Is it really the best substitute for traditional theories? In B. D. Slife, R. N. Williams, & S. H. Barlow (Eds.), *Critical issues in psychotherapy: Translating new ideas into practice.* Thousand Oaks, CA: Sage Publications.

Slife, B. D., & Williams, R. N. (1995). *What's behind the research? Discovering hidden assumptions in the behavioral sciences.* Thousand Oaks, CA: Sage Publications.

Slife, B. D., & Reber, J. S. (2005). Comparing the practical implications of secular and Christian truth in psychotherapy. In A. Jackson and L. Fischer (Eds.), *Turning Freud upside down: Gospel perspectives on psychotherapy's fundamental problems.* Provo, UT: BYU Press.

Valenstein, E. S. (1998). *Blaming the brain: The truth about drugs and mental health.* New York: Free Press.

Wallach, M. A. & Wallach, L. (1983). *Psychology's sanction for selfishness: The error of egoism in theory and therapy.* San Francisco, CA: W. H. Freeman and Company.

Yalom, I. D. (1980). *Existential psychotherapy.* New York: Basic Books.

Yanchar, S. C., & Slife, B. D. (1997). Pursuing unity in a fragmented psychology: Problems and prospects. *Review of General Psychology, 1*(3), 235–255.

Lane Fischer

On the Need to Acknowledge Good and Evil

The existence of good and evil is largely ignored by current models of psychotherapy. Although it is ignored, it is inextricably tied to (1) the nature of moral agency, (2) the process of development, and (3) the nature of being. It is intimately tied to some of the fundamental questions that underlie psychotherapy. Good and evil can't be ignored. If we are to develop a psychotherapy based on the restored gospel of Jesus Christ, we must acknowledge good and evil.

On the Need to Acknowledge Good and Evil

The Nature of Agency

One important misconception of agency is that *agency* is synonymous with *choice*. Richard Williams's (1992) brilliant analysis of agency clearly argued that they cannot be synonyms. He showed that "the notion of freedom as choosing among alternatives is . . . unsatisfactory." Williams suggested that "there are three fundamental and interconnecting problems with equating choice and freedom (later termed *agency*). First, choice demands a chooser, and the nature and activity of such a chooser entails ontological problems. Second, there is a problem in establishing ground on which a chooser can make a free choice. Third, there is the problem of distinguishing between freedom and randomness." Williams analyzed each of the three problems, showed the inadequacy of the prevailing view that agency is synonymous with choice, and, rather than just dissect the prevailing view, he offered a persuasive alternative. Williams's alternative definition of agency and freedom is "having the world truthfully." He stated, "I am not really satisfactorily free unless I am free from error (i.e., unless the truth of the matter is available to me)." Furthermore, "freedom requires truth."

Williams (1994) expanded his analysis and critiqued both modernist (primarily Cartesian) and postmodernist approaches to the question of agency. Again, he showed that modernist notions of choosing among alternatives by purely rational, objective, putative apodictic knowledge is impossible. He also showed that the reactionary postmodern approach also fails because it fails to define good and evil. He said, "To the extent that postmodern accounts opt out of the moral discourse by assuming a relativist position, they opt out of the discourse on agency as well. Postmodernism has been, and continues to be, strong in its defense of volition from a non-Cartesian perspective (which perspective I personally favor), but so long as it embraces moral relativism as a satisfactory account of human action it cannot arrive at the heart of the question of agency."

Extrapolating from Williams, then, agency is inextricably dependent on acknowledging good and evil as we would acknowledge truth from falsity. And applying Williams's definition, it seems that I exercise agency and have freedom when I live truthfully or, in my words, when I pursue virtue.

Richard G. Scott (1996) articulated a nuanced understanding of agency. He stated in LDS general conference that "your agency, the right to make choices, is not given so that you can get what you want. This divine gift is provided so that you will choose what your Father in Heaven wants for you. That way He can lead you to become all that He intends you to be."

Let me propose a nuanced definition of agency that is consistent with both Elder Scott and Richard Williams. Think of agency as a particular kind of choice. Agency can be considered as the choice to pursue virtue, which is what Father in Heaven wants and invites us to do. Agency may be the choice to pursue good analogous to living truthfully. While we may be enticed by good or evil, perhaps we exercise agency only when we choose to pursue good. All other choices are simply choices, not necessarily an exercise of agency.

Relatedly, another common conception is that agency is an inalienable *right* to choose among equivalent options. It seems to me that we have always had the ability to choose, but we have not always had agency. It was given as a gift. If agency depends on the existence of good in the face of evil, then good, which emanates from God, and the opportunity to pursue the good (become all that God wants us to be, in Elder Scott's words) is the gift that Elder Scott was articulating. Agency was given to us as a spiritual gift from God. Agency is a gift (not a right) and opportunity to pursue virtue.

This is consistent with Lehi's conception. "Wherefore, the Lord God *gave* unto man that he should act for himself. Wherefore, man could not act for himself save it should be that he was enticed by the *one or the other*" (good or evil) (2 Ne. 2:16, emphasis added). It is consistent with Mormon's conception: "For behold, my brethren, it is *given* unto you to judge, that ye may know *good from evil*" (Moro. 7:15, emphasis added). It is consistent with God's statements to Joseph Smith: "Behold, I *gave* unto him that he should be an agent unto himself" (D&C 29:35) and "that every man may act in doctrine and principle pertaining to futurity, according to the moral agency which I have *given* unto him" (D&C 101:78, emphasis added). Furthermore, "the Lord said unto Enoch: Behold these thy brethren; they are the workmanship of mine own hands, and I gave unto them their knowledge, in the day I created them; and in the Garden of Eden, *gave* I unto man his agency" (Moses 7:32, emphasis added).

Agency and the Atonement

Under this conception, the gift of agency depends on the availability of good. It is somewhat clear that the gift of agency to choose good depends on the Atonement of Jesus Christ. Lehi taught, "They are free to choose liberty and eternal life, through the great Mediator of all men, or to choose captivity and death, according to the captivity and power of the devil; for he seeketh that all men might be miserable like unto himself" (2 Ne. 2:27). In fact, all of Lehi's great exposition in 2 Nephi chapter 2 centers on the Great Mediator and the Atonement of Jesus Christ as the linchpin in the whole plan of happiness. We often interpret Lehi's exposition on opposition and conclude that Satan is in opposition to the great plan of happiness (and so he is). We hear therefore that Satan fulfills a valuable function in the overall scheme of things. We hear that without Satan's opposition, mankind would not be free. But when I turn that logic around, the concepts clarify. If I conceive of evil as prior, then Lehi's discourse on the Messiah and the Great Mediator makes more sense to me. If evil was prior, then the emergence of the Messiah and good became the necessary opposition. Satan offered myriad choices, none of which led to virtue, good, or God. It was good that emerged as the opposition to evil! Satan does not provide opposition to good. The Atonement of Jesus Christ provides opposition to evil. When thus ordered, it becomes clear why Lehi focused on the Great Mediator and Christ's Atonement in his discussions of freedom. It is the presence of good and Christ's Atonement that provides freedom, not the presence of evil.

God is the source of light and good. Doctrine and Covenants section 88 is a powerful example.

> Which glory is that of the church of the Firstborn, even of God, the holiest of all, through Jesus Christ his Son—he that

> ascended up on high, as also he descended below all things, in that he comprehended all things, that he might be in all and through all things, the light of truth; which truth shineth. This is the light of Christ. As also he is in the sun, and the light of the sun, and the power thereof by which it was made. As also he is in the moon, and is the light of the moon, and the power thereof by which it was made; as also the light of the stars, and the power thereof by which they were made; and the earth also, and the power thereof, even the earth upon which you stand. And the light which shineth, which giveth you light, is through him who enlighteneth your eyes, which is the same light that quickeneth your understandings; which light proceedeth forth from the presence of God to fill the immensity of space—the light which is in all things, which giveth life to all things, which is the law by which all things are governed, even the power of God who sitteth upon his throne, who is in the bosom of eternity, who is in the midst of all things. (D&C 88:5–13)

Similarly, the Savior declared multiple times that he is "the light and the life of the world, a light which shineth in darkness and the darkness comprehendeth it not" (D&C 34:2). This construction does not support the idea of complimentary understanding in which the darkness comprehends because it is juxtaposed to the presence of light. It does not seem to be a complimentary relationship between darkness and light.

It is a misconception to think that Satan's evil provides freedom. Satan has never been interested in true freedom. As did Lehi, Moses also informed us of Satan.

> Wherefore, because that Satan rebelled against me, and sought to destroy the agency of man, which I, the Lord God, had given him, and also, that I should give unto him mine own power; by the power of my mine Only Begotten, I caused that he should be cast down; and he became Satan, yea, even the devil, the father of all lies, to deceive and to blind men, and to lead them captive at his will, even as many as would not hearken unto my voice. (Moses 4:3–4)

I have wondered exactly how Satan proposed to destroy the agency of man. If agency were an inalienable right, then it would be impossible to destroy it. Satan's stratagem would be a bluff.

Apparently, it wasn't an idle threat, because the attempt resulted in his expulsion. But if agency were a gift that was dependent on the existence of good and the Atonement of Jesus Christ, how could Satan have destroyed the agency of man? We must remember the purpose of the entire plan of happiness, which is "to bring to pass the immortality and eternal life of man" (Moses 1:39).

Satan's objective was to disable the plan of happiness by disabling agency. How? This is certainly not a settled question. Judd (1999) articulated two alternative models by which Lucifer sought to destroy the agency of humankind. The first is the commonly held belief that "his method was to selfishly force mankind to do right." Judd intoned a second, alternative understanding from Bruce R. McConkie (1982) and Robert J. Matthews (1990). Judd interpreted McConkie thus. Lucifer's plan "was to eliminate any distinction between right and wrong, allowing humankind to live any way that they desired, and that in the end, he (Satan) would redeem them." Of course, Judd is astute to note that Satan was a liar from the beginning and has never supported his followers. Whatever promise or guarantee that Lucifer gave, he would not have kept his promise. While the Savior's objective is for all to become joint heirs and receive all that Father hath with him, Satan's objective was to have it all for himself.

I offer an additional model by which Lucifer sought to destroy the agency of humankind. Consider how the plan was indeed enabled and how it could have been disrupted. In order for humans to be exalted, there had to be a path that led to God. Nephi called it the "strait and narrow path which leads to eternal life" (2 Ne. 31:18). Since no unclean thing can dwell in the presence of God (1 Ne. 10:21), walking the path to God would require an atoning sacrifice and cleansing. No wonder Nephi emphasized baptism as the gate into the path and following the Savior on the path. No wonder he concluded,

> my beloved brethren, after ye have gotten into this strait and narrow path, I would ask if all is done? Behold, I say unto you, Nay; for ye have not come thus far save it were by the word of Christ with unshaken faith in him, relying wholly upon the merits of him who is mighty to save. Wherefore, ye must press forward with a steadfastness in Christ, having a perfect brightness of hope, and a love of God and of all men. Wherefore, if ye shall

> press forward, feasting upon the word of Christ, and endure to the end, behold, thus saith the Father: Ye shall have eternal life. (2 Ne. 31:19–20)

This is all consistent with Mormon's exposition on good and evil (Moro. 7:12–13). In essence, good comes from God and leads to God (and exaltation). Evil leads away from God (and away from exaltation). I think Satan tried to destroy the agency of man by disabling the path that leads to God and eternal life. Lehi is clear that in order for agency to exist, the path that leads to God must exist. If only one path led to God and all others did not, then disabling the path that leads to God would *de facto* destroy the agency of man to choose good. There would be no *good* path to choose.

According to Lehi and Nephi, the path that leads to God exists only because of Christ's Atonement and his role as the Great Mediator. If Satan could stop Christ's Atonement and destroy the Great Mediator, then there would be no path of goodness to God. It wouldn't matter at all what path men were to choose. Alternative to other conceptions, Satan's plan was not a plan to force man to obey or to eliminate the distinction between good and evil. I think that Satan's plan was to remove the path to God such that it didn't matter at all what choices were made. There would be no force involved at all. Simply no path would lead to God. Consider all the ways Satan sought to forestall Christ's Atonement. As one example, he inspired Herod to order the slaughter of all the babies and toddlers in an entire region of his kingdom (Matt. 2). He would stop at nothing to block the Atonement. When Christ's Atonement was effected and the universal resurrection was accomplished, it was finished. All that is left for Satan is to try to make men miserable like unto himself (2 Ne. 2:18).

It is a misconception to think of agency as an inalienable right to choose among equivalent options. Moral agency is a gift to choose good, which gift is made possible by the loving sacrifice and Atonement of Christ. The Atonement of Jesus Christ either created the path to God or opened the gate to it. If not for the Atonement of Jesus Christ and the path to God, there would be no agency. The misconception emerges in therapists' language when they say things like, "I am neutral. My role is to facilitate the exploration of options and to enhance choosing," as though "choosing" were the therapeutic objective and that the goodness of the choice were irrelevant. It is a misconception to think that "choosing," in itself, is healthy, rather than "choosing good" or pursuing virtue. We should be clear that agency is not synonymous with choice and that that agency is a gift to choose good. Agency is the opportunity to pursue virtue. Therapists should not be neutral. Therapists should invite clients to pursue virtue (Fischer, 2005).

The Process of Growth

When we rationalize choosing evil as part of God's educational plan, we clearly misunderstand the nature of good and evil. When we claim that there must be opposition in all things and that we must, of necessity, experience evil in order to understand good, or that there is heuristic value in walking in the dark in order to understand the light, we clearly fail to understand the Savior's life. I don't think they are complementary heuristics.

One of Satan's most subtle lies was that we need to experience evil and good in order to grow. The lie is found in the simple conjunction *and.* Satan lied when he claimed that we must know good *and* evil (see Gen. 3:5). Most of the references in the scriptures use a different conjunction. The prophets tend to say that we must know good *from* evil (2 Ne. 2:5, 26; Hel. 14:31; Moro. 7:15–19). There is significant difference in meaning between those two phrases, "good *and* evil" and "good *from* evil." Satan would convince us that we must participate in evil in order to understand the light. Satan would argue that we must disobey Father in Heaven in order to gain knowledge. Satan's argument that we must experience evil to understand good is a dangerous lie.

I don't think it works that way. I think there is complete asymmetry in the instructive power of good and evil, light and dark. I think we understand the light only when we ingest the light. Curiously, we also understand the dark only when we ingest the light. We understand neither the light nor the dark when we ingest the dark. The light teaches us about both the light and the dark. The dark teaches us about neither. Good and evil are not complementary, one informing us about the other. They are completely asymmetrical.

This is not to say that any of us stand in total light. We are working toward brighter and brighter light. Each step into greater light helps us better discern good *from* evil. Alma was crystal clear on how light and dark work within us. He said:

> It is given unto many to know the mysteries of God; nevertheless they are laid under a strict command that they shall not impart only according to the portion of his word which he doth grant unto the children of men, according to the heed and diligence which they give unto him. And therefore, he that will harden his heart, the same receiveth the lesser portion of the word; and he that will not harden his heart, to him is given the greater portion of the word, until it is given unto him to know the mysteries of God until he know them in full. And they that will harden their hearts, to them is given the lesser portion of the word until they know nothing concerning his mysteries; and then they are taken captive by the devil, and led by his will down to destruction. Now this is what is meant by the chains of hell. (Alma 12:9–11)

As we progressively ingest the dark, we become darker and darker. We do not understand the light by ingesting the dark. We don't expand freedom by choosing to walk the path of darkness. Walking any path other than the path of light leads us to become less discerning, less free, and more captive. Satan lied to Eve when he said we needed to know good *and* evil. We need to know good *from* evil. And we do that by ingesting the light. The dark teaches us nothing.

Arguing that we only understand the light after ingesting the dark raises a very serious doctrinal complication. It argues that Jesus had to ingest evil (sin) in order to understand good. Jesus never ingested evil. He lived a perfect life, progressively ingesting the light until he comprehended all things including all light and all dark. By only ingesting the light, he could discern the good *from* the evil. Understanding the asymmetry of light and dark is my best way to understand Jesus's perfect life. Satan's lie was yet one more way to deny the Christ and the Atonement. In order for Christ's Atonement to be effective, he had to be sinless. If Satan can convince us that we must ingest evil to understand good, then Jesus must have done the same, and therefore he could not have been sinless, and the Atonement is a myth.

If we resist Satan's slanderous claim that the Savior could not have been sinless, he comes up with another lie. Satan will then argue that

Jesus was a special case and that the rest of mortals, must, of necessity, sin and ingest evil in order to understand the good. This is also a lie. We never have to ingest evil at all. We grow from light to greater light. And the scriptures testify that it is possible for us to never sin.

> For they that are wise and have received the truth, and have taken the Holy Spirit for their guide, and have not been deceived—verily I say unto you, they shall not be hewn down and cast into the fire, but shall abide the day. And the earth shall be given unto them for an inheritance; and they shall multiply and wax strong, and their children shall grow up without sin unto salvation. (D&C 45:57–58)

Not only was it possible for Jesus to live a sinless life, but, for those wise souls who have bound Satan by their righteousness, their children will grow up without sin unto salvation. Humans can do this. We can do this. We don't need to ever ingest the dark. Our task is to pursue virtue. These things are possible. We can ingest only light.

Good and Evil and the Nature of Being

Jackson (2005) addressed a relational ontology in our first volume, *Turning Freud Upside Down.* Clearly, for Jackson, the nature of moral agency is inextricably bound up in relationships. A moral act is moral because of how the act functions within a relationship. A moral act may occur in relationship with God or in relationship with other human beings. The first and second great commandments are clearly embedded in relationships (Matt. 22:36–39), and, extrapolating from King Benjamin, there may not even be a real distinction between the two commandments (Mosiah 2:17). I would like to briefly consider the pragmatic impact of good and evil on our fundamental being.

The simple question is, how does the nature of good and evil impact the nature of a human being? Perhaps it takes a longer view than this mortality to see the answer. In the premortal existence, we were housed in bodies of spirit. Lucifer was there and likewise housed in a body of spirit. In our current, mortal sphere, we are housed temporarily in composite bodies of spirit and flesh and bone and blood. Lucifer is still housed in a body of spirit and will never experience the more complex composite body. There is now a fundamental difference between us. Why?

From Abraham, we learn of the beginning of our current ontological state:

> Now the Lord had shown unto me, Abraham, the intelligences that were organized before the world was; and among all these there were many of the noble and great ones; and God saw these souls that they were good, and he stood in the midst of them, and he said: These I will make my rulers; for he stood among those that were spirits, and he saw that they were good; and he said unto me: Abraham, thou are one of them; thou wast chosen before thou wast born. And there stood one among them that was like unto God, and he said unto those who were with him: We will go down, for there is space there, and we will take of these materials, and we will make an earth whereon these may dwell; and we will prove them herewith, to see if they will do all things whatsoever the Lord their God shall command them; and they who keep their first estate shall be added upon; and they who keep not their first estate shall not have glory in the same kingdom with those who keep their first estate; and they who keep their second estate shall have glory added upon their heads for ever and ever. And the Lord said: Whom shall I send? And one answered like unto the Son of Man: Here am I, send me. And another answered and said: Here am I, send me. And the Lord said: I will send the first. And the second was angry, and kept not his first estate; and, at that day, many followed after him. (Abr. 3:22–28)

Moses identified the "second" one:

> And I, the Lord God, spake unto Moses, saying: That Satan, whom thou hast commanded in the name of mine Only Begotten, is the same which was from the beginning, and he came before me, saying—Behold, here am I, send me, I will be thy son, and I will redeem all mankind, that one soul shall not be lost, and surely I will do it; wherefore give me thine honor. But, behold, my Beloved Son, which was my Beloved and Chosen from the beginning, said unto me—Father, thy will be done, and the glory be thine forever. Wherefore, because that Satan rebelled against me, and sought to destroy the agency of man, which I, the Lord God, had given him, and also, that I should

> give unto him mine own power; by the power of my mine Only Begotten, I caused that he should be cast down; and he became Satan, yea, even the devil, the father of all lies, to deceive and to blind men, and to lead them captive at his will, even as many as would not hearken unto my voice. (Moses 4:1–4)

The nature of Satan's current body was determined by his rejection of good and pursuit of evil. As he pursued evil, ingested evil, and gloried in evil, he "kept not his first estate." He was not allowed to enter the next estate to be housed in the more complex composite body. His very body has been determined by how he pursued evil. Humans, here in this mortality, kept their first estate. Our bodies have become more complex and developed primarily because of how we pursued virtue, ingested light, and labored for the good. At an ontological level, our being has been shaped by good and evil.

Can we see the differences among us now according to how we pursue virtue? It is subtle, but I believe that differences in being can even be detected across this short mortality. James E. Faust (2004) gave an example of observing his friend who had pursued virtue over a lifetime. "As part of the oath and covenant of the priesthood, the Lord makes several promises to His faithful sons 'which he cannot break.' First, the priesthood holders 'are sanctified by the Spirit unto the renewing of their bodies.' I think President Hinckley is a great example of this. He has been renewed in body, mind, and spirit in a most remarkable manner." Similarly, President Hugh B. Brown (1963) quoted D&C 89:33 and testified, "Brethren, I bear testimony to the fact that that promise has been realized in the life of President David O. McKay, that he has been sanctified by the Spirit unto the renewing of his body, and some of the rest of us are better off today than we were many years ago so far as physical health is concerned—and we attribute that fact to his blessing" (p. 90). The nature of our being within this life may even be impacted by how we deal with good and evil.

Certainly, there will be significant differences in our bodies and being after the end of this second estate. The differences will be more stark than they are now. Joseph Smith taught us of these differences:

> For notwithstanding they die, they also shall rise again, a spiritual body. They who are of a celestial spirit shall receive the same

> body which was a natural body; even ye shall receive your bodies, and your glory shall be that glory by which your bodies are quickened. Ye who are quickened by a portion of the celestial glory shall then receive of the same, even a fulness. And they who are quickened by a portion of the terrestrial glory shall then receive of the same, even a fulness. (D&C 88:27–31)

Those bodies celestial and bodies terrestrial will be of different ilk with different faculties primarily because of how we pursued virtue in our first and second estates. If a fundamental question in psychotherapy is, what is the nature of a human being? then it is foolish to ignore the influence of good and evil. There are stark differences in our bodies between estates and subtle differences within this estate. Although the differences in this mortality are subtle, they are nonetheless important and presage the stark differences in the long term. To ignore the influence of good and evil in the process of psychotherapeutic helping seems foolish. Our pursuit of virtue will shape our very being. The invitation to ourselves and clients to pursue virtue is perhaps the most important thing we can do as therapists.

Good and Evil in Psychotherapy

As I proposed in *Turning Freud Upside Down* (2005), humans are nested in a series of ecologies that are characterized by qualitatively different but hierarchically more adequate laws. Psychotherapists can understand and accept the level of law that a client chooses to bear, but they can also gently invite them to greater virtue. Although we talk about good and evil in dichotomous terms, the restored gospel has refined our understanding. Successive ecologies in the hierarchy are more encompassing and more virtuous than the previous ecologies. A therapist doesn't have to dichotomize or demonize. We can gently and lovingly invite clients to pursue progressively greater virtue. But we cannot ignore the reality of good and evil.

References

Brown, H. B. (1963). Participation: The way to salvation. In *One hundred and thirty-third annual conference of The Church of Jesus Christ of Latter-day Saints*, (pp. 89–92). Salt Lake City: The Church of Jesus Christ of Latter-day Saints.

Faust, J. D. (2004, November). The key of the knowledge of God. *Ensign*, 52–55.

Fischer, L. (2005). The nature of law: Universal but not uniform. In A. P. Jackson & L. Fischer with D. Dant (Eds.), *Turning Freud upside down: Gospel perspectives on psychotherapy's fundamental problems* (pp. 36–50). Provo, UT: Brigham Young University Press.

Jackson, A. P. (2005). Relationships. In A. P. Jackson & L. Fischer with D. Dant, (Eds.), *Turning Freud upside down: Gospel perspectives on psychotherapy's fundamental problems.* Provo, UT: Brigham Young University Press.

Judd, D. K. (2005). Moral agency: A doctrinal approach to therapy. In A. P. Jackson, L. Fischer, & D. Dant, (Eds.), *Turning Freud upside down: Gospel perspectives on psychotherapy's fundamental problems.* Provo, UT: Brigham Young University Press.

Matthews, R. J. (1990). *A Bible! A Bible!* Salt Lake City: Bookcraft.

McConkie, B. R. (1982). *The millennial Messiah.* Salt Lake City: Deseret Book.

Scott, R. G. (1996, May). Finding joy in life. *Ensign,* 24–26.

Williams, R. N. (1992). The human context of agency. *American Psychologist, 47*(6), 752–760.

Williams, R. N. (1994). The modern, the post-modern, and the question of truth: Perspectives on the problem of agency. *Journal of Theoretical and Philosophical Psychology, 14*(1), 25–39.

Matthew R. Draper
and
Mark S. Green

The Ideals of Pistis, Elpis, and Agape

Implications for Counseling in Diverse Settings

We share a fundamental assumption with many of our colleagues who are therapists by profession and Christian by faith: we are ultimately not alone in the world. Indeed, we share the assumption that we have the loving companionship of the Holy Spirit to help guide our efforts to ease the suffering of others. The Holy Spirit is a gift to all those who are faithful, which can provide great comfort and guidance to us. As the Lord counseled Thomas B. Marsh, who had just been called on a mission, "Go your way whithersoever I will, and it shall be given you by the Comforter what you shall do and whither you shall go" (D&C 31:11). The "Comforter" in this verse is the Holy Spirit, who assists us—like Thomas Marsh—on our journey and prompts us whithersoever the Lord needs us to go and whatever he needs us to do.

The Greek term for "Comforter" as used in the New Testament is *paraklete.* A *paraklete* not only gives comfort, but also helps, assists, and advises others (Draper, 2002, p. 149). It is important for us to remember the multifaceted nature of the Comforter, because we are invited to serve a similar role to his in this world with those we meet. As Alma asked new members of the church who were being baptized in the Waters of Mormon, "Yea, and are [ye] willing to mourn with those that mourn; yea, and comfort those that stand in need of comfort" (Mosiah 18:9). Like the *paraklete,* this comfort comes in the form of help, assistance, and advice as we strive to comfort those around us. We are best able to comfort those around us in this broad sense if we embody certain characteristics, which facilitate our receptivity to the Holy Spirit.

Although there are many characteristics that would make such receptivity possible, in this chapter we will outline why these characteristics are crucial in the world today and will define three of them. We will then discuss how these characteristics would help therapists and counselors in difficult settings, with an example from a supermaximum security prison. We will also posit that counselors' embodiment of these characteristics can facilitate their clients' embodiment of them as well, even in secular settings and in secular ways. All singular first person accounts are related by Matt Draper.

Our Individualistic Age

The Savior prophesied that in the last days "iniquity shall abound" and that "the love of many shall wax cold" (Matt. 24:12). One of the reasons why love "waxes cold" is because people "shall be lovers of their own selves" (2 Tim. 3:2). They put their own wants and desires above the needs of others, both singularly and collectively. When such selfishness abounds, the Spirit cannot abide (Maxwell, 1975). Paul, for example, in his first letter to Corinth spoke very pointedly about a member of the church there who persisted in an incestuous affair with his own stepmother (1 Cor. 5:1–6). As concerned as he was about the affair itself, he felt doubly concerned that others had done nothing to counsel the man, and instead "insisted that they were correct in supporting his right to choose" (Draper, 2001, p. 74).

Our individual rights to choose are dear, precious, and fully supported by the Lord, who gives us agency in all things and holds us accountable for our choices, "that every man may act in doctrine and principle pertaining to futurity, according to the moral agency which I have given unto him, that every man may be accountable for his own sins in the day of judgment" (D&C 101:78). Insisting on our collective right to choose, however, without also contemplating the needs of others breeds a selfishness that started festering long ago in our history. Early in the nineteenth century, for example, Alexis de Tocqueville defined individualism as "calm and considered feeling which disposes each citizen to isolate himself from the mass of his fellows and withdraw into the circle of family and friends; with this little society formed to his taste, he gladly leaves the greater society to look after itself" (1969, p. 506). This withdrawal into a self-created world we tailor to our own wants, however, often continues until all we have left, at the bottom of it all, is ourselves.

I am reminded of a client who sat in my office sobbing disconsolately. She was a young woman in years, but appeared much older. There had been a time in her life when she felt deeply connected to family, community, and church. As she grew, however, she gradually severed the meaningful moral ties to others and pursued a life she felt she wanted. After she had tailored her life to the point that she could always do whatever she wanted with no one objecting, she looked around herself and, in a moment of existential crisis, realized that she felt completely alone in the world.

Sadly, her experience mirrored her reality. She had few people who loved her enough to sacrifice meaningfully for her, and she felt such love herself for equally few. As she began to calm herself, she looked up at me with tearstained cheeks and chuckled, "Well, only you can make you happy," without humor, and began sobbing once more.

Upon reflecting on her experience, I realized that it demonstrated individualism gone awry. Her pursuit of her own desires to the exclusion of her relationships with others left her bereft of the relationships that would provide meaningful moral guidance, support, and ongoing meaningful connection. As de Tocqueville stated, individualism "threatens, at last, to enclose him entirely in the solitude of his own heart" (1969, p. 506). My client found that once enclosed in the solitude of her own heart, her life felt meaningless without the profound connections to others she had once enjoyed.

When individuals feel, as my client felt, that they are the center of their own world, they often discover they have severed the ties of interdependence that would provide a deeper sense of connection and could protect them from the vicissitudes of life (Richardson, Rogers, & McCarroll, 1998). When the problems of life assail those who feel well-connected to others, those individuals have others they can turn to for emotional support and moral guidance. They are not the only ones who can make themselves happy—a statement that would appear ludicrous to them—because they have others upon whom they rely and who rely upon them in turn (Richardson, Fowers, & Guignon, 1999).

However, to the individual who has enclosed himself in the solitude of his own heart, his suffering is his fault alone; only he can make himself *not* suffer, and feel happy. He has an over-inflated sense of his own emotional autonomy, having only himself to blame for what he feels. Some experiences are outside of individual control and reasonably lead to suffering, such as the sudden death of a loved one, termination of a job due to recession, or a chronic illness. Because of this, the individualistic ethos eventually leaves people to "oscillate between an exaggerated sense of personal autonomy and a sense of being the victim of forces beyond their control" (Richardson, Fowers, & Guignon, 1999, p. 29).

Another unfortunate effect of individualism gone awry is the inability to understand certain emotions based in social interaction and relationship, namely, shame and guilt. These emotions served a very valuable purpose historically, when human beings derived a sense of worth and a deeper sense of meaning, intertwined in mutual moral obligation for one another (Wolfe, 1989). An experience of shame served a social regulatory function, helping the individual recognize when he or she was inadequate to social standards. An experience of guilt also served a regulatory social function, indicating to individuals that they were behaving inappropriately in a particular setting or context. One prompts growth by helping us change who we are; the other prompts growth by helping us behave within social guidelines.

However, the negative effect of these emotions, both historically and currently, is found when shame and guilt are experienced to a paralytic or neurotic degree. In our modern individualistic society, wherein the interconnected sense of meaning and worth has eroded, these emotions have become nearly impossible to understand and respond to and have thus increased to a pathological degree. When individualism becomes overemphasized as an ideal (as the Savior predicted), individual problems are understood as individual and due to inadequacy of the persons themselves. This understanding reflects a culture that is shame-based without the growth that shame had the potential to prompt in individuals historically (Lewis, 1992). Shame could prompt growth because shame entails a feeling about the self-in-relation (who I am to myself and others) while guilt entails a feeling about actions (what I have done to myself or others). Shame can prompt us to transform who we are, guilt to transform what we have done and will do. Shame can cease having a corrective power in an individualistic society because everything becomes about the self, when in nonindividualistic societies people may change to better relate to others. As Richardson, Fowers, and Guignon (1999) reflected when discussing the effect of individualism, "individuals tend to feel that they must attain an almost impregnable autonomy or are inadequate, vulnerable, or ashamed" (p. 29).

This shame, in general, can pull us away from relating to others, regardless of whether we come from collective or individualistic cultures. In an individualistic culture, our self-worth is self-generated and self-informed, so we are the cause of and victim of our own shame. This seems to double the shame and unfortunately increase the self-focus that created the shame to begin with. Unfortunately, this serves to shake the foundation of self-worth as well as communal connection as the person feeling the shame distances him- or herself from others. Guilt, likewise, is hard to understand and feels pathological when examined through the lens of radical individualism. If deeper moral and emotional ties are tenuous at best, guilt seems neurotic and unnecessary. Whereas historically guilt would prompt us to do what we could to be redeemed when we have sinned against another, in our selfish age we are no longer sufficiently deeply connected to allow for such interpersonal redemption. Instead, without these deep connections, guilt can take on a pathological tinge, becoming pervasive and difficult to cope with and understand. Feelings of both shame and guilt then become present in the therapy setting, as people try to process and deal with emotions that have lost some of their social regulatory function.

Worldly Therapy: Perpetuating the Problem

The process of psychotherapy not only reflects the values of the broader culture, but it can magnify them as well (Fancher, 1995). Unfortunately, the value of individualism is notably pervasive both in our broader culture and in modern psychotherapy theory and practice (Bellah, Madsen, Sullivan, Swidler, & Tipton, 1985; Cushman, 1995). One value often perpetuated in psychotherapy is the value of creating "individuated" selves for our clients (and the assumption that therapists are individuated selves as well). The individuated self that mainstream psychotherapists seek to perpetuate is one where the individual demonstrates "more effective individual behavior, enhanced self-realization, or a kind of personal authenticity in which one chooses one's own values and directions in splendid isolation from the pull of tradition or society" (Richardson, Fowers, & Guignon, 1999, p. 5).

In our personal experiences as therapists, we have encountered many cases where both we and our colleagues habitually try to help an individual be free from the arbitrary constraints of the moral authority of others (e.g., adults free from the harmful authority of their controlling parents, spouses free from the arbitrary authority of one another). Although this can be highly valuable when the moral authority of others is questionable or harmful, the process of individuation can also be taken too far without deeper value commitments undergirding and informing the process. One of the consequences is a form of selfishness that is harmful to the individual as well as to the fabric of social and moral commitments.

Philip Cushman (1990; 1991; 1995) described some of these problematic elements of the psychotherapy process when too much emphasis is placed on the individual relative to deeper commitments to others. According to Cushman, therapy has become, in part, a process by which we help our clients "function in a highly autonomous, isolated way . . . to be self-soothing, self-loving, and self-sufficient" (1990, p. 604). One can imagine such a person, self-focused in a way that his therapist assured him would be helpful. He would find over time, however, that without any fundamental reason to get out of himself and into the shared world of other people, his self-focus would fail him. He would find his very being collapsing into a narcissistic black hole, where his will, his energy, and his values revolve around himself. The autonomous self can only function for so long, and under only a certain amount of strain, before he collapses.

As therapists, we occasionally see the outcome of such a collapse. Our clients feel fragile, empty, and worthless, seeking our help: to help them help themselves feel better. Like a black hole, these people feel profoundly empty, and seek therapy to fill the void. This "empty self" feels grandiose at times when life goes his way, assuring himself that his being is up to him. Yet he also feels worthless at other times when he feels terrible because his life is outside of his control (Cushman, 1990, p. 604).

Unfortunately, the process of therapy can perpetuate this problematic cycle when the values informing the process are individualistic and selfish. An individuated self will tend to collapse and become an empty self when she lives a life devoid of deeper commitments and meaning. Because psychology promises "higher individual functioning," "better self-esteem," or "happiness," she will seek out a psychotherapist to heal the void in her soul. The psychotherapist, reflecting society's individualistic values, will help her focus on those attributes that will help her feel better about herself, as well as assist her in developing self-soothing and self-coping skills. Relieved, she is once again an individualized self, until the pressures of being autonomous to that degree cause a collapse once more, prompting her to return to therapy.

The Gospel-Centered Solution

Selfishness, in the form of individualism taken too far, breeds emptiness in human experience. Such emptiness is due (in part) to "an absence of communal forms and beliefs" as well as the interpersonal obligations, commitments, and relationships that used to enrich our collective lives (Cushman, 1990, p. 604). In order to prevent the self from becoming empty, it is important that we, as counselors, help people to get outside themselves, to value their relationships and sensible moral commitments to others. This is not to imply that we should counsel others to lose their sense of identity in relationships, but rather the idea that becoming more fully yourself may very well mean to become more fully in-relation with others. For example, a father becomes more fully himself, not by looking out for his own preferences and desires at the expense of his spouse and children, but rather he becomes more fully himself by embracing how he, uniquely, enriches the role of fatherhood as he relates deeply to his spouse and children.

Although we work with people from diverse backgrounds and of diverse beliefs, we have many reasons to believe that such an approach would be helpful. As the Savior commanded at the temple in Jerusalem, "Thou shalt love thy neighbor as thyself" (Matt. 22:39). When we can feel such love, it leads to a great protective power in our hearts against the uncertainties of life and the anxieties they bring. "There is no fear in love; but perfect love casteth out fear: because fear hath torment. He that feareth is not made perfect in love" (1 Jn. 4:18). Such love is admittedly difficult for us, and may be only imperfectly realized, but striving for such an ideal can prove both rewarding and healing.

An important first step toward this realization is to assist others in getting out of their selfish and individualistic ways, to reconnect them with the world of others, to prompt them to value the other as much as the self. Such valuing of others allows us to cultivate in ourselves not only love and interest in others, but also a genuine curiosity—the kind of love that seeks to know. G. K. Chesterton asserts in his book *Orthodoxy,* "how much larger your life would be if your self were smaller in it; if you could really look at other men with common curiosity and pleasure . . . you would begin to be interested in them. . . . You would break out of this tiny tawdry theatre in which your own plot is always being played, and you would find yourself under a freer sky, and in a street full of splendid strangers" (1995, p. 25).

Gospel-centered counselors can help those they work with break out of their "tiny tawdry theatre[s]" by modeling specific characteristics that, when taken up by the client, will connect them with others in a way that will combat the selfishness from individualism, and the consequent empty self.

Three Ideal Counselor Characteristics

Three characteristics are addressed by the various authors of the New Testament and are described as those ideals that are key to the good life, to living as the Savior would want us to live. We present these three ideals in the original Greek of the New Testament era: πίστίς, ἐλπίς, and ἀγάπη. While these terms are roughly translated as the widely recognized virtues of faith, hope, and love, we wish to discuss their connotations that are likely to be lost in translation. Πίστίς (Pistis) connotes having faith in another, both her capacity and her potential. Ἐλπίς (Elpis) implies holding hope for the other, her condition, and the outcome of her suffering. Ἀγάπη (Agape) is love for another, caring for her as much as for the self.

Pistis. Pistis implies a very strong feeling of faith, one that does not necessarily show as impassioned speech, but rather as the firm bedrock of belief. When we have this feeling for others, our faith in them can feel inspiring, and can prompt them to have faith in themselves as well as those they know. Such faith, when taken up by our clients, "enables people to withstand the worst of humanity. It also enables people to look beyond themselves. More importantly, it enables them to forgive" (Faust, 2007). Sometimes our belief in others, the heartfelt and authentic expression of that belief, can provide comfort in times of pain and a flickering light during very dark times.

Not only does this type of faith allow us to forgive others, but it can also connect us to them during difficult times in life. In the book of Enos, for example, we read that Enos and his fathers were granted promises because of the intensity of the faith they had in their progeny. Enos and his fathers had such great faith that their progeny would follow Christ that the Lord told Enos, "Thy fathers have also required of me this thing; and it shall be done unto them according to their faith; for their faith was like unto thine" (Enos 1:18). The ancestors of Enos had great faith in the Lord, but also had this faith in their children, so much so that the Lord allowed them to require these profound blessings of him.

I am reminded of two separate individuals I have worked with, both of whom prompted me to feel this type of faith, which in turn helped them have this faith for others. One was a young man in his late teens who came from a chaotic family with absent affection and a great degree of turmoil. When I first met with him, he had very little faith in himself and believed himself to be worthless. He doubted his own abilities and his relationship with his struggling parents and his squabbling siblings. I noted, however, that despite his liabilities, he possessed a keen mind and a sensitive heart—one he sought to shelter from others. I possessed Pistis for him, and felt it unwavering. I could share, when appropriate, reasons why he could have faith in himself and in his situation: he possessed strengths of which he himself remained unaware. Eventually, he began to recognize these strengths, and became more involved in the life of his family in a supportive way. As he felt the bedrock of my faith in him, he learned to feel it for himself and others, in a way that connected him deeply to them.

Another client was struggling in his relationship with his teenage daughter. Their relationship became increasingly characterized by rage-filled fights followed by long periods of sullen silence. The more she would assert herself, the more he would attempt to restrict her behavior, prompting her to assert herself more. Each pathological cycle heightened greater verbal combat. I noted the intensity and reality of the commitment and obligation he felt for his daughter, which prompted a feeling of Pistis within me. Although he had lost faith in himself and his daughter, I felt strongly that he could regain lost ground. I asked him questions like, "How is your daughter a good person?" and "In what ways do you see success in how you're raising her?" Because I felt such strong Pistis for him, he began slowly to feel the same for his daughter, which strengthened their rocky relationship.

Neither this father's case nor the teenager's story ended with a simplistic "cure." However, in both cases, the clients became better connected to others in their lives through the faith they had in others as well as their newfound faith in themselves.

Elpis. Elpis implies holding hope for another, even when they have lost it for themselves. This hope encompasses the temporal hope that the pain and suffering of others is temporary, that there is a light that can be sought in the darkness of their lives even if it cannot be immediately seen or felt. When we feel Elpis for others, they can often draw strength from our expressions of hope.

For example, in supervision with my students and in conversation with colleagues, I have noted a theme through the years in the stories they tell about their clients. Many clients report that their counselor is their "rock," the person who is always steady and steadfast, upon whom they can rely even in dark and uncertain times. The counselors in turn report seeing the silver lining in the otherwise bleak lives of their clients, which provides hope, and with hope they can provide strength to others during such times.

Likewise, Mormon offers a powerful example of the importance of hope during times of trial and tribulation. As he sought to lead his armies in the defense of his people, he grieved: "But behold, I was without hope, for I knew the judgments of the Lord which should come upon them; for they repented not of their iniquities, but did struggle for their lives without calling upon that Being who created them" (Morm. 5:2). Without hope and without the strength that comes from it, his ability to lead his people crumbled. So too can we feel challenged counseling others when we lose hope for them. Many of us have had the feeling that we did not know where to proceed in our work with our clients, where to go next or what to say. All avenues of treatment felt blocked or sabotaged by the client, and it was when we lost hope that we lost our power to effect change.

Such a situation happened to me quite recently. I had an ecclesiastical leader who sought my counsel at the recommendation of his superior in his church. His referral came about because he perpetuated cyber-affairs: trysts with women online. He justified his behavior to himself and to his church superior by stating that they weren't "real" affairs because he wasn't "really doing anything in real life that was wrong" and that "adultery requires the physical presence of another person." His marriage had collapsed; his wife threatened to divorce him if he did not change. He thought that if he went through the motions of counseling he could assuage the concerns of his superior and mollify his wife sufficiently to regain access to his congregation and the preaching job he loved so much.

As we met, I noted that to me his approach felt passively defensive, reserved, guarded. He would not admit to wrongdoing and assured me that although he felt his behavior was not a problem, he had desisted in his online behavior. I felt frustrated by the lack of progress in the session and thought that because he had no desire to change, he effectively wasted our time. My feelings of hopelessness became intense when I learned that although he had given up his Internet connection at home, the public librarian caught him using library computers to speak to his cyber-mistress. She called my client's wife, who called her husband's superior, who, in turn, called him and informed him that he would not be getting his congregation back. His wife, in turn, left him and threatened divorce proceedings.

Only then, in the darkest of times, did my client's passive façade crumble. He arrived at my office already crying real tears of suffering, of realization of despair. Then, and only then, did our real work begin. As Paul wrote to the Romans, "We glory in tribulations also: knowing that tribulation worketh patience; and patience, experience; and experience, hope: And hope maketh not ashamed; because the love of God is shed abroad in our hearts by the Holy Ghost" (Rom. 5:3–5). Only by going through tribulations can we gain the patience and experience that brings hope. It is our experience as counselors that often permits us to see the larger picture of our clients' condition and to feel the hope for the outcome of their suffering.

In the case of this client, it was when he felt totally bereft of hope that he needed some of mine. Ironically, it was only when he had no hope that I felt inspired to regain the hope for him that I had lost. When we express such hope for our clients, it does not come out in the form of simple platitudes, but rather in a steadfast vision of what is possible for them and a steady willingness to prompt them in that direction. Such prompting helped this client feel hope for his own situation, and this hope permitted him to engage in service once more, both to his wife and to the members of his church, this time as a fellow congregation member. Through this hope, he reported, he once again had true "joy in labor" because he served out of true hope for others rather than out of authority.

Agape. Agape connotes the fundamental valuing of the other as much as the self. Such love often culminates from the previous two feelings. If we truly have faith in the other, and hope for the other, then we are likely to feel Agape for him as well.

Such feelings of genuine affection for the other are very difficult to understand and to work with in a worldly framework for psychology. My LDS supervisees often struggle to understand and reconcile their feelings for their clients and colleagues within a worldly psychology that presents love to clients and colleagues as unethical and as a sign of neurosis or poor boundaries. Mainstream psychology presents the only love that our mainstream culture seems to understand, the love of personal desire. This love is an inherently selfish one that demands that the person feeling the love meet his needs for physical or emotional affection at the expense of the person he "loves." But the love that my supervisees feel for their clients and colleagues is not one of personal need, one that would prompt them to use others for their own benefit. Rather, this form of love is one that prompts them instead to behave with the highest attention to ethics and to serve their clients and colleagues in the most professional and forthright manner possible, because they value their clients and colleagues as much as themselves. When we define this feeling in supervision as Agape, the supervisees often feel relief, that there is a word for their experience that is a moral and ethical feeling: a feeling that prompts them to look after the needs of others first in the most professional manner possible. This feeling has direct implications for the field of counseling and serves as a counterforce to the individualism prevalent in our field (Adams, Draper, & Hairston, 2005).

As mentioned earlier, one of the consequences of radical individualism is clinical shame and guilt. Many people in our society narcissistically experience the moral guidance of others as slights to the core of their being, and hence withdraw from those who would seek to guide them so they no longer have to feel ashamed or guilty. Eventually, they are withdrawn into the "solitude of their own hearts," fearing the connections to others that might feel injurious to them. Agape, however, is the antidote to the toxin of fear, for where such love is, fear cannot abide: "[P]erfect love casteth out all fear" (Moro. 8:16).

We believe—as oversimplified as it may seem—that the antidote to certain forms of depression and anxiety is service, and some empirical researchers have noted the same effect (Layous et al., 2012; Weinstein & Ryan, 2010). By serving others, we step out of our own skins and into the lives of others; and by stepping empathically into their lives, we can better value them. When we value others, our selves feel less important, and as we focus on ourselves less we are paradoxically strengthened. A paradox Christ noted when he said, "He that loseth his life . . . shall find it" (Matt. 10:39).

I've noticed this pattern in my work with couples. Many times when couples seek my counsel, it is due to one or both partners are feeling dissatisfied about the marriage because they have certain wants or needs that are not being realized. More often than not, I find that the selfishness of one or both partners is exacerbating the dissatisfaction between them. One exercise I have these couples complete is learning about the wants and needs of their partners in a manner that is noncombative and nonshaming (which is often a challenge). Once they have done so, we also work together to have each partner seek to meet the needs of the other. This is possible only when both parties are engaged, and it often remains a challenge to remind them that their service to their spouse comes without a demand of reciprocity. Then, when each partner performs this service, the partner who is served responds with gratitude. We practice this pattern in session, and then the couple is required to proactively seek opportunities to meet the needs of his or her spouse throughout the week. This increases, in turn, their feeling of Agape for one another, and when that feeling builds, marital disputes often decrease as well.

As a caveat, feeling Agape for others creates a certain risk for us as counselors. When we allow others to truly matter to us, when we value them as much as ourselves, we leave ourselves vulnerable to disappointment. We then seek to limit our feeling of Agape only to those close to us—those we believe will not disappoint or hurt us. Although this reaction is understandable, we are commanded to "be not partial towards them in love above many others, but let thy love be for them as for thyself; and let thy love abound unto all men" (D&C 112:11). Advantageously, when others are aware of how we value them, it communicates to them clearly that they are *worth caring for.* When they feel that they are worth caring for, they are strengthened against their own struggles in life and are better able to value others. Agape, in this sense, is contagious. Often when people are truly valued, they begin to more fully value others. By our loving them, they learn to better love themselves and through this love are better able to love others.

There are many ways in which we as counselors can model Agape for their clients. The first is emotionally, by truly attending to the client and communicating nonverbally that the client matters to us personally. We do this through our attending skills, our empathic responses, and our evident desire to know more about their suffering and their situation. We do this when we first see them, showing with our smile and our expressions that we are glad to see them. We also do this when they leave a session with our reminders of what they would like to accomplish for the week and our desiring success for them. Our Agape for them is even more evident when they suffer setbacks and greater trials, and our love for them strengthens us and allows us to remain in the helpful role. Contrary to selfish models of empathy, which prompt us to feel what the client is feeling, a model of empathy that truly values the other can strengthen us in difficult emotional times because it allows us to "experience another's suffering precisely as his suffering, in the category of the other, and my reaction to him is not a cry of pain but a word of consolation and a gesture of assistance" (Morson & Emerson, 1990, p. 185).

Pistis, Elpis, and Agape in Difficult Settings

The principles of Pistis, Elpis, and Agape may seem more challenging to apply outside of gospel settings working with Christian clients. These principles, however, can provide some strength to counselors working even in the most difficult settings with some of the most frustrating clients.

One such setting where both my coauthor Mark Green and I worked proved one of the most inimical to the Spirit, and to the characteristics of Pistis, Elpis, and Agape. At Wabash Valley Correctional Facility, there is a supermaximum security wing called the Segregated Housing Unit (SHU): a place so notorious that it has been featured both on Discovery Channel's program *Inside Supermax* and

MSNBC's *Lockup*. I worked at Wabash Valley as a psychologist for two years, and one of my rotations was the SHU. This facility houses the most violent, dangerous, or unstable prisoners in solitary confinement; many of them are stored for years at a time in solitary cells. Each wing of the SHU comprises two stories of cells on one side facing a plain concrete wall on the other. There is a control pod at the center, with each wing radiating outward. The first senses struck upon entering the SHU are smell and sound. The smell is one of human waste, disinfectant and stale air. The sound is an oppressive white noise from the ventilation system, punctuated by occasional screams or loud swearing. Everything in the SHU appears dingy, lit by grey light filtered down from the occasional skylight in the ceiling, or yellow light from the solitary cyanide-argon light bulbs in the dark cells. It is the feel of the place that is the most poignant, however, a feeling that is difficult to describe. Often, when the two-inch-thick steel door would roll back to grant me access to the central pod, the air would blow past me in an effort to escape. At times, I could feel my hope and faith fluttering out of me in that potent breeze as I entered the unit. The air felt dense with intensely palpable anger and hatred. In such an environment, concentration proves difficult, and feelings of personal security are diminished greatly. Consequently, feelings of Pistis, Elpis, and Agape are very hard to muster.

I received a referral one day for a new client in the SHU, a man whose physician diagnosed him with Schizoaffective Disorder. His condition required regular monitoring from "Psych" (the local colloquialism for professional mental health services), so I added him to my caseload. When I first met Mr. Wrack (not his real name), I introduced myself and shook his hand through the slot in the plate steel door to his cell. He refused to speak to me, other than to briefly answer my questions and to let me know he didn't trust Psych. For over a month our meetings would be very brief—I would greet him warmly, shake his hand, and perform a behavior assessment. I would always ask if there was anything else he wanted to talk about; he would merely grunt and reply, "No."

Eventually, however, Mr. Wrack asked that I have him pulled out of his cell so he could speak to me outside of the earshot of his fellow inmates (each cell abuts the other in a long row for both stories, offering very little privacy). So, the officers, per policy, chained his hands and feet and escorted him to the holding cell. Once the officers left, Mr. Wrack virtually exploded, his normally apathetic demeanor vanishing. He described to me in great detail his betrayal at the hands of his older brother. The reason for his incarceration was the drug-fueled crime he and his brother committed together, but when they were arrested, his brother turned state's evidence against him and received a much shorter sentence in his agreement with the prosecution. I listened empathically, responding to his anger and his feelings of betrayal, and asked him why this was an issue today. Mr. Wrack reached inside his waistband and withdrew a crumpled letter, which he threw at me through the cell door. I unfolded the note and read while the client continued to rage about the "S.O.B. that snitched" on him, the brother he had not heard from in ten years. In the letter, written in a clumsy and shaking hand, his brother asked him for forgiveness. He described the trials of his own incarceration, his becoming sober, finding a job, and finding a wife. He offered to visit Mr. Wrack and do whatever he could to be forgiven. In that moment, my tenuous hold on Pistis, Elpis, and Agape returned. I could finally see a way to potentially help my client.

To show these characteristics to Mr. Wrack, I first validated his feelings of anger and betrayal. I knew that the reason those feelings were so powerful was because of his love for his brother—love he had lost, but could regain. I finally had faith that this hardened man could change. With that faith came hope for him, and for his situation. Through the feeling of hope coupled with the feeling of faith, I could value him even in a setting that prompts self-protection above any intimation of empathy. My expressions of Agape, however, proved to be what prompted the change. Many times, people in correctional settings are treated as untouchable, so an honest handshake is powerful. The inmates are often not listened to, so truly listening to them also communicates a valuing of them that they experience in a profound way. Lastly, given that Agape is a feeling for-the-other, it frees the counselor to own his or her own reactions to the client's affect and behavior. Although I knew Mr. Wrack was a violent offender, and I needed to be careful, I could own those feelings while also serving him to the best of my ability. I could also own my feelings of frustration with him as *my* feelings, and not make my feelings *his* problem.

Mr. Wrack learned slowly to trust me, because (I think) he could sense the Agape I had for him, and the trustworthy behavior it engendered in me. As he learned to trust me, he learned to trust my guidance. I suggested that he respond to his brother, and describe to his brother how he felt about the betrayal. Mr. Wrack tried to write a letter on his own repeatedly, but gave up in frustration. Eventually, I suggested that I take dictation, and he could tell me what to write to his brother, and he would send the letter. We did so, and the client dictated two rage-filled letters that I then handed him at the end of our meeting, should he choose to send them. I found later that he did send one of them, and received another very contrite letter from his brother, once again asking for forgiveness.

After a series of exchanges like this, Mr. Wrack's heart softened somewhat toward his brother. I would offer process comments, sharing my own experience of learning to believe in Mr. Wrack and forgiving him for the minor slights he offered in fits of rage, then asking him what that meant to him. I would then point out that he had the opportunity to do the same for his brother, who had wronged him far more grievously. As Mr. Wrack did so, he began to learn about the difficulties his brother faced with finding a job, starting a family, and trying to stay sober. He started to feel faith in his brother and his process of becoming a better person. He felt hope for his brother, that there would be a positive outcome in the many trials he faced. Most importantly, he felt Agape for his brother; his brother once more mattered as much to him as he did to himself.

As Mr. Wrack felt the faith that allowed him to forgive his brother, the consequent hope and love provided him with an anchor in the storm of his difficult life outside of himself. His new sister-in-law began to correspond with him as well, sending pictures of their new baby, and their new home, and Mr. Wrack proved eloquently supportive in his letters to her during her distress over their life circumstances. Gradually, Mr. Wrack ceased acting out against custody staff and other inmates. He described how he had a purpose in life beyond his own rage-fueled suffering. He had to get out of the SHU so he could see visitors, once more embrace his prodigal brother, and embrace for the first time his sister-in-law and beloved niece. His hard work paid off, earning him a transfer out of the SHU back to maximum, and from maximum to high medium where he could once again see visitors.

Conclusion

Life is challenging. For many it perhaps feels difficult beyond hope. These difficulties are harder to overcome in our time and in our society because our moral obligations to one another have grown thin. Individualism in our age can be taken to a radical extreme, wherein people are left bereft of the morally grounded nurturing and support that existed more commonly in previous eras. Unfortunately, as we practice psychology we can at times perpetuate this problematic trend. However, as gospel-centered counselors we have tools that allow us to prompt people to focus on others as much as the self in a way that can reground them in nurturing relationships with others. The three tools we offer in this chapter—Pistis, Elpis, and Agape—will serve gospel-centered counselors well, even in difficult settings. Pistis prompts us to have faith in others, both in capacity and potential. Elpis is the hope we feel for others even in the face of great suffering, that such suffering is temporary and can be ameliorated. Agape is the consequent feeling, valuing others as much as the self. This feeling prompts us to the heights of ethical service to our clients. We, as counselors, can model each of these feelings. Then our clients can embody each in turn as they learn to feel such faith, hope, and love for others. These tools can serve us well, even in challenging settings working with difficult populations.

References

Adams, M., Draper, M. R., & Hairston, C. (2005). Emulating the perfect counselor: Bringing love and joy into counseling. *Journal for the Association of Mormon Counselors and Psychotherapists, 28*, 20–24.

Bellah, R., Madsen, R., Sullivan, W. M., Swidler, A., & Tiption, S. M. (1985). *Habits of the heart: Individualism and commitment in American life*. Berkeley, CA: University of California Press.

Chesterton, G. K. (1995). *Orthodoxy*. San Francisco: Ignatuis Press. (Original work published 1908.)

Cushman, P. (1990). Why the self is empty. *The American Psychologist, 45*(5), 599–611.

Cushman, P. (1991). Ideology obscured. *The American Psychologist, 46*(3), 206–219.
Cushman, P. (1995). *Constructing the self, constructing America: A cultural history of psychotherapy*. Reading, MA: Addison-Wesley.
Draper, R. D. (2001). *The Savior's prophecies: From the fall of Jerusalem to the second coming*. American Fork, UT: Covenant Communications.
Draper, R. D. (2002). *A Fulness of Joy*. American Fork, UT: Covenant Communications.
Fancher, R. (1995). *Cultures of healing: Correcting the image of American mental health care*. New York: Freeman.
Faust, J. E. (2007, May). The healing power of forgiveness. *Ensign*, 67–69.
Layous, K., Nelson, S. K., Oberle, E., Schonert-Reichl, K., & Lyubomirsky, S. (2012). Kindness counts: Prompting prosocial behavior in preadolescents boosts peer acceptance and well-being. *PLOS ONE, 7*(12), e51380.
Lewis, M. (1992). *Shame: The exposed self*. New York: Free Press.
Maxwell, N. A. (1975). *Of one heart*. Salt Lake City, UT: Deseret Book.
Morson, G. S., & Emerson, C. (1990). *Mikhail Bakhtin: Creation of a prosaics*. Stanford, CA: Stanford University Press, California.
Richardson, F. C., Fowers, B. J., & Guignon, C. B. (1999). *Re-envisioning psychology: Moral dimensions of theory and practice*. San Fransisco, CA: Josey-Bass Publishers.
Richardson, F. C., Rogers, A., & McCarroll, J. (1998). Toward a dialogical self. *The American Behavioral Scientist, 41*(4), 496–515.
Tocqueville, A. D. (1969). *Democracy in America*. New York: Anchor Books.
Weinstein, N., & Ryan, R. M. (2010). When helping helps: Autonomous motivation for prosocial behavior and its influence on well-being for the helper and recipient. *Journal of Personality and Social Psychology, 98*(2), 222–244.
Wolfe, A. (1989). *Whose keeper? Social science and moral obligation*. Berkeley, CA: University of California Press.

Timothy B. Smith

The Foundational Principle of Faith

The Foundational Principle of Faith

Members of The Church of Jesus Christ of Latter-day Saints believe that the gospel of Jesus Christ applies to all aspects of social life: "His teachings established standards of human behavior" (Wirthlin, 1998, p. 25; see also Benson, 1985). With that understanding, gospel principles become a foundation, the only solid foundation, for work in the mental health professions. Although the gospel encompasses all truth, regardless of its origin (Young, 1854), principles revealed through God's anointed prophets stand preeminent (Benson, 1988; Hunter, 1994). Thus, therapists can improve their work by seeking inspired principles that illuminate how God works with his children in distress and by applying those principles to their own imperfect attempts to facilitate mental health.

Any parallel of the gospel of Jesus Christ with contemporary mental health practices is necessarily multifaceted. There are dozens of relevant gospel principles, with countless possible implications. For example, principles of forgiveness and gratitude have received sustained attention in the research literature (Emmons & McCullough, 2004; Worthington, 2005). Given the breadth of topics available in the gospel—with nearly all pertaining to well-being, directly or indirectly—it seems reasonable to give particular attention to those principles most prominent within the divine cannon. Accordingly, this chapter will restrict its focus to the singular topic of *faith*, a topic which itself is broad enough to fill several volumes but has heretofore received scant attention among mental health practitioners.

The Principle of Faith

Faith is "the assurance of things hoped for, the evidence of things not seen" (JST Heb. 11:1); in other words, "faith is to hope for things which are not seen, but which are true" (Bible Dictionary, s.v. *faith*). Faith presupposes truths. In the gospel of Jesus Christ, faith in the Lord receives primary emphasis (A of F 1:4).

Faith is not merely belief; it is belief that guides action. One may believe in something intangible (e.g., freedom) or believe in some unseen future event (e.g., pending retirement) yet do nothing. Belief alone has insufficient motivational force unless circumstances impel. However, faith needs no circumstantial constraints: Volition itself is sufficient. Faith is an act of asserting one's internal beliefs onto the external world.

Thus, one may believe in God yet lack faith in him. Such a person may share a vocabulary with religious counterparts but may not necessarily undertake personal sacrifices necessary to know him (*Lectures on Faith,* 1985). Faith enables personal sacrifice because its assurance rests on the ends, not on the means. That is, faith enables work and endures pain because the unseen end condition is believed to be better than the present moment. With faith, people act "as if" the goal is at hand despite circumstances that seemingly indicate the opposite. Faith is a response to all things blatantly, and supposedly solely, material. Faith is the principle necessary for receiving that which truly is, rather than that which merely seems to be.

Conscious human behavior entails faith: Action is based on guiding belief. Except in cases of thoughtless reactivity or incapacity (e.g., severe mental illness), faith or its absence is relevant to individual actions of all types, from pathology to prayer, from therapy to theophany. Faith is a principle more entwined with individual well-being than poverty or pleasure—useful concepts that overly saturate theories of social work and psychology. Faith is a foundational principle for any attempt to understand and improve human conditions.

The remainder of this chapter will first review several components of faith that are relevant to mental health, followed by descriptions of several considerations for strengthening faith and discussion of some psychological consequences or fruits of faith. Implications for mental health interventions based on the principle of faith are then described, with direct applications to therapists provided in the conclusion. This chapter aims to demonstrate that applying the principle of faith to mental health practice enhances our ability to work effectively as therapists. Stated more pointedly, faith in correct principles is not only essential for religious devotion, but it is also essential for personal well-being. Therapists would do well to align their practice with that reality.

Components of Faith: Acting on Belief in Principles

Do mental health professionals believe they help clients? This question seems banal, yet it illustrates how belief in an unseen future (e.g., improved client functioning) motivates therapists—and by extension to other settings, everyone. Constructive actions are based on beliefs about improved future conditions. Belief in an unseen event, person, or principle precedes positive actions. "Without faith you can do nothing" (D&C 8:10).

Faith is a relatively simple concept: "belief that leads to action," but neither belief nor action are simplistic concepts, let alone their juncture. So faith entails some explication, considering it from multiple angles so as to better understand it and its implications for mental health and mental health services. The following three considerations offer some clarification about what faith is and what it is not.

Calm Belief without Reactivity, the Antithesis of Fear. Although faith precedes constructive action, not all human actions are constructive. We live in a world of great uncertainty. Because people do disappoint us and betray our trust, we can come to fear uncertainty. Fear can make dysfunctional coping strategies (e.g., despair, anger) seem preferable to faith. Thus, adults often suspend faith through a variety of alternative coping strategies, such as consistent, predictable patterns of living, as in the following case:

> Joan has experienced generalized symptoms of anxiety and mild depression for several years. She was raised in a home in which her father did not hold a steady job and her family suffered from economic struggles throughout her childhood and adolescence. Upon leaving home to attend college, Joan at first felt a sense of liberation, but upon graduation she found herself increasingly disillusioned. She returned for graduate study but subsequently floundered again in her attempts in the workplace. She has no close relationships, but she does maintain contact with former classmates in graduate school. Her daily routine has become increasingly rigid as she attempts to combat loneliness with repetitive household tasks.

Fear of uncertainty can inhibit not only our sense of safety (trust) but also the accuracy of our evaluations about reality. As illustrated in the case of Joan, internalization of fear can manifest itself in symptoms such as conservative avoidance and structured repetition that do reduce uncertainty and exposure to pain but at the same time inhibit other emotional experiences, particularly intimacy and a sense of fulfillment.

Whereas some people cope with uncertainty through internalizing strategies such as withdrawal or compulsivity, others tend to favor externalizing strategies, such as aggression and blaming others rather than taking personal responsibility for consequences. Attempts to deal with uncertainty that are not based on faith, whether by externalization or internalization, seek to impose control or predictability. If we cannot predict pain, responses of the common "natural man" (1 Cor. 2:14; Mosiah 3:19) are *reactive* (withdraw or attack).

Humans react to uncertainty in a variety of highly nuanced ways, not merely through internalization or externalization; table 1 provides several examples. Typically, these reactions interact cyclically: intellectualization fuels skepticism, skepticism prompts anger, and so on. Individuals can react differently in different circumstances, but general themes play themselves out over time, repeating in variant form. People typically exhibit preferred habits of confronting discomfort and uncertainty, so the responses listed in table 1 can be useful to mental health professionals working with clients whose reactive coping methods warrant replacement with faith, trust, and proactivity.

Despite the apparent variety across the reactions listed in table 1, they share similarities. They all oppose faith. They attempt to create or maintain a sense of comfort or control amid the profound complexity of reality. Nevertheless, all lack sufficient depth or breadth to adequately manage that complexity.

When used in combination, reactive coping strategies (table 1) can patch up a makeshift belief system adequate for most daily tasks. Thus, people can manage uncertainty without much faith. However, this lack of trust comes at a cost: unfulfilled emotional longing and previous emotional damage insufficiently repaired will inevitably impact quality of living (notable under distressing circumstances when not apparent otherwise). One can rationalize only so far as circumstances allow; eventually confrontation occurs, whether by agents external (e.g., police) or internal (e.g., elevated blood pressure). Circumstances are uncertain. The only viable solution to uncertainty is faith.

Belief in Correct Principles. People most often make decisions based on their evaluations of the circumstances: who is present, what resources are available, what consequences are likely, etc. However, circumstances change, people change, and the law of entropy

Table 1

Common nonoptimal reactions to uncertainty

- Naïve Optimism
  Problem = shallow roots easily ripped when mismatches with reality occur repeatedly
- Criticism/Skepticism
  Problem = nonconstructive; circular spiral to pessimism; satisfying only to conceit
- Anger/Aggression
  Problem = destructive; pushes other people away; foments others' fears
- Despair/Paralysis
  Problem = self-destructive; diminishes potential
- Intellectualization/Rationalization
  Problem = self-sufficient, therefore limited in success across contexts
- Blind Belief
  Problem = vulnerable to manipulation; sheltered from personal responsibility
- Aloofness ("worldly-wise," "street-smart")
  Problem = lack of fulfillment, intimacy
- Compulsivity
  Problem = premature foreclosure; avoidant of uncertainty; reinforces self-gratification

is constant. Faith placed in anything temporary will eventually fail (e.g., Matt. 6:19). Hence faith founded on situations, people, or material things can prove disappointing or even damaging.

To yield consistent beneficial effects, faith must be founded on correct principles, taught by God through his authorized representatives, anointed prophets. Table 2 lists examples of correct principles. According to the teachings of the Lord Jesus Christ, love is the paramount motive and virtue that facilitates other principles (e.g., Matt. 22:36–40). Love necessarily allows for the expression of agency (second on the list), albeit with restrictions when impinging on others' agency or well-being. These several principles (table 2) are best interpreted in light of the other principles, rather than separately. For instance, the two principles of love and honoring agency, when

Table 2

Examples of correct principles from canonized LDS scriptures

- Love, the Paramount Virtue
- Honoring Human Agency
- Revelation from God to Prophets and to All People through the Holy Spirit
- Accountability and Obedience to God's Commands (once understood)
- Repentance and Progression through God's Grace
- Hope and Optimism
- Family Unity and Brotherly Kindness for All People
- Knowledge and Remembrance of Truth
- Patience
- Mercy, Forgiveness, and Generosity
- Justice and Fair Treatment
- Humility and Desiring Improvement
- Self-mastery and Temperance
- Integrity and Honesty
- Virtue, Chastity, and Fidelity
- Proactive Planning and Diligence to Enact Plans
- Peace and Order
- Gratitude
- Reflection and Wisdom
- Provision for and Protection of the Innocent and Defenseless

considered simultaneously, would indicate that human interactions should optimally involve methods of behavior change that are closer to the spectrum of influence than the spectrum of coercion (D&C 128:37–45). Similarly, the principles of accountability, justice, and obedience qualify that all actions have consequences, hence the need for self-restraint and so forth. Each principle provides an essential context for the others, with motives optimally rooted in the paramount virtue, love.

Correct principles do not change, despite changes in circumstances, people, or material conditions. Therefore, utilizing correct principles to guide belief and action is far preferable to utilizing circumstances. This precept has been taught most clearly by Elder Richard G. Scott:

The Foundational Principle of Faith

> There are two patterns for making decisions in life: (1) decisions based upon circumstance and (2) decisions based upon eternal truth. Satan encourages choices to be made according to circumstance. That is: What are others doing? What seems to be socially or politically acceptable? What will bring the quickest, most satisfying response? . . . With this approach there is no underlying set of values or standards used to consistently guide those decisions. Each one is made for what appears to be the most attractive choice at the moment. Those who choose this path . . . are left to their own strength and to that of others influenced to act in their favor. Sadly, most of God's children make decisions this way. That is why the world is in such turmoil.
>
> The pattern of the Lord is for His children to make decisions based upon eternal truth. This requires that your life continue to be centered in the commandments of God. Thus, decisions are made in accordance with unchanging truths, aided by prayer and the guidance of the Holy Ghost. . . . Your actions will be predictable and will bless the lives of all in the circle of your influence. You will have a meaningful life of purpose, peace, and happiness. (January 2007, p. 13)

Congruence with the teachings of Jesus Christ and his prophets is the standard for determining the veracity of a given principle (Kimball, 1979; Moro. 7:13–18; 10:6; D&C 1:38). Divine laws, coupled with guidance from the Holy Spirit, inform action (D&C 88:36–38; Wirthlin, 1998). Hence, individuals with faith in correct principles can have complete confidence, acting with full assurance, irrespective of circumstance[1] (Job 13:15; Alma 38:5; Hinckley, 1995; Uchtdorf, 2014).

---

1. For instance, the prophet Joseph Smith (1971) stated, "The object with me is to obey and teach others to obey God in just what He tells us to do. It mattereth not whether the principle is popular or unpopular, I will always maintain a true principle, even if I stand alone in it" (vol. 6, p. 223).

With correct principles as its foundation (Scott, 2003), faith differs radically from ungrounded mysticism. Faith is not a naïve belief in everything supernatural, nor is it a belief in anything purported to improve circumstances (e.g., "cures" promoted by the charismatic). For example, modern medicine has incrementally improved treatment effectiveness over time because it is based on rigorous research methods (correct principles of observation and deduction), which methods are clearly superior to claims and treatments based on anecdotal or "expert" explanations. Despite the obvious improvements and countless lives saved from medical research, we often see mental health clients who are disillusioned by modern medicine (which is progressing but flawed) turn to an alternative method for healing, reverting back to the unscientific standard of anecdotal evidence. Later, when that alternative treatment also fails, they turn to yet another alternative recommended by someone else. In such cases, the underlying naïve and perhaps desperate belief is in the possibility of *being healed by something,* not in a true principle associated with healing yet undiscovered. People may believe a variety of things, but only beliefs in correct principles yield reliable results.

Belief alone is insufficient. As agnostics point out and as followers of mysticism or folk superstitions eventually discover, belief alone has no value. Beliefs detached from experience lack motivational force. However, faith is not merely belief. It is not merely desire. It is a belief and a desire that engage a person in action, which action leads to experience.

Acting on Beliefs. Faith motivates effort. In that respect, it is completely unlike reactive methods to maintain comfort (table 1). Reactivity is easy, instinctual, thoughtless. It is the equivalent of credit card spending on whatever one needs most at the moment; reactivity yields instant results yet accumulates personal losses. In contrast, faith requires substantial initial investment. Like opening a new savings account when personal funds are minimal, faith entails immediate sacrifice. Yet when the savings account is held open consistently over time, despite market instability, dividends accrue. Faith is an emotional investment to live purposefully, planning and acting for the future, not merely for the present.

In scripture, faith is often described metaphorically as sowing seeds in a field (Alma 32; Matt. 13; Mark 4). Planting crops requires real labor and subsequent vigilance if one is to obtain a harvest. Initially, faith is the opposite of comfort. One must sacrifice several meals of grain to obtain much more after a season of growth (Ether 12:6). If the labors are performed, the harvest is assured (Ps. 126:5; D&C 6:33). In the end, faith is rewarded by abundance—comfort and security beyond anything possibly obtained by immediate personal consumption (1 Cor. 2:9).

This notion relates directly to mental health and well-being. Attributes conducive to mental health require planned action. Traits such as self-mastery or resilience to stress do not spring up spontaneously; they need to be cultivated.

Developing Faith: How Faith Can Be Strengthened

Comparisons of faith to the process of agricultural cultivation emphasize the multiple steps and prolonged efforts involved (Alma 32; Matt. 13; Mark 4). Anyone plowing, planting, watering, and weeding can attest to the labor—and to the inevitable harvest. The fruits of faith also appear after the requisite preliminaries (Alma 32:41–42). This section contains descriptions of nine considerations (table 3) conducive to the development of faith through exertion over time.

Acting on Principles Requires Faith; Acting on Correct Principles Strengthens Faith. As alluded to previously, adhering to correct principles demonstrates greater faith than relying on circumstances (exigency, utility, etc.) in choosing a course of action. Circumstantial demands are obvious: When we are hungry, we seek sustenance; when we experience social pressures, we conform. Circumstantial demands are the part of the equation that appears "known" or real, whereas the relevant principles remain abstract and distant compared with immediate pressures (e.g., endurance of hunger when fasting to obtain spiritual communion). Hence correct principles require faith to enact.

This is not to say that circumstances should be ignored. Exigency can be evaluated; utility can be considered: fires must be put out, and financial market conditions can change our investment portfolios. Evaluation and consideration denote judgment, not reactivity. However, such judgment must be guided by correct principles to yield fruitful results over time. House fires can be prevented, and

Table 3

Considerations for Strengthening Faith

Identify specific principles (table 2) that are pertinent to the situation at hand.
Consider prophetic teachings and seek the Holy Spirit to discern which combination of correct principles can inform a course of action.
Identify and work through doubts and fears inhibiting the determined course of action.
Seek answers to sincere questions as they arise.
Recognize personal suffering as a catalyst for increased enlightenment, rather than feeling embittered.
Focus attention on desired future outcomes.
Acknowledge personal rationalizations and affirm that correct principles supersede personal inclinations.
Seek to understand and acquire God's attributes by reflecting on scriptural descriptions of his actions and on the actions of his disciples.
Recognize and express gratitude for spiritual experiences and blessings, including: • personal character development • strengthened interpersonal relationships • divine intervention, peacefulness, and compensating power

disciplined investing accounts for market fluctuations. In contrast to thoughtful evaluation and judgment, exigency and utility are weak guidelines—too variable and subjective to implement consistently. Thus, faith entails consideration and judgment, a purposeful choice to value an abstract principle over a particular circumstance. When acting in faith, preferring the abstract to the immediate, we do not discard common sense. Rather, we have the sense to consider contexts beyond those immediately apparent.

Acting on correct principles strengthens faith because evidences inevitably accrue to our benefit. For instance, when we restrain anger (acting on the principles of humility and brotherly kindness when our initial urge is antithetical to those principles), we can experience closer interpersonal relationships. And over time, closer relationships provide us with additional emotional support and sources of satisfaction. Thus the fruits of our actions become obvious with time. A person who has repeatedly engaged in self-mastery, as difficult as that can be, earns the trust and respect of others, and a positive cycle ensues. As evidences of positive benefits accumulate over time, they strengthen our resolve to rely on correct principles (table 2), rather than on our initial impulses (table 1). The more we act in faith in correct principles, the more we recognize the positive confirmations, the fruits of our faith (Alma 32).

Discerning Which Principles to Enact. Individuals skeptical of religious faith still believe in something. All sorts of principles influence actions, from individualism and intellectualism to hedonism and humanism. And the principles believed yield corresponding actions (no pacifist has yet begun a war). Religious faith involves the purposeful affirmation of values taught by God's prophets over those taught by others, not because the values happen to align with our cultural and religious heritage but because they can be confirmed by spiritual experiences and can also be demonstrated to benefit everyone.[2]

A basic consideration therefore involves the relative validity of the principles believed. Principles have varying merits and limitations. For example, incentives for gain (utility) are more motivating long term than consistent duress (exigency), as demonstrated by turnover rates of employees offered bonuses for performance versus those pressured to achieve. Both utility and exigency yield results, but one approach is clearly superior to the other. Some principles are preferable to others.

The Lord Jesus Christ taught that not every law has equal weight (Matt. 23:23). Adherence to certain principles will foster more expansive personal and collective wellbeing than other principles (1 Cor. 12:31–13:13). In particular, the Lord's teachings emphasized motives

2. Joseph Smith taught: "God will not command anything, but what is peculiarly adapted in itself, to ameliorate the condition of every man under whatever circumstances it may find him, it matters not what kingdom or country he may be in" (Smith, 1840, p. 54).

(e.g., Matt. 6:1–4). Thus, the degree of personal and collective development we experience as humans depends not only on our actions *but also on the principles we believe as we act.* Belief in correct principles taught by God's prophets (such as table 2) yields the highest returns. The actions we take may be identical (e.g., helping someone in need), but the benefits accrue differentially based on our underlying values, the reasons for acting in that way (e.g., to impress others versus to alleviate guilt versus to promote the welfare of the person helped versus to uplift an offspring of Deity)—hence the essential need to base faith on correct principles.

Real life situations are complex, so multiple gospel principles (table 2) may be relevant in any given situation. For instance, when we learn of a new major life challenge, the principles of patience, gratitude, remembrance of truth, and so forth all apply, but different challenges may require different approaches. Sometimes acting decisively is necessary, and other times, we should first seek for additional information. We have the opportunity to consider which combination of principles best fits our present circumstances. The principles remain the same, but their application optimally occurs in combination with related principles.

Problems can result when we latch onto one correct principle without consideration of others that may also pertain to the circumstances. For instance, a parent justifying overlooking a child's repeated problematic behavior may justify inaction in terms of love or patience but could also consider principles of accountability, progression through overcoming personal limitations, and responsibility to teach correct principles and repentance (D&C 68:25). A child repeatedly corrected will resent authority, but a child left uncorrected will experience suboptimal growth and inevitable problems. Clearly, children benefit from both patience and correction. No single principle (table 2) provides optimal development; principles work best when working together.

In dealing with life's complexities, we have two aids: (1) multiple sources of scriptural teachings and prophetic interpretations of those teachings, and (2) the guidance of the Holy Spirit (and the light of Christ, or conscience). The better we understand the breadth of prophetic examples and counsel (e.g., dilemmas navigated by individuals in the scriptures), and the more we come to discern the impressions of the Spirit accurately, the better we are able to handle complexity.[3]

To be clear, acting with faith in correct principles and in God's guidance about how best to apply them does not diminish complexity. Rather, through experiences—failures and successes—we grow in our ability to carefully consider among alternatives, including incompatible alternatives (e.g., patient silence versus immediate correction). Following scriptural examples and following guidance from the Spirit will help us identify which combination of principles is optimal in a given context and also help us to remain vigilant in other circumstances that require other combinations of principles. Hence, the repeated prophetic emphasis on seeking spiritual guidance, distinguishing spiritual promptings, and acting accordingly (e.g., Ezek. 13:3; John 14:26; 2 Ne. 32:5).

We need not be paralyzed when we do not immediately identify an optimal solution to complex problems. Although there can be a *best* alternative among the many good options facing us (Oaks, 2007), sometimes God cares more that we act in faith, irrespective of the direction we choose, so long as our motives are pure (D&C 80:3). Elder Richard G. Scott (May 2007, p. 10) counseled that when we have weighed the relevant principles but have received no divine confirmation about the best option among many alternatives, we are to move forward in faith:

> What do you do when you have prepared carefully, have prayed fervently, waited a reasonable time for a response, and still do not feel an answer? You may want to express thanks when that occurs, for it is an evidence of His trust. When you are living worthily and your choice is consistent with the Savior's teachings and you need to act, proceed with trust. As you are sensitive to the promptings of the Spirit, one of two things will certainly occur at the appropriate time: either the stupor of thought will come, indicating an improper choice, or the peace or the burning in the bosom will be felt, confirming that your choice was correct. When you are living righteously

3. "Keep the commandments of God; and then you will be able more perfectly to understand the difference between right and wrong—between the things of God and the things of men; and your path will be like that of the just, which shineth brighter and brighter unto the perfect day." Smith, 1971, vol. 5, p. 31.

and are acting with trust, God will not let you proceed too far without a warning impression if you have made the wrong decision.

God trusts us to act and invites us to develop our capacity to act (D&C 58:26–29). And when we move forward with faith in the particular combination of principles that seems best, "*all* things work together for good to them that love God" (Rom. 8:28, emphasis added). Thankfully, the phrase *all things* includes our mistakes. Thus, when we have done our best but still err, we will not ultimately fail, because God will make up the difference and enable our growth through the temporary setbacks. Trusting in him results in improvement, sometimes because of our temporary discomfort. And we will receive an eventual confirmation that the way we initially selected was appropriate or deserves reconsideration. In faith, we move forward without initial confirmation, but the eventual confirmation is certain.

Overcoming Doubt to Produce Constructive Results. Just as faith is a principle of action, fear and doubt can foster inaction. Paralysis can result from mild suspicion just as well as from utter panic. Thus, fear is the opposite of faith. "Where doubt and uncertainty are, there faith is not, nor can it be. For doubt and faith do not exist in the same person at the same time" (*Lectures on Faith,* 1985, p. 71, lecture 6, par. 12). Although we may initially vacillate, hesitating with fear, constructive action occurs when our faith overcomes fear.

Living with faith entails an active vigilance against doubting God's teachings and fearing the consequences of those teachings. God counsels us, "Doubt not, fear not" (D&C 6:36; see also Morm. 9:27). That is strong counsel. Doubt *not* what God has spoken. Fear *not* the consequences of implementing his teachings. The counsel to choose faith in God's counsels and reject fear of consequences ("Look unto God with firmness of mind," Jacob 3:1) requires substantial vigilance and effort but enables emotional stability and personal peace.

In part because of the effort required to overcome natural human inclinations, the counsel to choose faith in God's teachings (table 2) can be mocked in a society that accepts or promotes natural inclinations. To skeptics of religious teachings, reliance on abstract principles can seem illogical and simplistic. Skeptics want facts (but then doubt them too). Worldly wisdom honors skepticism informed by relativity. In intellectual circles, criticisms of religion abound. The overall climate has become so antithetical to religious faith that Church members influenced by skeptics can doubt core scriptural teachings. If they persist in doubt, they may soften claims of truth and qualify their beliefs. They may sort out doctrines possibly offensive from those benign enough to be acceptable to critics. The metaphorical thorns springing from seeds of doubt choke seeds of faith (Matt. 13:22). Similar to the continual weeding of a garden, persistent belief in truth requires the removal of fear and doubt.

If truth exists and can be known, then the counsel to avoid fear and doubt is patently reasonable: once we understand a correct principle, we should trust it to be correct. Truth is truth. When we trust it, we apply it—facing ambiguity with faith. Facing ambiguity with faith entails replacing doubt with the certainty that if we apply the correct principles, we have done what we should—and those actions are sufficient, regardless of the apparent or actual outcome.

Living with faith is difficult because doubt and fear come easily and often. Human knowledge is based on experience and reason, both of which are fallible (BonJour, 2001; Crane, 2005); there is no certain empirical or philosophical foundation for what can be known. Everything that we think we know can be doubted (e.g., Descartes, 1641). When pushed to logical extremes, we cannot easily defend any belief—scientific or spiritual. Infinite reasons, even if improbable, can be proposed to undermine any position—rational or religious. Reason and experience are necessary but insufficient in the face of uncertainty. And uncertainty is everywhere. Thus, the profound need for faith in correct principles.

By definition, faith does not provide knowledge in the face of uncertainty. Rather, it provides direction when the details remain unknown. When we trust in correct principles (table 2), we can take positive action in the face of ambiguity. We may remain ignorant of many specifics, but we remain confident enough to move forward because we see other evidences confirming the reality of the underlying principles. For instance, scientists concede that the phenomenon of gravity (gravitation) has been imprecisely understood (most notably at extreme values; Rovelli, 2007); nevertheless, scientists have aligned with the general principle of gravitation to produce results that people lacking the same depth of understanding would consider miraculous (e.g., magnetic resonance imaging, rocket propulsion). Trust in overarching principles yields positive outcomes even though we may suffer from imprecision. To give an example pertinent to mental health, a woman who has been mistreated may not know exactly how to forgive and move forward with her life, but every step taken toward forgiveness (a correct principle) will illuminate a path to personal peace, whereas reactive resentment and revenge will impair emotional well-being and delay the needed healing. *When we are uncertain about precisely how to apply a correct principle but do our best to apply it anyway, we demonstrate faith.* And that action necessarily entails overcoming doubt and fear.

Seeking Enlightenment by Asking Genuine Questions. Skeptics may question the value of suspending doubt, which is a core precept of both philosophy and scientific inquiry. However, suspending doubt denotes neither placated ignorance nor abated curiosity. Rather, seeking answers to unanswered questions *is the very essence of faith.* Doubt yields no solutions, but faith seeks answers.

When we ask an honest question, we openly admit our ignorance but simultaneously seek to dispel it. By asking honest questions, we say, in essence, "I do not know, but I know what I can do and will do: I will seek and ask." For instance, a fourteen-year-old boy had real questions, profound questions that challenged established precedents, but until he received an answer, Joseph Smith continued seeking (JS–H 1:8–10).

As with all things, the value of a question depends on the motive behind it. Honest questions seek enlightenment (Alma 27:7; 34:5) and enact faith (1 Ne. 15:11; Matt. 7:7–11). However, questions designed to undermine belief can be posed (Mosiah 12:19; Alma 10:13), and questions arising from motives such as cynicism (and other reactions in table 1) can challenge faith. For instance, motives of cynicism often (1) prompt premature alignment with an incorrect solution (e.g., "that cannot be possible"), (2) diminish the desire to seek deep explanations that entail prolonged effort, and (3) give rise to sweeping rejections, discarding whole topics when encountering a few irregular particulars (throwing out the proverbial baby with the bathwater when every drop of bathwater so obviously requires disposal). When asking questions, motive matters. Motives of anger cloud reason ("Why did you do that again?"), as do motives of despair ("Why me?") and personal ambition ("Why not?"). Motives of naïve optimism preclude the whole process ("Why ask at all?"). Honest questions are motivated by the possibility of increased enlightenment, even when that enlightenment entails personal discomfort and when initial responses prove unsatisfactory and prompt additional seeking.

Seeking knowledge is itself an act of faith (Gen. 18:23–33; Ether 3:1–13). Avoiding reactions (table 1), such as premature foreclosure when answers are not forthcoming, is also an act of faith. When answers are not obtained, faith prevents discouragement because it is rooted in a greater desire than the desire for certainty: trust in God. The salve of the Spirit ("look unto me in every thought," D&C 6:36) is the only remedy for our natural inclinations to reject things that cannot be explained at this time. Eventually, after this life, we will acquire all knowledge. Persistence in the process of enlightenment requires trust. When the presently unknown or unknowable are seen as temporary conditions, we persist in seeking.

Experiencing Pain Challenges or Channels Faith. Mental health clients tend to accurately describe pain—it hurts. There is no mistaking the sharp jabs felt from criticism or the suffocation felt from neglect. Suffering is not synonymous with mental illness; it is a universal human condition, typically temporary but notably persistent among those seeking therapy.

Pain is a condition. In that sense, pain is morally neutral. It motivates action, but it does not determine the actions taken. Pain is a signal and a catalyst. It demands attention, resolution, and subsequent learning, either enflaming fear or invigorating faith.

Mental health professionals frequently differentiate wellness and dysfunction according to discrepant exposure to adverse events. People experiencing prolonged pain often experience emotional malaise. The association is so obvious that we assume it to be causal. It is not. Painful events precede but do not result in dysfunction. Mental illness and well-being are far more complex than that simplistic formulation. We notice adverse symptoms such as binge eating or physical aggression because underlying pain motivated visible actions, but their more proximal causes were previously unobservable potentials within the person (e.g., thought patterns, neurological functioning, prior learning, present values). For instance, either excessive weight loss or extreme irritability may be associated with latent struggles with self-worth, hyperthyroidism, patterns of irrational thinking, etc., that repeated pain made obvious by overwhelming optimal psychological and physiological functioning. Individuals use a variety of coping methods, most of which work most of the time. When current coping fails to reduce pain, individuals invoke other strategies, for better or worse.

Dysfunction can arise from incorrect interpretations and thoughtless reactions about how to proceed as a result of the pain. Repeated pain can beat down on some individuals to the point that they feel little else. Yet the same pain inflicted repeatedly upon others may steel resolve to the point of permanent positive character transformation (e.g., the Prophet Joseph Smith, Mohandas Gandhi, Viktor Frankl, Nelson Mandela). Pain is so powerful that when handled reactively (through reflexive, unconscious processing; see table 1), it perpetuates continued pain (e.g., internalization leading to cycles of self-doubt and self-blame; externalization leading to cycles of victimization and antisocial dysfunction). However, when people cope with pain using correct principles (table 2), the cycle of increased pain can become manageable or be replaced with peace: it is blatantly irrational to perpetuate pain. Faith in correct principles enables internalization of the suffering to enhance self-knowledge, resolution, and humility; externalization based on correct principles can result in compassion, service, and mercy.

Personal suffering can be a catalyst for destruction or healing. Reactivity perpetuates pain. Faith, acting upon correct principles (table 2), diminishes pain for oneself and others.

Looking to the Future Enhances Faith. Human suffering is bad enough once, but its impact multiplies when we relive it again and again in memory. When our thoughts repeatedly return to our sorrow, it can seem as if there is no future at all; but when our vision is fixed on the future, memory can help us learn from the past (e.g., planning to avoid previous errors).

Elaborating on the biblical account of Lot's wife, who perished when she looked back to Sodom, Elder Jeffrey R. Holland clarified, "It isn't just that she looked back; she looked back longingly. In short, her attachment to the past outweighed her confidence in the future" (2009, p. 3). Attachment to the past confines us. It narrows our engagement with the present. It can disconnect us from potential alternatives in the future. We cannot arrive where we need to be with our backs turned toward the intended destination.

For many individuals in distress, the past continues to be destructive in the present. A crucial function of therapy is to proffer a future worth considering, worth facing, worth seeking. Seeking a better future involves learning from the harmful events of the past and then setting them aside. Elder Holland has counseled, "Dismiss the destructive and keep dismissing it, until the beauty of the Atonement of Christ has revealed to you your bright future. . . . God doesn't care nearly as much about where you have been as He does about where you are, and with His help, where you are willing to go" (2009, p. 6).

In the New Testament, Saul of Tarsus sorrowed that he had persecuted the followers of God (Philip. 3:6–7). A changed man, Paul the disciple learned to forget the past and face the future: "This one thing I do, *forgetting those things which are behind, and reaching forth unto those things which are before,* I press toward the mark for the prize of the high calling of God in Christ Jesus" (Philip. 3:13–14, emphasis added; see also 1 Cor. 15:9–10). Mental health interventions will be most effective when they encourage clients to do likewise—cease rumination (Nolen-Hoeksema, Wisco, & Lyubomirsky, 2008), look optimistically to the future (Seligman & Csikszentmihalyi, 2000), and cease comparisons with other people (Ellis, 2001).

Trusting Not in Man. To consistently act on correct principles (table 2), we must trust those principles more than we trust anything else, including ourselves. Exclusive reliance on our own judgment demonstrates a lack of faith (rationalization, foreclosure, etc.; see table 1). Love for true principles stems from the same sentiment that acknowledges our own failings (e.g., 2 Ne. 4:19). We must recognize ourselves as limited, inconsistent, and dependent, in order to cling to the principles that make us strong (Ether 12:27).

Although we benefit from self-confidence, trust misplaced only in oneself provides a false sense of security (2 Ne. 28:31). Self-confidence does not necessarily equate with self-improvement. Our desires for confidence and certainty can cause us to lose patience with others who have different abilities or different worldviews. Feelings of certainty can foreclose other alternatives and stop progression. We can be certain but nevertheless incorrect. Certainty is not accuracy. It is human nature to more strongly desire certainty than truth.

Reliance on oneself yields immediate results, so in that sense it is preferable to apathy, withdrawal, or despair. Nevertheless, unintended negative consequences accompany attempts at completely autonomous functioning. Self-oriented living does not produce joy, even though we are more likely to obtain things that we desire. Obtaining what we desire is not the same as obtaining edification, unless the desires are for edification (Maxwell, 1996; Oaks, 2011). Motives centered in self yield so much less than motives based on universal beneficence. For instance, interpersonal strife results from selfishness, which selfishness denotes a lack of faith (heeding one's immediate desires rather than delaying personal gratification for the sake of collective benefit). Where there is little trust in principles, there is little trust in other people, and when we do not trust in other people yet seek our own will, conflict is inevitable. People seeking their own will without trust in others believe that they must take matters into their own hands. Whether by verbal argument, passive resistance, or physical intimidation, sole reliance on oneself to obtain desired ends (2 Ne. 4:34) is contrary to faith—and to well-being. We are interdependent, not independent. What might have been ours through faith fails to edify when taken by our own force of will upon others.

This concept of self-reliance versus interdependent faith applies not only to individuals but also to social groups. A society succeeds to the degree that its members demonstrate faith in mutually sanctioned principles (i.e., procedures of governance, enforcement of law). Societies break down to the extent autonomy replaces mutual trust and adherence to shared principles (i.e., cultural mores, common decency). When we adhere to common values, we implicitly assume that others will do the same, but when we see others violate common values, it is easier to rationalize noncompliance in ourselves. When we rely on common principles, the collective is strengthened, and when we primarily take our cues from individuals, the collective is weakened.

Differences between the real and the ideal can lead to skepticism when human fallibility frustrates expectations. When people disappoint us, personally or collectively, we may feel abandoned or angry. Our mistrust deepens, not only in people but also in principles. When we see correct principles disregarded, we often disbelieve not merely the people but the principles. Hence, the need for mental health therapy to help restore confidence in correct principles (love, forgiveness, equality, protection of the innocent, etc.) such that people's actions become proactive, not reactive (*agentic*, see Warner, 2001).

The type of interpersonal trust that we call a virtue, the trust that people with compromised mental health typically could strengthen, is actually a trust in correct principles, not the result of perpetual one-on-one evaluations of each new person. People who exhibit the virtue of interpersonal trust do not mistrust everyone until trust is proven. Rather, they exhibit a benevolent trust in individuals because they trust in the general principle of human decency. Trust in the principle enables trust in particular people.

Of course, interpersonal trust based on the general principle of human decency is delimited; decency has boundaries. Faith in human decency is not gullibility. When generic trust is found to be misplaced in a specific instance (misattribution), individuals exhibiting the virtue of interpersonal trust do not ascribe the error to the principle but to the person. For instance, they do not lose faith in God when they are inevitably betrayed by their fellowman (Gen. 37:28; Luke 22:48; Alma 14:1–28).

Exercising Faith in God Enhances Faith in Correct Principles. Across the world, most people already believe in correct principles such as personal sacrifice, gratitude, patience, and others listed in table 2. Values such as these appear universal (Peterson & Seligman, 2004), and people benefit to the extent that they apply any of these principles (e.g., Emmons & McCullough, 2004; Lopez & Snyder, 2009; Worthington, 2005), whether or not they believe them to be the spiritual framework of the universe.

Nevertheless, additional benefit comes from believing that moral guidelines are of divine origin (e.g., Koenig, King, & Carson, 2012). Specifically, belief in God enhances belief in correct principles because God embodies and models all virtues (i.e., the recorded actions of Jesus Christ while on earth and when speaking with his people and prophets), which principles would otherwise be abstractions—diffuse ideals without exemplar. Although we observe virtuous actions in our fellowmen, no one actuates all virtues simultaneously or to such an extent as God. For instance, the social context of the concept *patience* typically means waiting perhaps a week or a month before changing course, but when we learn that "the God of patience" (Rom. 15:5) waits for as long as needed for our return to him, even if millennia (D&C 138), that elevates our understanding of the concept—enabling us to hold a much higher standard of patience for ourselves than would ever be possible by observing other humans. Sincere disciples of God model his attributes for others, and the process of elevated virtue influences others, all based on the original example set by God himself. As noted by the Apostle John, "We love him, because he first loved us" (1 Jn. 4:19). Learning occurs best through emulation (Bandura, 1977).

Moreover, the very thought of God prompts remembrance of his attributes. One who believes in God receives continual reminders of attributes worthy of aspiration. Thus, belief in God provides repeated promptings that strengthen the faith of those who seek to apply correct principles. And the more accurately we understand the attributes of Divinity, the stronger our faith (*Lectures on Faith,* 1985).

At the present time, many people in society acknowledge correct principles (table 2), even when they do not believe in God. They may believe in moral relativism, practicing many virtues but setting others aside when personal motives conflict with them. Such moral inconsistency can be minimized by a belief in God, who holds us accountable and who invites us to set aside self-justification. Thus, faith in God strengthens faith in moral principles.

Recognizing Spiritual Experiences Confirms Faith. Faith is confirmed not only through the eventual positive outcomes from applying correct principles but also from spiritual impressions. The Holy Ghost witnesses to individuals that their actions are pleasing to God (*Lectures on Faith,* 1985). These spiritual feelings confirm faith. We sense resonance with the Divine, and that impression guides action as much as if it were auditory, visual, olfactory, gustatory, or tactile.

This is not to say that faith lacks evidence experienced through the senses. Faith is also confirmed from witnessing outward spiritual manifestations—miracles that follow belief (Mark 16:17–18; Morm. 9:24; D&C 46:11–26; 63:9–11). Those with faith can see prayers answered by God. They experience real-world events that provide assurance. Thus, persistent faith results in knowledge (Alma 32:34–35); the desired outcomes of faith become apparent (Alma 32:41–43; Ether 12:19).

Fruits of Faith: Character Development, Interpersonal Well-being, Access to Divine Aid

As faith develops and people take corresponding actions, those actions result in consequences, the so-called "fruits of faith." Thus faith, once acted upon, has a foundation in the evidence from the outcomes.

The consequences of faith can be observed. Among others, three consequences of faith include personal character development, interpersonal well-being, and access to divine assistance.

Acting with Faith Promotes Personal Development. While unthinking reactivity based on the past diminishes character (table 1), faith promotes character development. "God uses your faith to mold your character. Character is the manifestation of what you are becoming. Strong moral character results from consistent correct choices in the trials and testing of life" (Scott, 2003, p. 76).

When we believe in a principle and act on that principle, we experience internal congruence, which results in self-confidence, trust in others, etc. For example, even though we can foresee immediate personal discomfort by telling the truth in an embarrassing social situation, if we have faith in the principle of honesty, the dissonance reduction felt by being honest will compensate for the temporary embarrassment. Although reactive dishonesty might be to our immediate advantage (e.g., anxiety reduction), the principle of truthfulness cuts across all situations, self-incriminating or otherwise. Reactive attempts to cope with adversity that focus on circumstances (avoidance, skepticism, etc.; see table 1) can fail because they attend only to external consequences, not to the person's internal state of congruence. Inner peace results from living congruently with personal values. Confidence increases when choosing to act on correct principles and receiving internal and spiritual validation for doing so.

Character development cannot occur without faith. If a person does the right thing (remains honest in a self-incriminating situation) but for the wrong reason (to gain favor with a third party who might share the same viewpoint), the perceived consequences will depend on the response of other people (the third party). Positive character traits develop haphazardly so long as other people remain the standard against which those traits are measured. People who measure themselves against social perceptions remain oblivious to the benefits of having lived in accordance with a higher principle (honesty for the sake of personal integrity) and thus cannot feel the increased self-confidence that comes to people who act for the sake of that principle. Character development comes not from doing the "right thing" but from doing it for the right reason. We achieve personal growth when we believe that we *should* act in a certain way and then act accordingly.

Faith Promotes Healthy Interpersonal Relationships. Interpersonal relationships involve both trust and mistrust. Appropriate trust, even when tentative at first, can increase over time. In that sense, interpersonal relationships are built initially on faith and then qualified based on experiences (or at least perceptions of experiences). The belief that past experiences can be trusted in evaluating other people is a mild form of faith commonplace in society. Earned trust does enhance relationships; accurate mistrust can protect from continued injury. We believe others' past actions will predict their future actions, and we act accordingly.

However, this common form of interpersonal trust is limited for at least three reasons. First, past behavior is a useful but imperfect predictor of future behavior, because people are both inconsistent and swayed by circumstances. People we trust based on past experiences can nevertheless injure us, and people we mistrust can benefit us. Self-protection requires conditional trust while ascertaining others' current motives, not merely past behaviors. By relying solely on past experience, a person will inevitably experience betrayal of trust or missed positive opportunities.

Second, interpersonal trust based solely on past experience is often reactive. It typically involves a "tit for tat" type of exchange: If you appear relaxed around me, I will relax around you; if you forgive me, I will forgive you. To forgive someone who has already forgiven us demonstrates merely reciprocity, not responsibility. Genuine intimacy requires an abiding commitment between people; in contrast, reactive trust ("I'll trust you so long as you . . .") precludes enduring intimacy.

Third, interpersonal trust based on past observations does not account for experiences unobserved or for other contextual factors, including the flaws of the evaluator. Humans often evaluate others too critically and evaluate themselves too generously (Alicke, Dunning, & Krueger, 2013). We fail to see the multiple layers of context preceding actions (Smith, 2004). Implicit faith in the predictive validity of past experience is highly pragmatic yet imperfect. Accumulated experience can inhibit interpersonal intimacy when reliance on that experience overrides more profound truths. In sum, interpersonal relationships involve trust, with that trust limited by evaluations of past behavior, perceived reciprocity, and immediate observations about motives.

More beneficial than interpersonal trust based on past experience or reciprocity is faith in God and his teachings, which can be applied to the particulars of interpersonal interactions. For instance, God asks that we forgive others for their actions that have harmed us (D&C 64:10; Luke 17:3–4). The principle of forgiveness requires genuine faith to enact, particularly when the other party has shown no sign of reciprocation or remorse. When offered in the face of likely rejection, forgiveness has little to do with interpersonal trust. A person would scarcely even consider forgiving an unrepentant perpetrator if the base motive involved a desire for the other person's reciprocity. Rather, the reason for acting despite mistrust depends on faith in a correct principle—forgiveness—and faith in God who exemplifies that principle. By itself,[4] the principle of forgiveness seems antithetical to reactive inclinations based on past experiences; it seems unreasonable and undesirable. Nevertheless, forgiveness proves much more beneficial to personal wellbeing than continued antipathy (Worthington, 2005). And the stark

4. As indicated previously, no principle should be considered alone. Decisions optimally occur in light of other principles. Hence, Robert Gleave (see chapter 3 of this book) advocates that forgiveness necessarily entails justice, another correct principle. Without justice and accountability, forgiveness is problematic for reasons that he provides.

reality is that without the leap of faith required by forgiveness (i.e., trust in others' capacity for reformation, even after contradictory evidence), almost every human would be isolated from every other within weeks. Forgiveness requires a leap of faith, but that faithfulness turns out to be necessary in all interpersonal relationships. To become close enough to other people to know them, to have a truly strong relationship with them, we need to first see them with the eye of faith—willing to extend undeserved forgiveness while remaining wise in extending trust.

Similarly, seeing other people as basically good contradicts the blatant facts of human frailty, yet that belief inspires mercy and goodwill where passive neutrality would seemingly be more logical. Sacrificing one's own desires for others seems foolish within materialistic culture, yet giving to others promotes personal happiness (Brooks, 2006). Faith in principles of self-reliance, fidelity, preparedness, etc., as taught by God and his servants results in greater benefits than mere trust in others based on their past actions. Hence interpersonal relationships improve when people look beyond the immediate particulars of their interaction to the principles undergirding all relationships.

Faith Allows Us to Benefit from Divine Intervention. Just as faith is essential in interpersonal relationships, faith precedes and characterizes interactions with all things spiritual. We must act on a belief in God in order to recognize that God is already acting on our behalf. A relationship with Heavenly Father presupposes belief in him, a correct understanding of his attributes, and realization of his approval (*Lectures on Faith,* 1985). Although God may be reaching out to us in countless ways, we benefit most from divine intervention when we recognize the hand making the offering. With faith, we recognize the benefits of divine interventions (2 Kgs. 6:17; Luke 24:32; D&C 76:12).

Our spiritual nature yearns to know God. Yet this hunger can be sated temporarily by indulging other senses—not only passions but especially the ego, the self-contained intellect. A desire to know God can persist across our lives, gently returning when we are reflective, but when we become continually fixed on other intents, our consciousness furrows a rut deep enough to make spiritual paths seem impractical. Patterns become engrained; spiritual atrophy occurs. Shut down often enough, our spiritual sense eventually decays to the point of disbelieving prior spiritual experiences; resentment of all things spiritual can extend to the former self, recast as gullible and deluded. A fruit, once sweet, may naturally rot from lack of attention—and rottenness is easy to disdain. No longer appealing, the putrid fruit nevertheless contains within it the seeds of a potential tree ready to produce when planted. The penitent recognize the need for planting and nourishing the seeds of faith (Alma 32).

Just as heavy tobacco use can dull our ability to taste food, when we repeatedly take in anything besides the Spirit, that thing will eventually diminish our ability to enjoy that which provides us nourishment. Faith may be replaced by alternatives (table 1), but our spiritual health, like our physical health, depends on enacting correct beliefs. Our body and our spirit were both designed to function through faith. Too often we rely on what we can see, when what we really require cannot be known without belief.

Ultimately, faith is a gift to be sought and developed (Heb. 11:1–12:2). God grants faith and then spiritual sight to those who desire to see the end from the beginning (Ether 3:25; D&C 76:12; Moses 1:4, 8; Abr. 3:1–14). He teaches those who wish to be taught (contrast Matt. 13:13 with John 16:29). He gives to those who receive (Matt. 25:29; D&C 39:4; 132:3). Like distracted children playing far from home, we must first desire to hear our Father before his call becomes audible above the clamor of our peers. His voice is heard by those who listen (John 10:27; 3 Ne. 11:5).

Thus, faith is the first step of spiritual progression: the motivation to enact precept upon precept (2 Ne. 28:30; Ether 12:3–31). It is the vision to climb upward when others clamber down, or walk around the corner when others wait against the wall. In short, faith sees a destination. It sees what might be attained, providing both purpose and persistence. With faith, life has meaning, progression without end. When one peak is scaled, one even higher can be seen afar off. There is always more to creation (Moses 1:4; D&C 132:20).

Our own spiritual development entails alignment with God's plan. With such alignment, we benefit from his interventions already prepared for us, most notably the Atonement wrought by

Jesus Christ (Alma 12:33). Although we cannot see *how* God's plan for us will be fulfilled, we can believe *that* his plan for us will be fulfilled (Morm. 5:23). "We can accept His will with peace and assurance, confident that His infinite wisdom surpasses our own ability to comprehend fully His plan as it unfolds a piece at a time" (Scott, 2003, p. 77). With such trust, we spiritually see the future in the present, not having to wait for some distant heaven to experience a portion of it here and now.

Implications of Faith for the Practice of Mental Health Therapy

Mental health practitioners have developed trust in a variety of principles: professional standards for ethical practice, professional licensure and oversight, theories of human personality, explanations for the causes of mental illness, and so on. Some of these principles are more accurate than others. Some may need to be replaced altogether (Williams, 1998). Applying the concepts of faith detailed in the previous sections of this chapter can help that winnowing process and strengthen our practices as we better align ourselves with correct principles.

All therapy, if it is therapeutic, promotes faith. Therapists can strengthen their clients' abilities to overcome doubt, blame, etc. by strengthening their faith. Acting with faith in clients' abilities to improve their own conditions, therapists would never take over clients' decisions, even implicitly, nor would they limit clients' learning from pain by only attempting to remove it. Humans are remarkably resilient, and the role of a therapist is not one of healer but of facilitator, counselor, coworker. Therapists who work by faith exhibit genuine trust in the process of recovery, without minimizing the work involved and without denying the client the privilege and benefit of that work.

The following descriptions of counseling integrate principles associated with faith. The approaches described are by no means exhaustive; dozens of applications of faith to counseling could be identified for mental health settings. These approaches are not sequential; individual clients require different interventions at different moments. They are not validated; they require revision and refinement. Nevertheless, approaches like these may be useful in generating ideas for a variety of practice settings and in moving mental health professions toward greater applications of faith.

Helping Clients Recognize Applications of Faith in Concrete Terms: Identifying Specific Examples in Their Own Lives. A basic step toward fostering clients' faith is to help them understand the principle itself. Faith is most readily applied when it is understood. Rather than assume that a client understands the principle of faith, therapists can explicitly portray the link between beliefs and actions. For instance, in conversation a therapist can draw out examples of people the client considers successful in a way he or she desires to succeed. The link between the individual's belief and action could be explained using common terminology, not necessarily the language of cognitive psychology; the principle itself (belief associated with action) is sufficiently universal and amenable to client intuition. Nevertheless, clients typically must see how the principle of faith works in other people's lives before they realize how the principle can apply to their own particular dilemmas. Their faith can increase when they hear examples of faith (see Rom. 10:17). Consider the following case example:

> Raymond has been stuck in a pattern of self-destructive substance use and addiction. Years of rejection by his father were compounded by limited social competence that resulted in similar rejection from peers. Recently released from jail, Raymond seeks to remain clean but has limited external supports. The therapist spent much of the second session eliciting examples of people who Raymond considers role models or people who have coped successfully with adversity. Then together Raymond and the therapist identified specific, concrete actions and associated beliefs of those individuals. The therapist emphasized how the outcomes achieved by those individuals were not certain—yet the individuals acted "as if" the outcomes were certain. They concluded the session by finding examples of how similar beliefs helped Raymond on two occasions.

Many clients may have gone awry by following examples of people who obtained what they desired by acting in ways antithetical to faith (e.g., "taking control" of situations through aggressive manipulation). Fewer and fewer role models of living with faith are touted. Identifying specific examples of individuals who succeed through faith can instill hope; if acting with faith worked for people they admire, it could possibly work for them. Clients' beliefs about the future begin to change as they come to recognize viable alternatives.

Helping Clients to Create a Vision of an Improved Future. Therapists working with troubled individuals attempting to cope through reactive methods (table 1) encourage faith even when the immediate prospects are disconcerting or downright frightening. Much of the initial work in therapy involves helping clients develop confidence that they can improve their condition. Clients must envision improvement before they take steps to enact that vision.

> In a subsequent session, Raymond appeared ambivalent about continuing therapy. Observing that their previous conversations frequently involved incidents of rejection, the therapist openly mused whether Raymond might be concerned about the therapist rejecting him. Raymond responded with anger but revealed that without a stable job, he felt incapable of financial solvency. He had accrued substantial debt that included court fees and the additional expense of mandated counseling. Raymond had little confidence in his immediate prospects and had only vague ideas about how to proceed. The therapist provided a referral to a local agency offering financial counseling. Raymond identified contacts who he believed could help him locate more stable employment. Together, the therapist and Raymond discussed his concerns about debt reduction strategies. Now recognizing concrete methods, Raymond identified steps he would take prior to the next session.

Initially, most clients want to reduce pain, a diffuse ambition without strategy. Rather than focusing on the pain (e.g., cycles of rejection, anger, despondency) as in Raymond's therapist's initial foible (making an overly personalized interpretation), it is often more useful to attune clients to positive, desirable outcomes (e.g., sustained employment, confidence in social settings, emotional intimacy in marriage) while recognizing that pain and discomfort may continue. Clients' vision of the future should be realistic: not to be free from pain but to manage pain when it occurs.

Clients are more likely to believe that improvement will occur when they recognize specific solutions. Specific solutions instill hope. Once clients have acquired a positive vision of the future, therapy promotes a reorientation to that future.

Helping Clients to Replace Past Patterns with a Focus on the Future. Clients in distress often feel stuck. They try new solutions but remain in ruts that prevent real change. Yet the pull of the past can be overcome by strong desires for improvement. Therapists can help clients let go of past patterns by looking to the future.

> When Raymond became discouraged, his therapist helped him recollect his deepest desires: to remarry, to open his own restaurant, and to help his younger brother who had recently divorced. The therapist continued to encourage him to emulate his identified role models. Raymond's passions remained partially submerged until his brother responded to his repeated invitations and moved in with him. Raymond cleaned his apartment and seemed to take on the responsibilities of an older brother.

A vision for the future lacks power until it becomes more compelling than the otherwise ever-present past. Faith's magnetism reorients our direction completely; a spindle floating in water becomes a compass once it is fixed, grounded. Not merely changing behavior, faith directs one's whole outlook.

Helping Clients Recognize and Appreciate Correct Principles. A key step in therapy involves helping clients personalize and internalize correct principles. To do so, therapists can help identify those principles and then foster clients' faith in them. For example, most people appreciate others' forgiveness or gratitude. After client recognition of the benefits when other people live according to principles, the subsequent work of therapy involves helping clients perceive those principles as desirable guides for their own actions. For instance, with sufficient recollection, clients can see how showing gratitude has been generally more effective than basing their actions on reactivity. Despite the specific ways in which the internalization is achieved (Acceptance and Commitment Therapy, Reality Therapy, CBT, etc.), the objective is to help clients truly value the principles most likely to improve their abilities to deal with a variety of complex situations.

> In a subsequent session, Raymond and the therapist discussed the issue of interpersonal approval, specifically noting the blatant honesty characteristic of the role models he had initially described. In contrast, Raymond admitted to frequently exaggerating his accomplishments to solicit social attention and lying to former associates about the reason for his absence during his

time in jail. Rather than focus on Raymond's self-disgust, which initially fueled much of the conversation, the therapist redirected Raymond to times when he had openly acknowledged his own weaknesses. Although these times had often resulted in the expected rejection, Raymond described feeling greater personal satisfaction when he had been forthright.

Many principles can help clients experience reality more accurately: humility (openness to learning) without self-denigration, fidelity, awareness of others' needs, moderation in zeal, and so forth. These principles are rarely articulated in traditional therapy, yet they underlie well-being. Applicable across circumstances, they are more useful templates than circumstance-specific ways of responding. Hence, therapists can speak openly about such principles and solicit from clients examples of how the application of those principles has been more satisfying than reactivity. Therapy can foment desires to develop those attributes. When we keenly desire an attribute, we are more likely to act upon it, irrespective of circumstance.

Helping Clients Act on Correct Principles. Individuals already feeling overwhelmed by distress may feel incapable of action. In a vicious cycle, clients experiencing anxiety attempt to prevent failure through inaction, which only perpetuates failure.

The requirement of effort is one reason why faith is so unappealing. Our natural inclination is to look for the easiest solution. It is not easy to delay immediate relief by taking actions that are only effective over time. It is not easy to envision a positive future when we hurt right now. It is not easy to apply abstract principles to concrete problems.

Raymond missed three months of therapy while in jail for violating the conditions of his parole. When confronted by his parole officer, he had disclosed a relapse into poly-substance use, which occurred after renewed contact with his former circle of friends. Previously, Raymond had been certain that he could avoid them, but he had felt flattered when one of them had sought him out. After re-engaging with his former associates, Raymond felt responsible for helping them benefit from the lessons that he himself had learned since becoming clean; he saw an opportunity to undo some damage he had caused previously—but past patterns returned. The therapist praised

Raymond's honesty with the parole officer and helped him identify ways to work through his shame about the past that had left him vulnerable to relapse.

Correct principles are the best guide for behavior, but problems occur when we have not yet learned how to apply a particular principle in a given setting, when we have not yet learned a principle needed for a new circumstance, or when we trust ourselves (or others) more than the principle. Therapy can help a client discover or restore trust in principles when trust has been misplaced in oneself or others (2 Ne. 28:31). Therapy can promote accurate responses to reality, building and reinforcing coping skills.

Self-mastery involves intense ongoing efforts. However, not all actions taken by the client or recommended by the therapist lead to improvement. The ultimate outcomes will depend on the steps taken. Much distress and even mental illness can result from seeking an intended outcome (e.g., acceptance by others) through incongruent means (e.g., assuaging guilt for wrongdoing rather than making amends). To promote healing, therapy must foster adherence to principles that guide optimal behavior.

Helping Clients Recognize Positive Outcomes That Come from Acting According to Correct Principles. Acting in accordance with correct principles, rather than merely reacting (table 1), requires tremendous mental, emotional, and even physical exertion. Typically, people struggle for self-improvement for a very short period of time before being dissuaded by easier alternatives or a false sense of self-adequacy. To persist we need reinforcement, recognition of the fruits that faith has generated.

Specifically, we need to know that what we are doing is what we should be doing—and that God is pleased with our actions: "Such was, and always will be, the situation of the saints of God, that unless they have an actual knowledge that the course that they are pursuing is according to the will of God, they will grow weary in their minds and faint" (*Lectures on Faith,* 1985, pp. 67–68). Optimally, clients will benefit from such spiritual confirmation, but even when they do not believe in God, they can come to see that acting on correct principles really works. They can come to know (not merely believe) that doing so will reward them with the intended desires.

In a subsequent session, Raymond reviewed events from the preceding months. Whereas in previous years his attempts to remain clean had typically lasted one week, for several months he had remained clean for all but six days, not including his time in jail. Through Raymond's personal involvement, his brother had not had to endure many of the hardships that Raymond had encountered during his own divorce. Raymond had begun dating a woman known by family members. His work situation remained tenuous, but with his brother helping to pay the rent, he could manage adequately. Taking stock of his progress filled him with hope at his immediate prospects, despite his lack of access to his children, large long-term debt, and recent shoulder surgery from which he had not entirely recovered.

Faith enacted enhances faith (see Alma 32:30–34). Clients who come to believe in correct principles (e.g., gratitude, forgiveness, love, accountability) and consistently act on those principles will experience permanent improvements in functioning. By overcoming doubt, shame, blame, etc., they see possible realities not previously apparent. Acting on belief in correct principles yields results; recognizing those results yields stronger belief. For this cycle of self-perpetuating improvement to continue, progress must be explicitly acknowledged. Progress without personal recognition tends to reverse direction. Enjoying the fruits of one's labors makes likely a return to labor.

Helping Clients Generalize Improvement across Many Aspects of Daily Living. Except in cases such as specific neurological trauma, symptoms of mental illness do not appear in isolation. Rather, they relate to one another as well as to other underlying beliefs and coping methods (table 1). Therefore, long-term symptom reduction requires genuine *lifestyle changes* to foster acquisition and maintenance of integrated patterns of improved beliefs and coping strategies.

Upon losing his job, Raymond relapsed into heavy substance abuse. He received a lenient sentence based on testimony of the therapist. When Raymond was released, he faced bankruptcy. The therapist reduced his customary fee so that Raymond could continue long-term therapy. Although this was the third time that Raymond had reached "rock bottom," with therapeutic encouragement his approach to recovery changed. He recognized his own incapacity to progress alone. He no longer felt like a victim. He held nothing back. His therapy and attendance at Narcotics Anonymous meetings no longer felt compulsory. Over time, he became a close mentor to two group members. He apologized to his former spouse and worked to forgive his father. He settled financial claims without filing for bankruptcy. He relocated to a city nearby and worked two jobs. He paid child support and regained visitation rights. He discontinued therapy upon termination of his parole.

Mental health therapy based on the principle of faith is the equivalent of a physician recommending regular exercise when the client requests medication for back pain—it is the most effective solution, but it appears completely undesirable. Lifestyle change, ultimately more conducive to health than symptom reduction, can be daunting when even desired at all. Clients require substantial support and assurance in making their personal leap into principle-centered living (table 4). Leaning into the winds of opposition, acting despite

Table 4

Considerations for mental health professionals

Help clients recognize applications of faith in concrete terms

- Briefly explain how beliefs result in actions.
- Identify examples of how other people have succeeded by acting on positive beliefs or principles.
- Identify instances in the client's life when she or he acted with faith despite obstacles.
- Instill hope that if acting in faith worked for others and for themselves in the past, it can work again now.

Help clients to create a vision of an improved future

- Help clients envision improvement in detail, including multiple steps over time.
- Rather than focus exclusively on the client's symptoms, attune clients to desired outcomes while recognizing that pain and discomfort may continue.
- Help clients develop realistic expectations (e.g., not free from pain but managing pain when it occurs).
- Help clients recognize specific strategies and beliefs that could facilitate improvement.

(cont.)

Table 4 *(cont.)*

Considerations for mental health professionals

Help clients to replace past patterns with a focus on the future

- Deepen recognition of past inadequate strategies (table 1) and foster desires for improvement.
- Facilitate a new worldview aligned with desired outcomes.

Help clients recognize and appreciate correct principles

- Identify correct principles (table 2) relevant to the client's desired outcomes.
- Review instances when those principles have helped the client and others.
- Help the client embrace the principles as necessary to obtain desired outcomes.

Help clients act on correct principles

- Identify how to apply abstract principles (table 2) to concrete problems.
- Bolster trust in a principle enough to experiment on it (at first, for a delimited period of a few days).
- Work through difficulties with initial experimentation to help clients practice living the principle, one day at a time, gradually for longer periods of time.
- Repair trust when damaged.
- Foster experimentation with additional correct principles and add coping skills.
- Facilitate client self-mastery.

Help clients recognize positive outcomes from acting according to correct principles

- Reinforce efforts and persistence.
- Review how initial doubts and fears have been replaced by positive actions.
- Consider the consequences of daily steps taken toward the desired outcome; acknowledge progress.

Help clients generalize improvement across many aspects of daily living

- Plan for long-term lifestyle changes.
- Identify additional areas for desired improvement and continue the improvement process.

discomfort, is the essence of faith that promotes development. Rather than settle for reduced uncertainty through repetitive living (e.g., the case of Joan) or settle for numbed insensitivity through disgruntled despondency (e.g., the case of Raymond), clients can face uncertainty and disappointment with faith, not in proximal insulation from pain but in principles of progression, learning and improving through the often harsh lessons of experience. Facilitating this transition requires an equally radical shift in therapeutic focus: from client symptoms to client potential, from circumstances to principles.

Conclusion: Applying the Principle of Faith in the Mental Health Professions

Constructive acts require faith. To the extent that we mental health practitioners attempt to assist people who struggle to cope with distress, we act in faith. We believe in a positive yet unseen future for them, and thus we do all in our power to help them realize that future.

However, the reality is that we mental health professionals do not always help our clients—and sometimes we unintentionally cause them harm (Lambert, 2010; Mays & Frank, 1985). Our work is not only flawed but occasionally damaging: some clients actually do worse because of therapy (Bergin, 1967; Mohr, 1995; Roback, 2000). Facing this thorny reality could cause uncertainty and paralysis for a practitioner, yet it does not—usually because we choose not to face it. We therapists, exactly like those we serve, avoid uncomfortable realities (e.g., our own failings) by implementing reactive coping strategies (table 1). Hence, our own abilities to help clients can sometimes be hampered by reactivity and defenses such as an implicit pride in our stature as professionals that covers personal insecurities or that privileges our own perceptions to the point that we misperceive the needs of those we purport to serve.

Applying the principles discussed in this chapter to our own clinical practice, to act with faith would involve shifting our focus from confidence in our own abilities to assurance in the power of God. Rather than place trust in ourselves ("I can help this client"), faith turns us to the only source of ultimate healing ("I know that God wants to help this person, and I know that I can be led to assist him in his work"). Our trust is no longer in our training or expertise, which are fallible; rather, our trust is in divine principles, infallible, to which we turn the client.

This shift from trust in our own abilities to faith in God's healing makes all the difference. It confers at least seven benefits to our practice. First, it allows us to acknowledge the reality of our own limitations—and therefore compensate proactively. When personal limitations are obvious, we are more likely to plan and prepare with care, which actually enhances the quality of our work ("For when I am weak, then am I strong," 2 Cor. 12:10).

Second, this shift from self to faith in God's healing breaks our reliance on our own formulaic prescriptions and channels our focus to understanding the person before us. We listen more actively and explore hypotheses more thoroughly before reaching conclusions. In short, we attune to reality, rather than to constructs of our own making, whether theoretical paradigm or counter-transference (reactivity).

Third, as our desire to assist God increases, we replace selfish motives with genuine concern for clients' well-being. We concern ourselves less about insurance reimbursements or office décor when we feel keenly, even painfully, the need to help a child of Deity to reclaim her or his potential presently masked by confusion or despair.

Fourth, our focus remains on long-term client well-being. We will see the larger picture of personal development and will be less likely to be misled by happenstance, such as misinterpreting a client's diminished external pressures as an increase in client coping skills. We will remain focused on the full potential of the person, not merely his or her temporary discomfort.

Fifth, we will experience decreased professional pessimism and "burn-out" as we work with challenging cases. Noble motives resting on a sure foundation flourish—rather than diminish—over time. Professional ruts never set in when we daily engage the sublime.

Sixth, turning to God helps us recognize the reality of divine interventions (see 1 Ne. 7:12). Rather than ignore spirituality or merely express silent prayers for divine assistance when facing a clinical challenge, we actively acknowledge the source of all healing with every client. We expect and witness miracles, from whispered remembrances to manifest outpourings of God's love. With this witness, we help clients recognize the source of their healing, whether implicitly through our actions or explicitly through our sharing what we have witnessed.

Seventh, by shifting our focus from ourselves to God, we draw closer to him in person and in personality. To seek the will of God in our daily labors makes us his servants, not merely laborers for wages on earth (Matt. 6:33; Luke 16:11–13). Our worship becomes part of our work (Alma 34:24–25), not merely part of weekend meetings. Our work becomes that of Adam and Eve: men and women who demonstrate through daily labors our desire to return to God's presence (Moses 5:1). Our pattern becomes that of the Savior, Jesus Christ, who desired only and always to do the will of his Father (Mosiah 15:7; 3 Ne. 11:11). Working selflessly to help people in need brings us closer to Deity (Matt. 25:34–36; 2 Ne. 26:30; Mosiah 4:26). We need but open the eyes of faith to recognize the profound privilege of serving clients in any capacity (Matt. 23:11; 25:40).

The principle of faith is as profound as anything ever contemplated by social scientists. The field is open for extended, systematic efforts to promote understanding of how faith underlies mental health and well-being. The field is ripe for questions. What questions will prompt *your* exploration in faith?

References

Alicke, M. D., Dunning, D. A., & Krueger, J. (Eds.). (2013). *The self in social judgment*. New York: Psychology Press.

Bandura, A. (1977). *Social learning theory.* Englewood Cliffs, NJ: Prentice Hall.

Benson, E. T. (1985, November). Born of God. *Ensign*, pp. 5–6.

Benson, E. T. (1988, September). In his steps. *Ensign*, pp. 2–6.

Bergin A. E. (1967). Some implications of psychotherapy research for therapeutic practice. *International Journal of Psychiatry*, 3, 136–160.

BonJour, L. (2001). Epistemological problems of perception. In E. Zalta (Ed.), *The Stanford Encyclopedia of Philosophy*. Retrieved from http://plato.stanford.edu/entries/perception-episprob/.

Brooks, A. (2006). *Who really cares? The surprising truth about compassionate conservatism*. New York: Basic Books.

Crane, T. (2005). The problem of perception. In E. Zalta (Ed.), *The Stanford Encyclopedia of Philosophy*. Retrieved April 23, 2009 from http://plato.stanford.edu/entries/perception-problem/.

Descartes, R. (1641). *Meditations on first philosophy.* Retrieved April 23, 2009 from http://oregonstate.edu/instruct/phl302/texts/descartes/meditations/Meditation1.html.

Ellis, A. (2001). *Overcoming destructive beliefs, feelings, and behaviors: New directions for rational emotive behavior therapy.* Amherst, NY: Prometheus Books.

Emmons, R. A., & McCullough, M. E. (2004). *The psychology of gratitude.* New York: Oxford University Press.

Hinckley, G. B. (1995, October). Faith: The essence of true religion. *Ensign,* pp. 2–6.

Holland, J. R. (2009, 13 January). *Remember Lot's wife.* Devotional given at Brigham Young University, Provo, UT.

Hunter, H. W. (1994, September). Come to the God of all truth. *Ensign*, pp. 72–73.

Kimball, S. W. (1979, July). Absolute truth. *Tambuli,* pp. 1–9.

Koenig, H., King, D., & Carson, V. B. (2012). *Handbook of religion and health.* Oxford University Press.

Lambert, M. J. (2010). *Prevention of treatment failure: The use of measuring, monitoring, and feedback in clinical practice.* Washington, DC: American Psychological Association.

Lectures on faith (1985). In Smith J. (Ed.), Salt Lake City, UT: Deseret Book Company.

Maxwell, N. A. (1996, November). According to the desire of [our] hearts. *Ensign,* pp. 21–23.

Mays, D., & Frank, C. (Eds.). (1985). *Negative outcome in psychotherapy and what to do about it.* New York: Springer.

Mohr, D. C. (1995). Negative outcome in psychotherapy: A critical review. *Clinical Psychology: Science and Practice,* 2(1), 1–27.

Nolen-Hoeksema, S., Wisco, B. E., & Lyubomirsky, S. (2008). Rethinking rumination. *Perspectives on Psychological Science,* 3(5), 400–424.

Oaks, D. H. (2011, May). Desire. *Ensign,* pp. 42–45.

Oaks, D. H. (2007, November). Good, better, best. *Ensign,* pp. 104–108.

Peterson, C., & Seligman, M. E. P. (2004). *Character strengths and virtues: A handbook and classification.* Washington, D.C.: APA Press and Oxford University Press.

Roback, H. B. (2000). Adverse outcomes in group psychotherapy: Risk factors, prevention, and research directions. *Journal of Psychotherapy Practice & Research,* 9(3), 113–122.

Rovelli, C. (2007). *Quantum gravity.* New York: Cambridge University Press.

Scott, R. G. (2007, May). The supernal gift of prayer. *Ensign*, pp. 8–11.

Scott, R. G. (2007, January). Living right. *Ensign*, pp. 10–15.

Scott, R. G. (2003, May). The sustaining power of faith in times of uncertainty and testing. *Ensign*, pp. 75–77.

Seligman, M. E. P., & Csikszentmihalyi, M. (2000). Positive psychology: An introduction. *The American Psychologist,* 55(1), 5–14.

Smith, J., Jr. (1840, February). [Letter to Isaac Galland, March 22, 1839]. *Times and Seasons,* pp. 51–56.

Smith, J., Jr. (1971). *History of The Church of Jesus Christ of Latter-day Saints.* B. H. Roberts (Ed.) (2nd ed., rev.) (Vols. 1–7). Salt Lake City: Deseret Book.

Smith, T. B. (2004). A contextual approach to assessment. In T. Smith (Ed.), *Practicing multiculturalism: Affirming diversity in counseling and psychology* (pp. 97–119). Boston: Allyn & Bacon.

Snyder, C. R., & Lopez, S. J. (Eds.). (2009). *Oxford handbook of positive psychology.* New York: Oxford University Press.
Uchtdorf, D. F. (2014, April). Grateful in any circumstances. *Ensign*, pp. 70–77.
Warner, C. T. (2001). *Bonds that make us free: Healing our relationships, coming to ourselves.* Salt Lake City, UT: Arbinger Institute.
Williams, R. N. (1998). Restoration and the "turning of things upside down": What is required of an LDS perspective? *MCAP Journal, 23*, 1–30.
Wirthlin, J. B. (1998, November). Cultivating divine attributes. *Ensign*, pp. 25–27.
Worthington, E. L. (Ed.). (2005). *Handbook of forgiveness.* New York: Routledge.
Young, B. (1854). Comprehensiveness of true religion. In *Journal of Discourses* (Vol. 1, pp. 334–339). Salt Lake City, UT: Church of Jesus Christ of Latter-day Saints.

Psychotherapy Vis-à-vis the Gospel

Aaron P. Jackson

The technical meaning of the French term *vis-à-vis* is face-to-face. It is sometimes used to mean *in relation to* (Vis-à-vis, n.d.). One of our purposes in this series has been to examine psychotherapy vis-à-vis the restored gospel. That is, we have worked to understand psychotherapy in contrast with, and in relation to, the gospel. Implicit in our project has been an assumption that psychotherapy and the gospel are each separate and valuable endeavors—obviously not equally valuable, but both valuable nonetheless.

In exploring psychotherapy vis-à-vis the gospel, there has been some temptation to go down a seductively simple path. We begin down the path by using the gospel light to expose the ambiguities, contradictions, and lacunae of the thinking behind psychotherapy. We can readily point out the reductionism, hedonism, individualism, biologism, etc. of the prevailing models of psychotherapy and discuss how these philosophical assumptions run counter to the gospel. While this is an important, satisfying, and sometimes even entertaining enterprise, it doesn't *necessarily* provide any insight into how the gospel might inform or reform the practice. The temptation is to simply critique without offering any constructive alternatives. This may lead some to conclude that psychotherapy is an inherently corrupt enterprise, which should ultimately be supplanted by the gospel. That is, replace psychotherapy with extant gospel practices, and thereby render it moot. I believe in this volume and its predecessor, we have wandered some distance down this path. While raising this point does not diminish the ideas presented here, I hope it does raise some important questions for the reader and provide implications for where we should go from here.

Before expanding on some of these ideas, I would like to acknowledge the possibility that our premise might be wrong. It may be that psychotherapy is not a valuable or legitimate enterprise in its own right. If, as Rieff (1968) predicted, psychology is taking the place of religion in helping people seek happiness and meaning and serves no righteous purpose, then perhaps we should simply critique psychotherapy into oblivion. However, I would like to argue against this approach. I do not think that psychotherapy needs to be in competition with the gospel—either philosophically or practically. I think psychotherapy and the psychologies upon which it is based can be useful and powerful complements to any religious practice, including that of the restored gospel. In order for it to be complementary, however, it must remain distinct. Which takes me back to the dangerous path.

The first part of the dangerous path is critique without alternative. We have all had the experience of being criticized without being given any constructive suggestions. It's not very helpful. When it comes to critiquing psychology, I am as guilty of this practice as anyone. I have spent a good portion of my career exploring and exposing the moral, philosophical, and practical weaknesses of mainstream psychology and psychotherapy. Following the well-trod path of pioneers such as Williams, Slife, Gantt, Richardson, and others, it has become a relatively simple thing to focus on the field's weaknesses and contradictions. However, it seems to me that the time has come for us to do more by way of providing alternatives. Several authors in this volume have done just that. They have courageously outlined tenets of gospel-friendly psychotherapy. These are giant leaps in the right direction. These leaps however, also expose the second part of the dangerous path.

The second part of the dangerous path is to simply supplant psychotherapy with gospel praxis. This path is much more subtle, even slippery. It seems straightforward enough to say we should take known gospel principles and call it psychology and known gospel practice and call it psychotherapy. For example, I could take the gospel doctrine of the soul and put it in place of philosophically corrupt notions like the ego or cognitive schema. I could take the doctrine of repentance and put it in place of psychotherapeutic constructs like corrective emotional experience or insight. While there may be some value to this process, it becomes dangerous for two reasons. First, by simply exchanging terms or constructs, I run the risk of losing the meaning of one or both. While this isn't much of a threat in psychology—where constructs run fast and loose anyway—there is a considerable danger in corrupting the meaning of gospel constructs like soul and forgiveness.

Second, there is the danger of losing the value of psychology and psychotherapy as distinct endeavors by simply subsuming them into obvious gospel knowledge and practice. Neal A. Maxwell (1976) made an important point in this regard. In discussing how we might work at the interface of the gospel and the behavioral sciences, he said, "LDS behavioral scientists must extract both the obvious *and hidden* wisdom embedded in the value system of the gospel of Jesus Christ" (Maxwell, 1976, emphasis added). I take his point to be that there are obvious aspects of the gospel that are relevant to the behavioral sciences. These might include faith, hope, charity, family relationships, repentance, etc.—all of which have clear implications for applied psychology. The contributors to this volume have expanded on a number of these. The danger here is to assume that because a gospel construct provides some explanation of a psychological phenomenon, that it is a sufficient explanation. I will try to illustrate this with some examples.

Tim Smith (this volume) carefully outlines the relationship of faith to mental health. In doing so, he makes statements like this one: "Clients who come to believe in correct principles (e.g., gratitude, forgiveness, love, accountability) and consistently act on those principles will experience permanent improvements in functioning" (p. 216).

In this case, and in several others throughout this volume, the naïve reader might interpret the author to be saying that mental health is essentially a function of adherence to gospel principles. In its most simplistic form, the formula is that righteousness = mental health and implies the converse, that poor mental health = unrighteousness. I do not think that any of the authors in this volume are subscribing to these simplistic notions. Nonetheless, it is easy to slip into language that might imply just that. It is problematic because there are some positive relationships between righteousness and mental health. However, these relationships are not comprehensive, simple, or clear.

Parallels

We might consider some parallels in trying to better understand the relationship between righteousness and mental health. For example, there is an apparent positive relationship between righteousness and physical health. However, most believers readily understand the complexity of the relationship. We understand that certain unrighteous acts might lead to physical health problems. At the same time, we also understand the importance of the word *might*, and we understand that physical health problems come from a variety of other *causes* such as genetic inheritance, pollution in the environment, accidents, etc. Only the most radical would suggest that a person disregard secular approaches to physical health and rely solely on gospel praxis such as living the Word of Wisdom and getting priesthood blessings when one is ill or hurt. While this parallel is useful, it is also limited. Physical health problems are limited to this life (Alma 11:43–44) and do not exist in the next life. It is not clear to me that mental health issues are resolved so readily. While the physical aspects of mental health problems may be solved by resurrection, because agency still operates and we are still learning in the next life, it may be that we will still have use for something like psychotherapy or counseling as one avenue by which we can learn and progress.

Another parallel that we might explore is the relationship between righteousness and education. Most would agree that there is some relationship between righteousness and being truly educated or wise. We can also see how education, without righteousness, can be spiritually destructive (2 Ne. 9:28–29). Even though we recognize this inherent risk in education, we also see education as an important aspect of righteousness. Again, only a radical few would argue that the whole of education should be eliminated or somehow subsumed by gospel practice. Likewise, very few would argue that our approaches to education should be limited to gospel praxis or that the entire cadre of effective teaching was illustrated by the Savior, so teachers should use primarily parables, references to previous teachers, and occasional direct confrontation and rebuke.

My point is that there are clear reasons to use secular physical and educational methods that go beyond those implied by the gospel. It stands to reason that the same may be true in the psychological realm. There may well be psychological interventions that are true and good, even though they are not explicitly inherent in the gospel. There are also less obvious aspects of the gospel that may have important implications. For example, the light of Christ and its relationship to insight and learning for all people (Reber, this volume, p. 142), or the subtle difference between agency and freedom and their relationship to determinism—in all its varieties (Williams, this volume).

Some of the work in this volume pushes us to clarify the critical semantic interfaces between psychotherapy and the gospel. For example, Smith (this volume) uses the term faith to mean "asserting one's internal beliefs onto the external world" (p. 183). While this notion of a leap of faith is common to many schools of psychotherapy as well as more commonsensical philosophies, we need to do more to clarify the differences and similarities between this notion and faith in the theological sense. Doing so would provide important bridges as well as distinctions between psychological faith and theological faith.

Reber (this volume) outlines several terms that require our attention as well. He pushes us to define constructs like the unconscious, altruism, and truth across the interface between the gospel and psychology. He begins to articulate these notions and their implication for mind-body dualism versus a more holistic approach. This seems a prime place for the "hidden wisdom" (Maxwell, 1976) of the gospel. We need to understand more fully what the gospel teaches us about dualism and holism as it applies to human beings. Reber also asserts that there are aspects of the human spirit that are unconscious. While it is easy to disparage Freud's hypothesized unconscious, it is much more challenging to articulate Reber's gospel-friendly unconscious.

Hansen (this volume) raises another important question. In her discussion of agency and extraspective versus introspective theorizing, she indicates that "relating requires understanding the tension or dialectic between agency and relational context" (p. 47). Perhaps this points us toward another unarticulated or "hidden wisdom" of the gospel. We might do well to consider Levinas's (2002) and Oliver's (2001) critiques of individualism. Maybe more relational approaches will help us to articulate agency in a way that more readily crosses the interface between psychology and the gospel. This is certainly what is suggested in my own chapter (Jackson, this volume). And for me, a more relational approach not only allows for a richer perspective on agency, but it also allows for the construct of love to be included in our theories—though what we mean by love in these contexts still deserves considerable attention.

Gantt and Knapp (this volume) bump up against individualism as well in their chapter. Their critique of egoistic perspectives on marriage leads the reader to wonder about the alternative. They suggest alterocentrism, or other-centeredness, as the philosophical solution. The related ideas of indebtedness and covenant relationships are excellent examples of the "hidden wisdom" (Maxwell, 1976) of the gospel. Williams (this volume, pp. 21–22) provides us with another example of how the hidden wisdom of the gospel can be used to clarify our semantics. He suggests that we deepen our understanding of the term agency by considering its ontological, phenomenological, and practical aspects. He pushes the idea of agency beyond its typically instrumental use in psychology (and the gospel) and asks us to consider the true nature of our interventions. His suggestion that psychotherapy is morally focused persuasion also deserves additional thought and explication.

Gleave's chapter (this volume) also illustrates the need for us to better define our constructs. As part of the foundation for his arguments about justice, he suggests that joy is an "individual goal that must be pursued first for ourselves and then afterward for others" (p. 64). He seems to contradict what the more relational authors in this series are suggesting—that we should construct alternative paradigms to the individualistic and egoistic philosophies that dominate psychology. Clearly, in order to better reconcile the gospel and psychology, we need to more fully address this fundamental issue. Gleave also leads us to consider the interface between gospel and therapeutic notions of forgiveness—another semantic struggle worth pursuing. Likewise, he broaches the question of anger—righteous and otherwise. This is yet one more construct that is in need of the gospel's "hidden wisdom" (Maxwell, 1976).

Like several other authors in this volume, Fischer (this volume) points us to ontological questions. He wonders whether agency is preeminent or a natural byproduct of the Atonement. This seems another way of asking about individual versus relational ontology—perhaps the most salient recurring theme in this volume. Draper (this volume) addresses this question head-on and wonders about our adoption of individualistic psychotherapeutic values such as autonomy. He takes an important step forward in showing how the gospel constructs of faith, hope, and charity can be further articulated to have direct application to psychotherapeutic science and practice. These are important first steps in our journey to better understand these rich doctrines and their implications for psychotherapy.

In conclusion, I will use another quote from Neal A. Maxwell (1986) to remind us of our responsibility to more fully understand and explicate the important constructs and beliefs discussed in this volume. He said,

> One of the unique features of the living church of Jesus Christ is its ever-expanding body of fundamental spiritual knowledge about man's identity and purpose, which enlarges "the memory of this people" (Alma 37:8). In fact, our ninth article of faith declares that God "will yet reveal many great and important things pertaining to the Kingdom of God." Thus nourished by a menu blending antiquity and futurity, Church members need never "faint in [their] minds" (Hebrews 12:3). Instead, we can be intellectually vibrant.

I hope this volume spurs us to the intellectual vibrancy Elder Maxwell envisioned.

References

Levinas, E. (2002). *Otherwise than being: Or beyond essence.* (A. Lingis, Trans.). Pittsburgh: Duquesne University Press.

Maxwell, N. A. (1976, July). *Some thoughts on the gospel and the behavioral sciences.* Retrieved from http://www.lds.org/ensign/1976/07/some-thoughts-on-the-gospel-and-the-behavioral-sciences.

Maxwell, N. A. (1986, November). "God will yet reveal." *Ensign 16*, p. 52.

Oliver, K. (2001). *Witnessing: Beyond recognition.* Minneapolis, MN: University of Minnesota Press.

Rieff, P. (1968). *The triumph of the therapeutic.* New York: Harper.

Vis-à-vis. (n.d.). Merriam-Webster online dictionary. Retrieved from http://www.merriam-webster.com/.

Vis-à-vis. (n.d.). Oxford English Dictionary Online. Retrieved from http://www.oed.com.erl.lib.byu.edu/.

Contributors

Matthew R. Draper currently works as a professor of psychology in the Department of Behavioral Sciences at Utah Valley University. He earned a doctorate in counseling psychology from the University of Texas at Austin and previously served as director of clinical training at Indiana State University. His research interests focus on the theology and philosophy of love and compassion and how these ideas can be applied both within a psychotherapy setting as well as in daily life. Clinically, he has worked in counseling centers, refugee trauma clinics, hospitals, and super-maximum-security prisons. He currently maintains a private practice to apply the principles he teaches and to inform his mentorship of his students in and out of the classroom.

Lane Fischer completed his doctoral studies at the University of Minnesota. He practiced child and adolescent psychotherapy as licensed psychologist in Minnesota until joining the faculty of BYU in 1993. He is a licensed psychologist in Utah and continues to work with children and families. He has served as the dean of students and as the chair of the Institutional Review Board for the Protection of Human Subjects at BYU. He has served as president of the Utah and Rocky Mountain Associations for Counselor Education and Supervision. He has served as the president of the Association of Mormon Counselors and Psychotherapists. He has served as the editor of the journal *Issues in Religion and Psychotherapy.*

Edwin E. Gantt is currently Associate Professor of Psychology at Brigham Young University and a visiting fellow of the Wheatley Institution. He received his doctoral degree in clinical psychology from Duquesne University, where he focused on existential-phenomenological psychology and qualitative research methods. He is the author of numerous scholarly articles and book chapters. He is coauthor (with Richard N. Williams) of

Psychology-for-the-Other: Levinas, Ethics, and the Practice of Psychotherapy and coauthor (with Brent D. Slife) of *Taking Sides: Clashing Views on Psychological Issues*. He is currently working on a book examining the impact of scientism in psychology. He teaches courses in the history and philosophy of psychology, personality theory, qualitative research methods, psychology of religion, and (his favorite) LDS perspectives and psychology. He and his wife, Anita, are the proud parents of four sons (Jared, Mark, Ben, and Stephen).

Robert L. Gleave is a psychologist and Clinical Professor Emeritus. He recently retired from Brigham Young University, where he held joint appointments in Counseling and Psychological Services and Counseling Psychology. He received a PhD in counseling psychology from Brigham Young University. His research interests include group psychotherapy and the application of religious and philosophical thought to psychotherapy practice. He has published book chapters and journal articles in both areas.

Mark S. Green received his undergraduate degree in psychology from Brigham Young University and a PhD in counseling psychology from Indiana State University. He currently works as a psychologist and prevention specialist at Wichita State University, in addition to running a small private practice in Wichita, Kansas. Mark and his wife, Emily, have eight children and enjoy the challenge of teaching them to seek and embrace truth, often settling for just not hurting each other. In addition to work and family responsibilities, Mark finds balance by singing, playing the piano, and trying not to get injured while exercising.

Kristin Lang Hansen, PhD, is a licensed clinical psychologist in private practice since 2001 and an affiliate research faculty member in the Department of Counseling Psychology at Brigham Young University. She also currently serves as the editor for *Issues in Religion and Psychotherapy.* She received her PhD in clinical psychology from Loyola University–Chicago in 2000 and completed an internship and postdoctoral work at Harvard Medical School. Correspondence should be directed to: Kristinlanghansen@gmail.com.

Aaron P. Jackson is Associate Professor of Counseling Psychology and Special Education at Brigham Young University. He received a BS in psychology and an MS in counseling from Brigham Young University and a PhD in counseling psychology from the University of Missouri–Columbia. His current research interests include exploring the role of values and bias in psychotherapy and psychotherapy training, and the interface of professional psychology and religion. He is the training director of BYU's counseling psychology doctoral program.

Stan J. Knapp is Associate Professor of Sociology at Brigham Young University. He received his PhD in sociology from Florida State University and has been teaching courses in social theory and family theory for almost thirty years. His work in family theory has centered on questions of how to theorize marital quality, the ethical or moral dimension of marriage and family life, and the practice of science and claims of expertise in the formation of knowledge claims about marriage and family. His work in social theory has examined the relation between rationality (in its various forms), the moral and ethical dimension of human life, and the way in which claims of expertise are formed and established.

Jeffrey S. Reber is Associate Professor and Chair of the Department of Psychology at the University of West Georgia. His PhD is in general psychology with a dual emphasis in theoretical/philosophical psychology and applied social psychology. He is also a practicing licensed professional counselor and the founder of Relational Counseling and Consulting Services (RCCS). Jeff's research, teaching, and counseling/consulting philosophies are informed by a relational approach to psychology that promotes critical thinking about the relationship between assumptions, implications, and alternative perspectives as they impact human sociality and consciousness. He has published twenty-one peer-reviewed journal articles, ten book chapters, and two books that exemplify his relational, critical-thinking approach to psychology. He also sits on the editorial boards of four academic peer-review publication outlets, and he served as the president of the Society for Theoretical and Philosophical Psychology (Division 24 of the APA) in 2014.

Timothy B. Smith is Professor of Counseling Psychology at Brigham Young University. His research focuses on spirituality and mental health, family and marital stability, cultural psychology, and social predictors of well-being and health. He is a licensed psychologist and a fellow of the American Psychological Association. He and his wife, Cindy, are the parents of five children, the joy of their lives.

Richard N. Williams received his PhD in psychological sciences from Purdue University. He is Professor of Psychology and currently Director of the Wheatley Institution at Brigham Young University. His scholarly interests include the conceptual foundations of psychological theories and the relationship between traditional and postmodern perspectives. Related to this topic, he has written *What's behind the Research: Discovering Hidden Assumptions in the Social Sciences* (with Brent Slife), Sage Press, 1995, and edited (with Edwin Gantt) *Psychology for the Other,* Duquesne University Press, 2002. More recently, he edited, with Daniel N. Robinson, *Scientism: The New Orthodoxy* (Bloomsbury, U.K., 2015). He has published in various scholarly journals—recently, with Edwin Gantt, "Moral Obligation and the Moral Judgment–Moral Action Gap: Toward a Phenomenology of Moral Life," *Journal of Moral Education,* 2012, and "Psychology and the Death of Aspiration," *Theory and Psychology,* 2014.

Cited Scriptural Passages

Names Index

Subject Index